Henry James and the Structure of the Romantic Imagination

Henry James
and the Structure of the Romantic Imagination

DANIEL MARK FOGEL

Louisiana State University Press / Baton Rouge and London

Manufactured in the United States of America

Designer: Albert Crochet
Typeface: Linotype Caledonia
Typesetter: Service Typesetters
Printer and binder: Thompson-Shore, Inc.

Portions of Chapter One were originally published, in somewhat different form, as "The Jamesian Dialectic in *The Ambassadors*," *Southern Review*, N.S., XIII (Summer, 1977), 468–91, and are reprinted here with the permission of the *Southern Review*.

The author wishes to acknowledge the following for their kind permission to quote extensively from published works:

W. W. Norton & Company for Henry James, *The Ambassadors*, edited by S. P. Rosenbaum (Norton Critical Edition, copyright © 1964).

Oxford University Press for *The Notebooks of Henry James*, edited by F. O. Matthiessen and Kenneth B. Murdock (copyright © 1947), and *The Tales of Henry James*, Volume I, edited by Maqbool Aziz (copyright © 1973).

Charles Scribner's Sons for *The Novels and Tales of Henry James*. New York Edition. Copyright 1907, 1908, 1909 by Charles Scribner's Sons, copyrights renewed; and Henry James, *The Art of the Novel: Critical Prefaces of Henry James*, ed. Richard P. Blackmur. Copyright 1934 by Charles Scribner's Sons, copyright renewed.

Published with the assistance of the Council on Research, Louisiana State University.

LIBRARY OF CONGRESS CATALOGING IN PUBLICATION DATA

Fogel, Daniel Mark.

Henry James and the structure of the romantic imagination.

Bibliography: p.

Includes index.

1. James, Henry, 1843–1916—Criticism and interpretation. I. Title.

PS2124.F56 813′.4

ISBN 0-8071-0789-1

81-4824

AACR2

For my parents,
Charlotte and Ephim Fogel

The spiral is a spiritualized circle. In the spiral form, the circle, uncoiled, unwound, has ceased to be vicious; it has been set free. I thought this up when I was a schoolboy, and I also discovered that Hegel's triadic series expressed merely the essential spirality of all things in their relation to time. Twirl follows twirl, and every synthesis is the thesis of the next series. If we consider the simplest spiral, three stages may be distinguished in it, corresponding to those of the triad: We can call "thetic" the small curve or arc that initiates the convolution centrally; "antithetic" the larger arc that faces the first in the process of continuing it; and "synthetic" the still ampler arc that continues the second while following the first along the outer side.

A colored spiral in a small ball of glass, this is how I see my own life.

—Vladimir Nabokov, *Conclusive Evidence*

The conscious American is apologetic, explanatory—a pessimist might sometimes say snobbish. But perhaps, after having traversed a certain phase by a sort of Hegelian unfolding, this type is on its way to become unconscious again. Extremes meet, and that is a symptom of great experiences as well as of great innocence.

—Henry James, "Americans Abroad"

circulations are moderations, currents triggered by extremes:
we must at all costs keep the circulations free and clear,
open and unimpeded: otherwise, extremes will become trapped,
local, locked in themselves, incapable of transaction

—A. R. Ammons, *Extremes and Moderations*

Contents

Abbreviations

Parenthetic citations in my text to the works listed below are to abbreviated titles, as follows:

AM	*The Ambassadors*
TA	*The American*
AN	*The Art of the Novel*
AA	*The Awkward Age*
GBI and *GBII*	*The Golden Bowl*
PLI and *PLII*	*The Portrait of a Lady*
RH	*Roderick Hudson*
TJ	*The Tales of Henry James*, ed. Maqbool Aziz
WDI and *WDII*	*The Wings of the Dove*

Acknowledgments

I want first of all to thank the teachers at Cornell University with whom I studied Henry James: Anthony Caputi, Jean Frantz Blackall, James Matlack (now of the University of Massachusetts), Arthur Mizener, David Shaw (now of the University of Toronto), and S. Cushing Strout, all of whom—especially Professors Shaw, Blackall, and Mizener—have offered valuable guidance as I have worked through my ideas about Henry James. I owe special thanks to M. H. Abrams, Arthur Mizener, and Walter Slatoff. In particular, Professor Slatoff helped to keep me alert to the complex nuances of the ethical questions James poses for us in his depiction of personal relationships; Professor Abrams aided me greatly in formulating my ideas about James's connection with Romanticism; and Professor Mizener, with whom I worked most closely, provided invaluable insights about ways to develop and refine virtually every phase of my commentary. I also want to thank Professor Dan McCall for his very helpful remarks; and, for their instructive comments, Professors J. A. Ward of Rice University and Walter Wright of the University of Nebraska, who read this book in manuscript for the LSU Press. All of these scholars have helped me to avoid many of the difficulties into which one is apt to stumble. The shortcomings that remain in this book are, of course, mine alone.

I am grateful, also, to Irwin Berg, former dean of the College of Arts and Sciences at Louisiana State University, and to Darwin Shrell, former chairman of the Department of English, for providing funds for the typing of the manuscript; to Ms. Sadie LeBlanc, my typist; to Margaret Dalrymple, a lucid, genial editor; to the National Endowment for the Humanities, for the summer stipend under which I completed the fourth chapter of this study; and, finally, to my wife, Rachel, for her sustaining love and for her careful reading of successive drafts of these essays.

Introduction

More than any other writer of the Victorian age, Henry James can be said to look forward in his own work to the theory and practice of fiction in the twentieth century. Yet precisely because what is forward-looking in James has been so widely and adequately recognized, the provenance of his work in Romantic literary tradition has been, comparatively speaking, overlooked. Despite a self-consciously cultivated nostalgia for the eighteenth century, James was very much a man of his own time; like many of his great contemporaries and near-contemporaries in England and America—and at once more cerebrally and more passionately than most—he was responsive to the rich literary heritage of the Romantic period.

Romanticism, as M. H. Abrams says, is a pesky word. In interpreting James as an inheritor of Romantic tradition, I mean to point quite specifically to his affinity with the writers of the Romantic period, particularly with the major English poets from about 1790 through 1830. By contrast, in the great majority of discussions of Henry James where the terms occur, *romantic* and *romanticism* refer not to a literary epoch but to attitudes and dispositions in the author or in his characters, whereas *romance* usually refers to a genre, either prose romance or a more broadly conceived literary type ranging, for example, from *The Faerie Queene* to *The Lord of the Rings*. Such are the general meanings James himself has in mind when he says that "it would be impossible to have a more romantic temperament than

Flaubert's Madame Bovary, and yet nothing less resembles a romance than the record of her adventures." Romance, James goes on to say, in a famous definition, has only one "*general* attribute," "the fact of the kind of experience with which it deals—experience liberated, so to speak; experience disengaged, disembodied, disencumbered, exempt from the conditions that we usually know to attach to it and, if we wish so to put the matter, drag upon it, and operating in a medium which relieves it, in a particular interest, of the inconvenience of a *related*, a measurable state, a state subject to all our vulgar communities." In a kindred vein, F. O. Matthiessen has observed that James frequently replaced the word *picturesque* with *romantic* in the final revision of *The Portrait of a Lady*. Similarly, in her recent discussion of Jamesian romance in such works as *The American* and *The Portrait of a Lady*, Elsa Nettels begins with a quotation from Clara Reeve's 1785 definition of romance as "an heroic fable, which treats of fabulous persons and things," picturing, Nettels adds, "the remote, the strange, the marvellous, the improbable." Now there are of course prominent elements of romance in the literature of the Romantic Age, and from time to time the Romantic poets strike what may be loosely called—with any number of meanings—romantic attitudes. For the sake of precision—the victim of these protean terms in many commentaries—I have referred throughout this study, as in the preceding sentence, to the Romantic and to Romanticism (upper case) whenever I am concerned with what James made of the literary legacy of the Romantic period and to the romantic and romanticism (lower case) whenever I intend a more general reference, such as Nettels' in her discussion of James or such as James's in his remark about Emma Bovary.[1]

My argument about the rootedness of James's fiction in Romantic tradition arises, then, from three general observations. First, the fictions of Henry James typically dramatize quests for experience. Involved in new situations and unprecedented dilemmas—most often by a transatlantic excursion—the Jamesian protagonist experiences an

1. M. H. Abrams, "Rationality and Imagination in Cultural History: A Reply to Wayne Booth," *Critical Inquiry*, II (1976), 450; Richard P. Blackmur (ed.), *The Art of the Novel: Critical Prefaces by Henry James* (New York, 1934), 33 (hereinafter cited in footnotes and parenthetically in the text as *AN*); F. O. Matthiessen, *Henry James: The Major Phase* (New York, 1944), 154–55; Elsa Nettels, *James and Conrad* (Athens, Ga., 1976), 81.

access of perception so profound that it transforms the self. Characters may actively undertake the quest, as do Milly Theale, with her poignant desire to live, and Isabel Archer, with her touchingly ardent belief in the possibility of limitless self-expansion. Alternatively, they may find the novel experiences that constitute the quest thrust upon them by others. Thus Lambert Strether, acting at Mrs. Newsome's behest and also under the comparatively undeveloped compulsion of the "curiosity in his indifference," discovers the necessity and congeniality of new modes of perception in his encounters with Maria Gostrey, with Little Bilham, with the Europeanized Chad, and, above all, with Madame de Vionnet. Similarly, Maggie Verver confronts, in her husband's adultery, a circumstance that forces her to rise beyond the lifeless innocence of her girlhood into the horrifyingly informed and organized innocence by which she triumphs over Charlotte Stant. Second, the structure of such quests for experience is fundamentally bipolar. Inexperience becomes experience, innocence knowledge, incomprehension insight. Third, the final attitude of the Jamesian protagonist is a synthesis of the polarities inherent in the quest. Strether, for example, despite his acquired European breadth of tolerance and an aesthetic discrimination undreamt of in Woollett, refuses Maria Gostrey's offer of marriage, "of exquisite service" based on "selection" ruled by "beauty and knowledge," in order to "be right"—but not, as he explains to Maria, "to have got anything for myself." Through a synthesis, Strether's limited Massachusetts propriety has evolved into a higher order of rightness, informed and enriched by all that he has taken in since his arrival in Europe. In much the same way, Milly Theale's spiritual triumph is the expression of transcendent innocence and benevolence, a transformation of her initial naïveté by the incorporation of new knowledge, the knowledge of deceit, of evil itself.[2]

The pattern in these instances, as in most of James's best fiction, parallels the Hegelian *Bildungsweg*, the structure of which M. H. Abrams summarizes thus: "the Idea (or to put it in an alternate way, anyone's mind thinking its way through philosophy) evolves through its component aspects, the 'fluid' thoughts, or 'concepts' [*Begriffe*], which inevitably move out of themselves to the extreme of their own antitheses, only to return into themselves on a higher level so as to

2. Henry James, *The Ambassadors*, ed. S. P. Rosenbaum (New York, 1964), 18 and 344; hereinafter cited in footnotes and parenthetically in the text as *AM*.

constitute 'self-movements, circles.' "[3] Goethe termed this typically Romantic design of the journey around and back, on a higher level, to the point of origin a "spiral" development. The goal is a synthesis incorporating the origin and its antitheses in a new whole that at once annuls, preserves, and transcends distinction. Abrams has shown the prevalence of this design in the literature as well as in the philosophy of the Romantic Age. It is prominent, he finds, in the speculation of Johann Gottlieb Fichte, Friedrich von Schelling, Georg Wilhelm Friedrich Hegel, and Johann von Schiller, among others, and in the thought and art of such figures as Blake, Wordsworth, Coleridge, and Goethe. Blake's description of the spiral dialectic as a motion from "innocence" through "experience" to "organized innocence" seems particularly useful for students of Henry James. But I would not argue for any particular attribution of influence—a man as widely read and as exposed to ideas as James (see, in this connection, René Wellek's "Henry James's Literary Theory and Criticism") would have felt the concept and design of the spiral return as a pervasive aspect of the thought of his age.[4] We need not tie James's own use of the synthesizing, circular ascent to such a possible single source as his early reading of Goethe.[5] As Dorothea Krook has observed, it is far more sensible to suppose that James took his "view of reality and its essential logic" from the "ambient air of nineteenth-century speculation, whose main current was the preoccupation with the phenomenon of self-consciousness" than to argue that he took it "from anywhere, or anybody, in particular."[6]

James's novels accordingly may be said to belong to a characteristically and generally Romantic genre with a built-in susceptibility to dialectical ordonnance. The characteristic structures in James's novels

3. M. H. Abrams, *Natural Supernaturalism: Tradition and Revolution in Romantic Literature* (New York, 1971), 226. For the discussions by Abrams drawn upon in the remainder of the present paragraph, see 172–95, 200–201, 225–28, 260–61, and 380–81.

4. René Wellek, "Henry James's Literary Theory and Criticism," *American Literature*, XXX (1958), 293–321. Wellek concludes this essay with the observation that "James alone in his time . . . in the English speaking world holds fast to the insights of organistic aesthetics and thus constitutes a bridge from the early nineteenth century to modern criticism."

5. See Cornelia Pulsifer Kelley, *The Early Development of Henry James* (Urbana, 1965), 38–58.

6. Dorothea Krook, *The Ordeal of Consciousness in Henry James* (Cambridge, Eng., 1967), 410–11. But for James on "Hegelian unfolding," see my epigraph.

are dialectical, and this is the case whether one looks at the structure of phrases, of sentences, of paragraphs, of chapters, of larger textual units, or of whole novels. James's integrity and power as an artist arise, according to this view, in large measure because he enacts in the constituent structures of his novels precisely the same dynamic that governs the consciousness of his major characters and because the structures themselves derive from a richly significant paradigm at the heart of what Abrams has shown to be the central tradition of English Romanticism.[7]

It may, of course, be objected that the design of spiral return can be discerned in works that antedate the Romantic period. But that one readily grants. A complex inheritance of philosophical and religious literature lay behind the Romantic exploitation of the spiral form as a mode of synthesis and of humanistic affirmation. Nevertheless, among Shakespeare's tragedies, for instance, only *Lear* and *Othello* may be aptly described as having such a form—in each the protagonist affirms in the end (disregarding, of course, Lear's last, distracted moments after Cordelia's death) a relation of organized innocence with the woman he loves, expressing an awareness far above and beyond the tragically inadequate, simple innocence of his original relation to her. But for the Romantics, the spiral return for the first time became the principal form of affirmation in work after work. The design, that is, cannot be said to be exclusively Romantic, but it is typically so, and since the Romantic poets who worked in it were the literary giants of his century, since James was steeped, moreover, in their work—by far the greatest number of explicit allusions in James are to the English Romantic poets—and since his own work reveals many similarities with theirs in theme and in the essential sensibility expressed, the notion that James's art may be usefully interpreted as drawing heavily on Romantic tradition rests on substantial foundations.

As has been remarked elsewhere, James's imagination thrived on "the Coleridgean principle of the reconciliation of opposites."[8] Ex-

7. See Wayne C. Booth's assessment of Abrams's achievement in *Natural Supernaturalism*, "M. H. Abrams: Historian, Critic, Pluralist," *Critical Inquiry*, II (1976), 411–45.

8. J. A. Ward, *The Search for Form: Studies in the Structure of James's Fiction* (Chapel Hill, 1967), 18.

perience is understood as a creative interplay of contraries. Sometimes the contraries in James's fiction are simply juxtaposed in bristling conjunction but with no clear medium of transaction between them. Sometimes, often in ways with important implications for interpreting the text, the oppositions are resolved. The resolution may be an Aristotelian mean between extremes, expressive, in part, of the novelist's preoccupation with balance, symmetry, and architectural proportion. At other times, it is a way of subsuming an antithesis in a primary term: thus, for example, Adam Verver sees myriad curves within his son-in-law's angular, Palladian outline. At still others, it is a fusion of polarities to create a new term. Its most condensed form is the oxymoron, a favorite Jamesian trope. Its most comprehensive expression is in the dynamic fusion achieved through the dialectic of spiral return. The variety of ways in which the ideas of opposition and of synthesis are built into the rhetorical, dramatic, and thematic structures of the novels might be thought of as threads interwoven to produce what I would contend is the central figure in James's carpet and a paradigm of moral as well as of formal significance, the spiral dialectic. James knows, to be sure, that drama subsists on contrast, but his enactment in his novels of the dialectical pattern is by no means merely an aesthetic compulsion, as we shall see, for example, when we come to *The Golden Bowl*, where the pattern of spiral return, a secular version of the traditional Christian schema of salvation (as Abrams shows in *Natural Supernaturalism*), helps establish criteria by which one can take stock of the moral value of the characters.

One can expect, in such narratives, to move from Edenic simplicity through a fall and experience of a fallen world and then on up to a recovery of the happiness of the first stage on a level that is higher because of the knowledge one has gained en route. The destination—the superior felicity one gains at last—justifies the intervening experience of loss and suffering.[9] We recognize in this traditionally significant narrative design the essential structure of Keats's theodicy in his "Vale of Soul-Making" letter and also in the history he gives in *The Fall of Hyperion* of the poet-narrator, who begins in an Edenic dream idyll, goes through a trial of self-doubt and mystic initiation in which

9. Again, I have drawn in the present paragraph on a variety of discussions by Abrams in *Natural Supernaturalism*. See especially 74–80, 122–29, 255, 278–92, and 299–307.

his very life is at stake, and emerges fully armed with assurance and with knowledge as the tragic poet of the epic. In *Prometheus Unbound*, Shelley goes to ingenious lengths to give prominence to the same narrative design. Prometheus, already converted from hatred to compassion, compels the Phantasm of Jupiter to repeat the hate-filled curse with which Prometheus had earlier defied Jupiter himself. Thus Shelley is able vividly to dramatize the preceding. antithetical stage of his hero's development, the stage of evil intervening between his first, frustrated efforts as a benefactor of mankind and his ultimate transcendent, millennial consciousness. Similarly, for a third and final example drawn from a wealth of such instances in Romantic texts, consider Wordsworth's having to go through a crisis in which he abandons imagination and takes up instead its antithesis, rational analysis, before he is able to resolve, in Book XIV of *The Prelude*, the dialectic of beauty and fear and to return to his initial affirmations of the imagination—an imagination, moreover, that beauty and fear had helped to bring into being in the comparatively unconscious spiritual integrity of his boyhood.

Blake's dictum that "Without Contraries is no progression" might well be taken as the motto of Jamesian art. Shelley's characteristic marriage of idealism and searching, ironic skepticism seems resonant with the play between idealizing lyricism and ironic criticism in the Jamesian dialectic. James himself appears to have felt a special affinity with Keats. But the analogy with Wordsworth seems to me to be especially and reciprocally illuminating. There have been numerous commentaries on the pervasive oppositions in Wordsworth's poetry. In a recent discussion, L. J. Swingle attempts to go beyond analysis of the "obvious chiaroscuro effect Wordsworth favors in his imagery and choice of subject matter: interweaving of light and dark, movement and rest, noise and silence," and so on, to explore "those curious and fundamental intellectual tensions manifest in the poet's writings" and brought to contemporary notice by the "iconoclastic" studies of David Ferry and others. Wordsworth, Swingle suggests, intentionally hovers, as it were, above bipolar alternatives so that we are "confronted with a crossroads," "allowing us to see the outlines of our own boundaries." But I would suggest more generally that in Wordsworth, as in James, we see expressed at every level of his art a preoccupation with duality and an oft-thwarted yet frequently satisfied urge to resolve it. Wordsworth's "chiaroscuro" effects, the "intellectual tensions" in his work, and the enactment in many of his poems of a synthesizing, circular ascent—notably in *The Prelude*, as Abrams demonstrates—are thus understood as being of a piece, the stylistic oppositions providing microcosms of the large thematic ones resolved in the overarching dialectic of the poet's account of the growth of his mind.[10]

More and more in the past two decades, scholars have drawn attention to the continuity of Romantic tradition and the literature of the twentieth century. This critical enterprise has concentrated primarily upon the connection between modern and Romantic poetry.[11] A few critics, however, have made important contributions to our understanding of the ways in which twentieth-century fiction assimilates significant Romantic elements. Herbert Lindenberger's study of Lawrence's Romanticism and David Thorburn's signal exploration of Conrad's are exemplary. Two very recent books about the relations between Romantic literature and post-Romantic fiction suggest, moreover, that interest in the topic is alive and growing.[12] The present study is offered in the hope that it will be a contribution to the growing appreciation of the influence and enduring vitality of Romanticism as well as a helpful guide for readers of Henry James.

A demonstration of the affinity of James's imagination for the Romantic dialectic of spiral return entails attention to two aspects of James's practice: his characteristic use of polarities and his inveterate (though sometimes thwarted) movement to synthesis. I am going to look chiefly at texts in James's late style because they seem to me to receive maximum illumination from this approach. A brief analysis of *The Awkward Age* in terms of the paradigm of spiral return intro-

10. David V. Erdman (ed.), *The Poetry and Prose of William Blake* (Garden City, 1970), 34; L. J. Swingle, "Wordsworth's Contrarieties: A Prelude to Wordsworthian Complexity," *ELH*, XLIV (1977), 337, 352, 353.

11. See, for example, Harold Bloom, *The Ringers in the Tower: Studies in Romantic Tradition* (Chicago, 1971); John Bayley, *The Romantic Survival: A Study in Poetic Evolution* (London, 1957); John Frank Kermode, *The Romantic Image* (New York, 1957); and Robert Woodrow Langbaum, *The Poetry of Experience: The Dramatic Monologue in Modern Literary Tradition* (London, 1957).

12. See Herbert Lindenberger, "Lawrence and the Romantic Tradition," in Harry T. Moore (ed.), *A D. H. Lawrence Miscellany* (Carbondale, 1959), 326–41, and David Thorburn, *Conrad's Romanticism* (New Haven, 1974). The two recent studies are Charles Schug's *The Romantic Genesis of the Modern Novel* (Pittsburgh, 1979)—about which more shortly—and Donald D. Stone's *The Romantic Impulse in Victorian Fiction* (Cambridge, Mass., 1980).

duces chapter one, which concentrates subsequently on the many levels of organization at which *The Ambassadors* embodies James's dialectic, from small stylistic detail to the overall pattern of Strether's development. Chapter two opens with a glance at some exemplary instances of James's use of polarities in *The Portrait of a Lady* (as revised for the New York Edition of his works) and goes on to explore the incorporation of the principles of opposition and synthesis in the dramatic organization of *The Wings of the Dove* and in the rhetoric and imagery of that novel. Chapter three focuses solely on *The Golden Bowl*, on the fulfillment by several of the major characters of the dialectic of spiral return, and on the significance of the dialectical pattern for understanding this most controversial of James's major works. Chapter four, finally, surveys James's use of oppositions throughout his career with special attention to the years of his apprenticeship (1865–75) and of his early period (1876–81), when he was first developing what would become regular methods for treating the polarities in his fictions.

It must be said that my overriding purpose in this book is to illumine James, not to prove that a case can be made for dialectic. I am interested above all in what James's protagonists achieve—or fail to achieve—in their quests for experience. And though the term *dialectic* is very apt for a process of reasoning, it doubtless does not fully convey what happens in a work of art, even though opposites are transcended. Like any convenient metaphor, the dialectic of spiral return may become a license for oversimplification. *Spiral*, after all, implies steady development, but for many readers the synthesis achieved "dialectically" in *The Ambassadors*, *The Wings of the Dove*, and elsewhere is not so much a uniform upward movement as a revelation, even though much action prepares for it. Similarly, Strether does not consciously say to himself, "Here is the thesis; here the antithesis: now, how do I synthesize?" Nevertheless, to view James's fiction in terms of the paradigm of spiral growth is to find various key elements of his art thrown into high, instructive relief. Unlike his characters, moreover, the novelist himself is a self-conscious dialectician in the proper, nonmetaphorical sense, as the vocabulary of rational discourse throughout his prefaces (stressing precisely such terms as *thesis*, *antithesis*, and *synthesis*) clearly shows. And if this last point is granted, then one might fairly say the same thing of James and of my approach to him in the following pages: *the fundamental object is the quest for experience, in which dialectical method is basic, but as a means, not as an end.* Throughout the following chapters, finally, my method is eclectic; the analysis of *The Ambassadors*, for example, is primarily psychological, in contrast to the later analysis of imagery in *The Wings of the Dove* and to that of structure and point of view in *The Golden Bowl.* I have pursued this eclecticism not merely because it is congenial to me or because the critical approach employed in each chapter seems particularly to illuminate the text at hand, but most of all because the variety of perspectives that disclose the Jamesian dialectic constitutes the strongest possible testimony to its centrality, to its lying at the heart of James's fictional method.

So far as previous James criticism is concerned, my argument expands a widely shared idea about James in two directions, toward more detailed demonstration in the body of the prose itself and toward a higher level of generality. That James arrays his themes in oppositions (for instance, American and European values, innocence and experience, idealism and pragmatism, appearance and reality) has been noted by many critics. To cite only a few representative instances, Leon Edel says that "contrast and comparison was . . . the law of his [James's] life"; S. Gorley Putt, following Edel, analyzes the "geminian" theme in James; Manfred Mackenzie discusses James's "binary form"; Ruth Yeazell sees "the dialectic of Jamesian talk" as mirroring "the tensions within the Jamesian consciousness itself"; Sallie Sears argues that James's vision is polar but that it allows no reconciliation of extremes; and, finally, Donald L. Mull makes James's imaginative conversions, the thematic syntheses the fictions achieve, central to his study of the novelist.[13]

13. Leon Edel, *Henry James: The Conquest of London, 1870–1881* (Philadelphia, 1962), Vol. II of Leon Edel, *The Life of Henry James* (5 vols.; Philadelphia, 1953–72), 193; S. Gorley Putt, *Henry James: A Reader's Guide* (Ithaca, 1967), 87; Manfred Mackenzie, *Communities of Honor and Love in Henry James* (Cambridge, Mass., 1976), *passim;* Ruth Bernard Yeazell, *Language and Knowledge in the Late Novels of Henry James* (Chicago, 1971), 15; Sallie Sears, *The Negative Imagination: Form and Perspective in the Novels of Henry James* (Ithaca, 1968); Donald L. Mull, *Henry James's "Sublime Economy": Money as Symbolic Center in the Fiction* (Middletown, 1973).

These remarks on previous criticism require a qualification. In my bibliography, I have listed all of the works consulted in the preparation of this study; they represent, however, only a fraction of the well over four thousand items that would have to be included in a complete bibliography of James studies to date.

I am most heavily indebted, of course, to the handful of critics who have linked James's contraries to his understanding and use of Romantic tradition. Adeline Tintner has persuasively shown that James uses a network of allusions to Keats to develop the conflicts that finally destroy Hyacinth Robinson in *The Princess Casamassima*. Richard A. Hocks, like J. A. Ward, sees James's imagination as Coleridgean.[14] Charles Schug's chapter on James in *The Romantic Genesis of the Modern Novel* arises from a very different understanding of Romanticism and of Romantic structure than that upon which the present study is based, and Schug develops readings of James radically different from mine; yet there is one respect (aside from Schug's several remarks about James's organicism) in which his discussion runs parallel to mine, his argument that James uses images and symbols in the late novels "in the manner of a Romantic Image; that is, they embody contraries, join opposites together." (But Schug, reading the late novels very much in the manner of Sallie Sears, finds that James offers only "an ironic reconciliation of opposites").[15] J. A. Ward's commentaries are the closest to my own. James's art, for him, is the fusion of "a Neo-Classicist James" and an "equally formidable Romanticist James, for whom the indispensable terms are 'germ,' 'organic form,' 'growth,' 'freedom,' and 'imagination.'" His major thesis is that the novels attempt to reconcile a tension between "free imaginative expansion" and "lucidity of design," an "open principle" and a "closed principle." He does not treat the details of James's prose in such terms, nor do they, in fact, play a prominent part in his subsequent discussions of partic-

---

It has been my conscientious effort, nevertheless, to speak to all of the best commentaries on James known to me to address the issues central to *Henry James and the Structure of the Romantic Imagination.*

14. Adeline R. Tintner, "Keats and James and *The Princess Casamassima*," *Nineteenth-Century Fiction*, XXVIII (1973), 179–93; Richard A. Hocks, *Henry James and Pragmatistic Thought: A Study in the Relationship Between the Philosophy of William James and the Literary Art of Henry James* (Chapel Hill, 1974), *passim.*

15. Schug, *The Romantic Genesis of the Modern Novel,* 123. The term *Romantic Image* is of course drawn from Frank Kermode's book of that title, cited in n. 11, above. (Having just spoken of my indebtedness to earlier critics, I should note that *The Romantic Genesis of the Modern Novel* was not yet out when *Henry James and the Structure of the Romantic Imagination* was accepted for publication, that there are therefore no further references to Schug's work in the following chapters, and that these few references to *The Romantic Genesis* are being penned even while the rest of my book proceeds through the publisher's production department.)

ular novels. Our arguments are, it seems to me, congenial to each other, distinct but complementary. Ward, for example, in considering the roundness of form in James's novels, talks about "circularity," an idea that is not contradicted but amplified by my notion that the circle ascends through antitheses (see the remarks on the structure of *The Golden Bowl* in chapter three, below). Most resonantly with my thesis, Ward has written of "the ascending spiral and thus the three related forms of Strether's growth: sudden illumination, recurrent pattern, and steady ascension."[16]

No one hitherto has argued in detail, at any rate, that dialectical models will illuminate every aspect of James's art. The extension of the idea of a dialectic in James's themes to the close analysis of polar structures in the stylistic details of his novels (in, for example, the structure of phrases, sentences, paragraphs, and chapters, and in the development of patterns of imagery) is new to James studies. So is the idea of the Romantic spiral as the major structural design in the fictions, to which the other dialectical elements are subsidiary. The disposition of James to dialectical ordonnance of his work, at least partly intentional, as his criticism, his notebooks, and the novels themselves make clear, places him, one of the great founders of twentieth-century fiction, squarely in a major tradition of nineteenth-century

16. J. A. Ward, "James's Idea of Structure," *PMLA*, LXXX (1965), 419; Ward, *The Search for Form*, 19, 25; J. A. Ward, "*The Ambassadors* as a Conversion Experience," *Southern Review*, n.s., V (1969), 368.

I have found two other very brief mentions of similar ideas about James. Ross Labrie describes James's epistemology as "a circular one" because "knowledge promotes interest; interest encourages attentiveness; attentiveness leads to knowledge, and so on. With each rounding of the spiral, a new level of consciousness is reached" ("Henry James's Idea of Consciousness," *American Literature*, XXXIX [1968], 526). Though he does not use the word *spiral*, James N. Wise's description of the end of *The Ambassadors* suggests that the form of Strether's experience is a circular ascent: "With his new knowledge Strether comes full circle by floating off at the novel's end, but he floats in one and the same motion on both a higher and a deeper level of understanding than ever before" ("The Floating World of Lambert Strether," *Arlington Quarterly*, II [1969], 110).

In *Henry James's Psychology of Experience: Innocence, Responsibility, and Renunciation in the Fiction of Henry James* (The Hague, 1975), Granville H. Jones develops a thesis superficially similar to mine. He sees the fictions as working toward syntheses in which the renunciation of the typical James protagonist represents a higher innocence than that with which the protagonist begins. Jones does not discuss the detail of James's style, does not connect James's practice with Romantic tradition, and—in contrast to my sense of the affirmative elements in James's dialectical procedure—he describes Jamesian structure as a "perfect circle of negation" (p. x).

Romanticism. Understanding James's relation to that tradition and the use he made of it is essential, as I hope to show, for discovering the meaning of his art.

CHAPTER ONE

Extremes and Moderations: *The Awkward Age* and *The Ambassadors*

I want to approach *The Ambassadors* by way of a brief comparison with *The Awkward Age*, the masterpiece of James's experimental fictions of the nineties. Although it was written only three years before *The Ambassadors, The Awkward Age* is strikingly different from the later work in the milieu it depicts as well as in narrative mode. One may well be far more struck at first with the contrasts between the two novels than with their similarities. The technique of *The Awkward Age* is severely objective. In it, James has pared authorial commentary to the bone. A series of dramatically presented "Occasions," almost wholly dialogue, supplants the author's characteristic use of a central observer.[1] The technique of *The Ambassadors* is lavishly impressionistic. In it, picture and scene alike are filtered generally—if not, to be sure, absolutely consistently—through the subtle meditative consciousness of Lambert Strether. In the earlier work, as in all of his major fictions of the nineties, James deals with English characters in London and its environs. In the later one, he treats American and French characters, primarily in Paris and its *banlieu. The Awkward Age* has left many readers in doubt as to where, among its personnages, James's sympathies lie. In *The Ambassadors*, few readers have failed to grasp James's deeply sympathetic relation to his protagonist, whose complex "process of vision" is an analogue for the creative artist's visionary apprehension of the world.[2]

1. Henry James, Preface to *The Awkward Age*, in *AN*, 110.
2. Henry James, Preface to *The Ambassadors*, in *AN*, 308.

Yet, despite these differences between the two novels, in both of them the formal enactment of a spiral dialectic is essential to James's affirmation of moral values. Several remarks in James's preface to *The Awkward Age* are indicative of the dialectical habit of mind—the story-teller, James suggests, "is terribly at the mercy of his mind"—that both underlies the plan of the novel and dominates his description of it. James confesses, using a favorite and oft-repeated figure, that the finished work had quite unexpectedly come to be "so considerable a mass" compared to "the germ sunk in it and still possibly distinguishable." This Coleridgean metaphor of "an unforeseen principle of growth" governing the development of the work of art is closely related to an assertion James makes later in the preface, that in *The Awkward Age* one may

> see the grave distinction between substance and form in a really wrought work of art signally break down. I hold it impossible to say, before "The Awkward Age," where one of these elements ends and the other begins. . . . They are separate before the fact, but the sacrament of execution indisolubly marries them, and the marriage, like any other marriage, has only to be a "true" one for the scandal of a breach not to show. . . . But his [the artist's] ground once conquered, in this particular field, he knows nothing of fragments and may say in all security: "Detach one if you can. You can analyse in *your* way, oh yes—to relate, to report, to explain; but you can't disintegrate my synthesis."

When James describes the plot of the novel—the story of the effects upon a sophisticated London set of the coming out of two marriageable young women—he speaks of a dynamic transaction between extremes: "Hence the charm of the dramatic struggle reflected in my book, the struggle somehow to fit propriety into a smooth general case which is really all the while bristling and crumbling into fierce particular ones." The diagram James drew of the ten books through which the intrigue is played out—a drawing, as he relates, of "small rounds" in "the neat figure of a circle"—implies the pattern of the spiral dialectic, rounding back on its point of origin (*AN*, 98–116). This pattern is precisely, in fact, the revolution James enacts by beginning with a book titled "Lady Julia," who is the evoked avatar of a bygone, idealized propriety and grace, and then by ending with a book titled "Nanda," who is Lady Julia's match as far as her moral sense goes but who has been rendered graceless and unmarriageable by her exposure to the scandalous goings-on of her mother's *salon*.

Nanda, whose unrequited but enduring love for Vanderbank mirrors Longdon's devotion to her grandmother, Lady Julia—to whom Nanda bears a striking physical resemblance—is herself a sort of Lady Julia, a Lady Julia on a different level, the great irony of the conclusion of the novel being that the direction of the spiral may seem to be down rather than up.[3]

Hindered by the systematic suppression of authorial commentary in *The Awkward Age*, readers are hard put to assess James's authorial viewpoint. One would expect to find him allied to Mr. Longdon, Nanda Brookenham, and the better self of the divided Vanderbank, yet James often appears, in this novel, to be laying feathers on either side of a finely adjusted balance. Viewed in the light of *Le Misanthrope*, *The Awkward Age*, for F. W. Dupee, is "the poetry of the London hostess," vindicating Mrs. Brook, whose redeeming traits—her energy, her role as an organizer of "amiability, proportion, beauty, wit"—stand opposed to the graceless imagination of Nanda, who expresses little more than "the moral sense gone bleak" "as a chimney-top when the fire's out." But for F. R. Leavis, the book is "a tragedy conceived in an imagination that was robustly, delicately and clairvoyantly moral" and Nanda is the central figure, "the tragic heroine." The narrator's remoteness not only opens *The Awkward Age* to such clashing interpretations but also casts the very plot of the novel and the chief motives of the characters into an obscurity only penetrable by rigorous and patient attention, though the rewards for scrutiny amply repay the effort.[4]

The Awkward Age, then, can never be an easy book. Its dizzying ambiguities, the apparent relativity of the moral issues it engages, and even its obscurities express, deliberately or not, James's subject: the crumbling of social values, the withering of the capacity for authoritative discrimination. For all of his amusement and sophistication, James sounds here and there in this novel notes of a deeper apprehension about the fate of society than he had hit in *The Prin-*

3. For a very different, primarily spatial (as opposed to temporal) account of the circular form of *The Awkward Age*, see Georges Poulet, *The Metamorphoses of the Circle*, trans. Carley Dawson and Elliot Coleman (Baltimore, 1967), 319, and also the critique of Poulet's analysis in Geoffrey Hartman, *Beyond Formalism: Literary Essays 1958–1970* (New Haven, 1970), 51–56.

4. F. W. Dupee, *Henry James* (New York, 1965), 121, 172–76; F. R. Leavis, *The Great Tradition: George Eliot, Henry James, Joseph Conrad* (New York, 1973), 170.

cess Casamassima, which dealt outright with the specter of revolutionary upheaval. The subversion in *The Awkward Age,* however less obtrusive, is perhaps more insidious, for now it is not the work of an ill-matched lot of anarchists but of modernity itself. "We've all come," says Nanda, quoting Mitchy, "to a pass that's the end of everything."[5] From James's *Notebooks,* we know that *The Awkward Age* first occurred to him as a possible short story when he was reading Brada's *Notes sur Londres.* James was particularly impressed by Brada's discussions of the masculinization of women and of the demoralization of the aristocracy in England. Brada also inspired James with the vision of "the great broad, rich theme of a large satirical novel in the picture, gathering a big armful of elements together, of the *train dont va* English society before one's eyes—the great modern collapses of all the forms and 'superstitions' and respects, good and bad, and restraints and mysteries—a vivid and mere showy general hit at the decadences and vulgarities and confusions and masculinizations and feminizations—the materializations and abdications and intrusions, and Americanizations, the lost sense, the brutalized manner—the publicity, the newspapers, the general revolution, the failure of fastidiousness."[6] This is the barely submerged nightmare in *The Awkward Age,* the theme of declension, which one glimpses in the repetition by various characters of figures that suggest James's anxiety, images, for example, of advertising posters (advertising is of course an object of enormous implicit loathing in *The Ambassadors*), of equestrian circus acts (used to describe Mrs. Brook and related to circus images employed for others of James's expert, self-serving intriguers, including Madame Merle and Maud Lowder), and of levitation (in which case the ever-present danger of rising to the heights of sophistication is that of an abrupt drop into crashing vulgarity).

Although it is designed to portray the dangerously fluid state of English social morality, *The Awkward Age* is at the same time structured to yield to close examination the authorial viewpoint that its narrator's withdrawal makes initially elusive. The ordonnance of "small rounds" around a center necessarily involves a system of mea-

5. Henry James, *The Awkward Age* (New York, 1908), Vol. IX of the New York Edition of Henry James (26 vols.; New York, 1907–17), 228; hereinafter cited parenthetically as *AA.*

6. F. O. Matthiessen and Kenneth B. Murdock (eds.), *The Notebooks of Henry James* (New York, 1947), 196.

surement and value. The constellation of books has as its central object not only what James calls "my situation, my subject in itself" (*AN*, 110) but also, implicitly at least, what he wants his readers to think and feel about that subject, the theme on which the "Occasions" of the story bear. James names each book in *The Awkward Age* for a character "whose influence or self-revelation is especially pertinent at that time."[7] Characters may vent sharply conflicting views in the course of an episode, but the titles give each book an overriding perspective, a prospect on the central object that becomes most clear when one correlates the title with the place of the "Occasion" in the overall plan of the novel.

Books One, Ten, Five, and Six have special prominence in the architecture of *The Awkward Age*. Book One, titled "Lady Julia," introduces James's major themes. These are all corrollaries to a decline in English society. Longdon's role is to intensify the reader's sense of the decline. We see later how his eighteenth-century home, Beccles, with its "old red surfaces" and "the long confirmation of time," suggestive "of panelled rooms, of precious mahogany, of portraits of women dead, of coloured china glimmering through glass doors, and delicate silver reflected on bared tables," is a "temple of peace," in opposition to Mrs. Brook's salon, the "temple of analysis." Longdon's note is above all his "beautiful" feeling for Lady Julia, who is set up in Book One as the standard of feminine grace and propriety according to which the masculinized modern women will be found wanting. Book Ten, "Nanda," balances Book One, for Nanda Brookenham, in spite of her shortcomings, rests at last in a devotion to Vanderbank every bit as hopeless and as fine as Longdon's devotion to her grandmother. "Any passion so great, so complete," says Mitchy, "is—satisfied or unsatisfied—a life" (*AA*, 224, 336, 349, 482). In her experience, her modernity, and her impressive way of knowing, she is very much her mother's daughter as well as a spiritual sister to Maisie, but in her proud, wounded retreat with Longdon she affirms the world figured by Lady Julia, to whom Longdon's adoption of Nanda is a memorial. The last episode thus, as mentioned earlier, returns upon the first at a different level, so that the novel is framed by Lady Julia's evocations and by a vision of Nanda as preeminently Lady

7. Jean Frantz Blackall, *Jamesian Ambiguity and "The Sacred Fount"* (Ithaca, 1965), 152.

Julia's granddaughter. Like Vanderbank's, Nanda's nature is divided, but in the end she validates her better self while Vanderbank betrays his.

Books Five and Six, "The Duchess" and "Mrs. Brook," are counterweights to the framing books. The Duchess is Mrs. Brook's foil, a consummate hypocrite who plays Arsinoé to Mrs. Brook's Célimène.[8] The Duchess raises her niece, Aggie, on the Continental system, which is opposed by James, in typical bipolar manner, to the English failure of system dramatized in the struggle of Mrs. Brook's set to deal with the emergence of Nanda. Such contrasts between the Duchess and Mrs. Brook are indeed important, but both women pursue strategies fundamentally inimical to the values represented by Lady Julia and Nanda. Juxtaposed at the center of the novel, they represent the far side of James's "neat figure of a circle," the extremes of its own antitheses—diagrammatically, the farthest point on the circle from its starting point—through which James's treatment of his subject passes before rounding back on its beginning.

Mrs. Brook's undeniable attractiveness derives chiefly from the wit and boldness with which she participates in the dismantling of traditional proprieties and also from her capacity for regarding herself in an ironic light. In his *Notebooks*, James approvingly cites Brada on the lamentable social declension of which Mrs. Brook's success is a clear symptom:

> 'Tel Gladstone, aujourd'hui Anglais jusqu'aux moelles, même dans une salutaire hypocrisie. Oui, assurément salutaire, et elle s'en va, elle disparait: encore quelques années et il n'en restera plus rien; et ce sera un grand dommage, car c'était une belle chose après tout, que de voir une puissante aristocratie, une société si riche et si forte, tant d'êtres divers tenus en respect par quelques fictions que suffisaient à défendre l'édifice social; c'était une salutaire illusion que de supposer toutes les femmes chastes, tous les hommes fidèles, et d'ignorer, de chasser résolument ceux qui portaient quelque atteinte visible à cette fiction. Ce respect des mots, cette pudeur de convention, provoquaient et developpaient néanmoins de réelles vertus: cela s'en va; dans certaines milieux cela a déjà disparu!'[9]

8. See Dupee, *Henry James*, 172.

9. Matthiessen and Murdock (eds.), *The Notebooks of Henry James*, 194–95. "Like Gladstone, English today to the marrow, even in a healthy hypocrisy. Yes, assuredly healthy, and it is going, it disappears: a few more years yet and nothing of it will remain; and that will be a great pity, for it was a beautiful thing after all to see a powerful aristocracy, a society so rich and so strong, so many

Readers today, too apt to overlook the seriousness with which James regarded the developments deplored here by Brada, are likely also to overvalue Mrs. Brook and to imagine that she embodies certain norms capable of competing with the values represented by Longdon, Nanda, and Lady Julia. We might, in this regard, take a cue from Mitchy's allusion to *I Henry IV* (see *AA*, 124). Mrs. Brook, like Falstaff, is a delightful, charming rogue. We warm to her as we never do to Nanda, who is too often graceless and cold. But, like Falstaff, Mrs. Brook embodies the corruption of the realm. She is a liar. She is treacherous. Her egotism and self-indulgence are prodigious. If for many readers she is the central figure of *The Awkward Age*, then that is at least in part because of the advantage in energy and in charisma that deviant characters in James frequently seem to have over morally straight, normative ones (Charlotte Stant's advantage over Maggie Verver, for example, and Kate Croy's over Milly Theale). The villains of many authors enjoy similar dramatic advantages (for example, Ahab's advantage over Starbuck, Edmund's over Edgar, Gloucester's over Richmond, Satan's over God in *Paradise Lost*, and so on). Nanda, on the other hand, may be thought of in relation to Prince Hal, for her virtue, like his, carries a chill. Yet bleak as Nanda may be, imaginatively impoverished and graceless as she surely is when she tells Vanderbank that her mother loves him, the wrong she suffers in her quiet, cruel struggle with her mother is far greater than any she inflicts. That, at last, is what James helps us to recognize by beginning the novel with a book named for Nanda's exemplary grandmother, Lady Julia, and by closing, in Nanda's book, with her impassioned outburst of tears.

"In spirit," Dupee says of *The Ambassadors*, "it recalls the urbane comedy of *The Awkward Age*, as if, having himself come to terms with the *femme du monde* in that novel, James was eager to show another elderly American accomplishing the same feat."[10] Dupee is

---

diverse beings held in respect by means of certain fictions that sufficed to uphold the social ediface. It was a healthy illusion to suppose all women chaste, all men faithful, and to ignore, resolutely to repel those who brought any visible taint upon that fiction. This respect for words, this modesty of convention, nevertheless provokes and develops some real virtues: it is on its way out; in certain quarters it has already disappeared!" [My translation].

10. Dupee, *Henry James*, 207.

thinking of Mrs. Brook as a prototype of Madame de Vionnet. There is something to be said for the comparison, though one ought to bear in mind that Mrs. Brook is a variety of *femme du monde* radically different from Madame de Vionnet, especially in that her peculiar roguish attractiveness depends precisely on her abandonment of the sort of *salutaire hypocrisie* that masks, for a considerable space of time, the sexual basis of Madame de Vionnet's passion for Chad and thus enables Strether to relax enough to appreciate her peculiar attractiveness and value. Strether's Countess is, after all, a creature of such high good taste that she could not possibly appear, as Mrs. Brook does to Longdon from the first, as the antithesis of the values Longdon associates with Lady Julia. The strongest parallel between the two women is unflattering to them both: they both compete with their daughters in affairs of the heart and dispose of the younger women, more or less ruthlessly, to their own advantage. But, though the situations are parallel, the intensities of the elements are very different. Nanda's commitment to Vanderbank is much more profound than Jeanne's to Chad, and Madame de Vionnet's passionate love for Chad is far deeper than Mrs. Brook's feeling for Vanderbank.

There is a far closer analogy between Longdon and Strether. Both are fifty-five years of age, single, and scrupulous to the point of fastidiousness. Both of them, furthermore, are provincials forced to uncover and to pass judgment upon the relations of a set of metropolitan sophisticates. Strether, though a much more subtle and complex being than Longdon, is at moments very like Nanda's guardian. In the beginning, for example, he is rigid in his denunciation of imputed vice ("She's base, venal—out of the streets"), and for some time he sees Madame de Vionnet in a glow of light not unlike the halo with which Longdon surrounds Lady Julia.[11] His feeling for Chad, when his faith in Chad is strong, and his feeling for Little Bilham as well, is of the same paternal, idealizing tenor as Longdon's response to Vanderbank, a figure finally perhaps even more disappointing than Chad turns out to be. The magnanimity with which Strether condones Little Bilham's "virtuous lie" implies something like the ethos of the genteel, bygone period Longdon harkens back to, the code of simply not saying, for the sake of sundry decencies, for the defense of *"l'édifice social,"* all that one, in a world of passion and pain, too inevitably

11. *AM*, 45.

knows. Each of these scrupulous gentlemen, moreover, commits himself to "save" others, Longdon declaring for Vanderbank and Nanda, Strether for Madame de Vionnet and Chad. In addition, Strether's New England conscience, though subtilized and rendered catholic by his initiation into European civilization, shapes his conduct right up to the final page of *The Ambassadors*, guiding him as Longdon is guided by the standards of his youth.

In many other regards, *The Ambassadors* admits of comparison with *The Awkward Age*. The symbolic relationship of Paris to Woollett is parallel to that between London and Beccles. The part played by the deceased Lady Julia is nearly as pervasive and as vivid as that of the absent Mrs. Newsome, who, like Lady Julia, defines an extreme of opposition to the metropolitan milieu. In both works, contrasting methods of conducting the social lives of marriageable young women are portrayed through the use of foils, Little Aggie's to Nanda, Mamie's to Jeanne de Vionnet. Nanda and Jeanne both lose in sexual rivalries with their mothers. The overall structure of the twelve books of *The Ambassadors*, moreover, enacts Strether's journey of spiral return—his limited Massachusetts propriety evolves through a synthesis into a higher order of rightness—and thus the form of his experience is parallel to the design I have just described in *The Awkward Age*.

The Ambassadors has especially lent itself to dialectical description by virtue of its famous symmetries. Its shape, E. M. Forster observed, is that "of an hour-glass," and in it, he argues, pattern is triumphant at the expense of "the immense richness of material which life provides." It was, comments F. O. Matthiessen, the "roundness of structure" of the novel that "caused James' preference for the book." It is also frequently recognized that the symmetries of *The Ambassadors* rest heavily on formal antithesis and on the thematic array of polar oppositions. R. W. Stallman, for instance, says that "*The Ambassadors* builds on contraries, contradictions, ambivalences arising from poles of opposition." Robert Durr, in an archetypal analysis of the novel, sees Strether as seeking "the power of an enlarged consciousness, the power to transcend the evil of antitheses by including them in a more encompassing vision." In a brief note on Strether's relation to his Balzacian namesake, James W. Gargano calls Balzac's *Louis Lambert* "a dialectical novel" and offers a summation of Strether's experience as the resolution of antitheses, for Strether achieves, he says, "a knowledge which recognizes the validity of spiritual values without denying the existence of man's earthy and physical nature." Frederick C. Crews, writing about *The Ambassadors*, defines the Jamesian "true hero" as the possessor of "an aesthetic sense of Life's vastness and diversity" and the Jamesian villain as, by contrast, "practical," so that "inclusiveness and practicality are the opposite poles in a moral world whose supreme virtue is an open mind." Two comments on the dialectic of *The Ambassadors*, finally, seem especially resonant with my geometrical figure for the form of the novel, the design of spiral return. Granville H. Jones describes Strether as returning to lost innocence by means "of pure negation, of total renunciation," thus bearing out Jones's thesis that James's typical fiction is a "perfect circle of negation." Far more congenial to my affirmative reading of Strether's history than Jones's transcendence by "pure negation" is J. A. Ward's suggestion that "Strether's growth of mind follows a dialectical structure," for Ward goes on to speak of an "ascending spiral" that expresses "the three related forms of Strether's growth: sudden illumination, recurrent pattern, and steady ascension."[12]

Like the preface to *The Awkward Age*, James's preface to *The Ambassadors* makes clear the dialectical structure of the novelist's conception. The "*situation*," he confides, "clearly would spring from the play of wildness and the development of extremes." Strether performs "a revolution"—the same circular term appears in James's original notebook entry about the novel, dated in 1895—passing in its course "through alternations of darkness and light." James's choice of narrative mode, his achieving, for Strether, "the double privilege of subject and object," suggests that the intricate ironies of the novel depend on the dialectical tension between subject and object, a tension impossible to keep up in conventional first-person narration, with its confusion of the terms, its "terrible fluidity of self-revelation." The

12. E. M. Forster, *Aspects of the Novel* (London, 1927), 196, 209; Matthiessen, *Henry James: The Major Phase*, 19; R. W. Stallman, "'The Sacred Rage': The Time-Theme in *The Ambassadors*," *Modern Fiction Studies*, III (1957), 54; Robert A. Durr, "The Night Journey in *The Ambassadors*," *Philological Quarterly*, XXXV (1956), 29; James W. Gargano, "*The Ambassadors* and *Louis Lambert*," *Modern Language Notes*, LXXV (1960), 211, 213; Frederick C. Crews, *The Tragedy of Manners: Moral Drama in the Later Novels of Henry James* (New Haven, 1957), 33; Jones, *Henry James's Psychology of Experience*, 261, x; Ward, "*The Ambassadors* as a Conversion Experience," 366, 368.

characteristic alternation, furthermore, of picture and scene is justified in this preface "for the charm of opposition and renewal"—"everything in it that is not scene . . . is discriminated preparation, is the fusion and synthesis of picture." And, James adds in his closing remarks, "it wouldn't take much to make me further argue that from an equal play of such oppositions the book gathers an intensity that fairly adds to the dramatic" (*AN*, 314–26).

James's themes in *The Ambassadors* may be expressed as a series of oppositions: America and Europe, Protestant and Catholic, Woollett and Paris, age and youth, business and leisure, exploitation and appreciation, repression and tolerance, purchase and inheritance, innocence and initiation, equality and hierarchy, matriarchy and patriarchy, and so forth.[13] Again and again, characters are dialectically opposed to each other: Strether to Waymarsh and to Chad, Chad to Little Bilham, Madame de Vionnet and Miss Gostrey to each other and also to Mrs. Newsome and Sarah, and Mamie Pocock to Jeanne de Vionnet. Thus, for example, in Book Eighth, Chad Newsome discovers Strether and Waymarsh together and "was doubtless to be struck . . . with the sharpness of their opposition," and, a few pages later, Strether himself observes something in Mamie Pocock that gives her, in relation to Jeanne, "intensity and purpose, as the symbol of an opposition." The precision and lucidity of such oppositions in *The Ambassadors* arise in large measure from the character of Strether's consciousness, particularly from his analytic clarity about his own internal divisions. That "he was burdened, poor Strether—it had better be confessed at the outset—with the oddity of a double consciousness" and that "there was detachment in his zeal and curiosity in his indifference" declare "the same secret principle" that prompts "Strether not absolutely to desire Waymarsh's presence at the dock" "delightful as it would be to find himself looking, after so much separation, into his comrade's face" (*AM*, 17, 18, 202, 210). Stressed thus from the opening pages of the novel, Strether's oddity is not merely significant of a burdensome, Puritan self-consciousness; it is also exemplary of the mental conditions essential to the vigorous development and exercise of imagination considered as a power that arises from oppositions

13. For the last two pairs of terms, I am indebted to Sallie Sears's discussion in *The Negative Imagination*, 105–51, a dialectical analysis of *The Ambassadors* in which the possibilities for synthesis are foreclosed.

and that encounters antitheses in order to resolve them. Strether, that is, is gifted with a Coleridgean secondary imagination. When Coleridge posits "opposite and counteracting forces" in intelligence that profoundly affect "the living principle" and "the process of our own self-consciousness," he is laying down the basis for his theory of the secondary imagination, which "dissolves, diffuses, dissipates, in order to re-create" and which "at all events . . . struggles to idealize and to unify."[14] Without his "double consciousness," Strether would have offered James neither "the opportunity to 'do' a man of imagination" nor the consequent occasion to revel in the "demonstration" of a "process of vision," a process that is "the precious moral of everything" (*AN*, 308, 310).

The idea of seeing in *The Ambassadors* is multifaceted. It denotes, first of all, simple perception. The actual look of things constantly informs Strether's sensibility. Miss Gostrey's "broad red velvet band," the appearance of Madame de Vionnet at prayer in Notre Dame, the emergence of Madame de Vionnet and Chad, "exactly the right thing," into a landscape reminiscent of Lambinet, all signal through Strether's visual apprehension distinct stages in his development (*AM*, 42, 307). James does not, of course, treat seeing as a purely physical phenomenon. It is also a requisite for and index to one's capacity for aesthetic appreciation. What Strether sees in Chad when he first meets him in Paris is revelatory of his own sensitivity, of the extent to which he can respond to refinements of style. Vision in this second sense is a power of discrimination; it involves the imagination as much as the eye. Without such discrimination, there could not come into play the third and most important aspect of the idea of seeing in the novel, the concept of vision as a moral process—James's humanistic belief in the obligations incurred by those who see. Having seen, having discriminated, one must judge and act. Strether's genius is his responsiveness in this special moral sense to what he sees, and that is why his drama becomes, "under stress, the drama of discrimination" (*AN*, 316). His changing perceptions of Europe and America, of Madame de Vionnet and Chad, and of himself and Mrs. Newsome necessitate continual alterations of his intentions. When the things he sees do not accord

14. Samuel Taylor Coleridge, *Biographia Literaria or Biographical Sketches of My Literary Life and Opinions*, ed. George Watson (New York, 1975), 156, 164, 167.

with his preconceptions, he feels it incumbent upon him to change his views, to reassess his objectives, and to revise his plans of action. Since, moreover, the capacity to see and judge and the desire to do well are not sufficient to account for moral heroism of the sort Strether attains, one must add that James does not limit the imperative to see to objects outside the self: the most difficult requirement for the Jamesian hero is that he must see truly into himself, must recognize his own limits and possibilities so that he may act conscientiously within them.

Meaningful seeing, then, should culminate in meaningful decision. Strether not only sees in James's fullest sense of the word but also makes choices on the basis of what he sees. He sees, for example, what he has missed in life. He knows that he is "too old at any rate for what" he sees. Because of this knowledge of himself, because of his understanding of the force and depth of Madame de Vionnet's love for Chad—and also because of his high moral need not to profit personally from his embassy—he chooses to exclude his own love for her from his considerations. When Miss Gostrey asks if he is "really in love with" Madame de Vionnet, he says that "it's of no importance I should know . . . it matters so little—has nothing to do, practically, with either of us." Strether does not deny his friend's implication, but he affirms the fidelity of his intentions to the facts as he sees them. He will not let his feelings for Madame de Vionnet blur his own astute location of himself (*AM*, 132, 291).

Chad, by way of contrast, sees only imperfectly. Insofar as he has become a polished gentleman, insofar as he displays the modifications of manner and presence that make him credible as Madame de Vionnet's lover, one can say that his is an educable sensibility. Certainly his capacity to see and change is far greater than that of his sister. Yet James makes us increasingly aware, throughout the novel, of Chad's insensitivity, his lack of imagination, a sort of stupidity that has the effect, finally, of profound moral cowardice. It comes out in Madame de Vionnet's observation that Chad puts "every effort off on the woman." Our sense of it grows as we see Chad put off on Strether decisions that should properly be his own. But we do not fully grasp the extent of Chad's limitations until we come face to face with his talent for self-deception. In Book Twelfth, when he declares that he is "not a bit tired" of Madame de Vionnet—to whose commitment, passion, and capacity for suffering he is stupidly oblivious—Strether can only stare. Strether knows that Chad is lying. We know it. But Chad apparently does not. Failing in insight, consequently incapable of being straight with himself, Chad illustrates by negative example that one must see all around and through an issue in order to act rightly upon it (*AM*, 148, 337).

The characteristic form of Strether's process of vision is dialectical, both in his consideration of particular objects of observation and in his slowly unfolding apprehension of the large general issues with which his embassy faces him. Strether's changing attitude toward Chad exemplifies the dialectical growth of his understanding over the long run. Initially, he thinks of Chad as the "wretched boy" of Woollett's reprobation. Thus, as soon as Chad appears, with the look and deportment of an accomplished man of the world, Strether has "to face with a mere strained smile and an uncomfortable flush" the "contingency" "that Chad should not be Chad." By the middle books of the novel, Strether has accepted the idea of a transformed Chad, the antithesis of his presupposition, a perception he defends, to the detriment of his personal prospects with Mrs. Newsome, as late as his great confrontation with Sarah Pocock at the end of Book Tenth. At last Strether comes to see that Chad's conversion is not intrinsic but that it is in part merely external and in part expressive of the value with which Chad has been invested by others. Madame de Vionnet

> had made him better, she had made him best, she had made him anything one would; but it came to our friend with supreme queerness that he was none the less only Chad. Strether had the sense that *he*, a little, had made him too; his high appreciation had, as it were, consecrated her work. The work, however admirable, was nevertheless of the strict human order, and in short it was marvelous that the companion of mere earthly joys, of comforts, aberrations (however one classed them) within the common experience, should be so transcendently prized.

This attitude, the perception that Chad has been the object of admirable work "nevertheless of the strict human order," is a synthesis of the extremes of Strether's view of Chad, moderating both his original denigration of his prospective son-in-law and his subsequent idealization of him (*AM*, 45, 90, 332).

Particular incidents of observation by Strether nearly always exhibit the "play of oppositions" so favored by his author. The prelude to his initiation in the European discrimination of types, for example, is his imagination of Mrs. Newsome as like Queen Elizabeth and of Miss Gostrey as like Mary Stuart, "an antithesis" in which he "could rest for an instant gratified." When he first observes Chad's apartment, Strether is drawn further than he has yet ventured into seduction by European values "by the presence of ornament as positive as it was discreet, and by the complexion of the stone, a cold fair grey, warmed and polished a little by life." In the following paragraph, he poses an architectural opposition to Chad's home, his own "admittedly secondary hotel" "all indoor chill, glass-roofed court and slippery staircase," which "expressed the presence of Waymarsh." Similarly, Madame de Vionnet first appears to him "dressed in black, but in black that struck him as light and transparent," and she so disarms him that he wonders if his idea of "going straight" is not in fact "already going crooked." In general, Madame de Vionnet's supreme mastery of harmony in variety is the note of her effect on Strether: "she was so odd a mixture of lucidity and mystery. She fell in at moments with the theory about her he most cherished, and she seemed at others to blow it into air. She spoke now as if her art were all an innocence, and then again as if her innocence were all an art" (*AM*, 43, 69, 70, 128, 230). Paris itself, for Strether, is a virtual chimera of oppositions:

> His greatest uneasiness seemed to peep at him out of the imminent impression that almost any acceptance of Paris might give one's authority away. It hung before him this morning, the vast bright Babylon, like some huge iridescent object, a jewel brilliant and hard, in which parts were not to be discriminated nor differences comfortably marked. It twinkled and trembled and melted together, and what seemed all surface one moment seemed all depth the next. (*AM*, 64)

The dualism of such perceptions depends only in part, however, upon Strether's double consciousness and his habit of looking all around a question, his open-minded willingness to entertain contraries. For James's fictions generally and characteristically bristle with the treachery of appearances. Whatever surface James presents is more likely than not to conceal perilous depths. Jim Pocock's description of his wife and mother-in-law might be taken as emblematic of this aspect of the oppositional element in *The Ambassadors*. They conceal their savage intensity in quietness: "they wear their fur the smooth side out," and "it's when they're prostrate that they most sit up" (*AM*,

215, 217). Sallie Sears comments effectively on the broad implications in James of this sort of deceptiveness:

> One of the main traits of James's symbolic world is indirection: of thought, speech, behavior, and feeling. It manifests itself in part in the persistent, almost ritualistic use of social masks and deceptive appearances, upon the uncovering of which so much of his ironic effect depends. Typically, the closest "friend" (Madame Merle, Kate Croy), unmasked, is the deadliest enemy; the "faithful" husband or lover in fact deeply attached to someone else; the affectionate mother (Mrs. Brook, Charlotte Verver) the most ruthless sexual rival. In these kinds of oppositions and reversals, and in the starkness of the conflict, the agony of betrayal so near to home, there is something reminiscent of the "ghastly premises," as Nietzsche characterizes them, lurking in the plot of classical tragedy.[15]

Strether encounters a world, then, in which the deceptiveness of appearances might be said to collaborate with his own characteristic knack for making out a doubleness in things.

Again and again Strether undergoes experiences that might be termed scenes of delayed recognition, incidents that aptly illustrate the interaction of his double consciousness with the misleading look of things. In Book Second, he sees a young man step out on Chad's balcony, and several moments pass before he concludes that the figure is not "Chad altered" but someone entirely new. In Book Third, "a gentleman, a stranger," enters the box Strether occupies with Miss Gostrey and Waymarsh at the Comédie Française, and a full paragraph elapses before Strether sees that they "were in presence of Chad himself." In Book Seventh, Strether for some time studies a woman praying in Notre Dame, imagining her to be "some fine firm concentrated heroine of an old story" before recognizing her, when she approaches him, as Madame de Vionnet. In Book Ninth, he enters Sarah Pocock's hotel room unattended, catches sight of a woman on the balcony—seeing only the color of her dress, for she was "so placed between the windows as to be hidden from him"—and concludes that the person is Sarah, discovering only after she moves into full view that it is Mamie. In Book Eleventh, finally, at the stupendous peripety of the novel, Strether recognizes Madame de Vionnet and Chad as the couple who have floated into his field of vision and who had first appeared to him as strangers, "figures, or something like them" who

15. Sears, *The Negative Imagination*, 129–30.

all day "had been wanted in the picture" (*AM*, 69, 89, 172, 247, 307).

In all of these cases, initial appearances are shown to be misleading. Strether sees, mistakes, then recognizes, always with the effect of a reversal of what he first supposed. Persons he first took to be strangers become those with whom he has most to do or, alternatively, an original, tentative identification yields dramatically to a new one. That James of course is very much of his particular moment in the history of the Romantic posture is apparent in his handling of these transformations of insight. Conrad's similar mode of dramatizing the psychological experiencing of the act suggests how centrally James's method represents the sensibility of his period. Compare, for example, Marlow's slow realization that the steamboat is under attack in "Heart of Darkness" or the moment in "Youth" when the ship blows up and Marlow's first thought as he flies through the air is that Chips is playing some sort of trick on him. One notes too that all of Strether's delayed recognitions, except the meeting with Mamie in Book Ninth, occur at moments when his imagination is engaged with one of the arts—with architecture when he considers the possibility that Little Bilham might be Chad, with theater when he discovers that the intruding stranger *is* Chad, with the novel of romance when he envisions Madame de Vionnet as a "heroine," and with painting when she and Chad float into the Lambinet-like landscape in which Strether has passed his day in the country.

This last example is particularly interesting because of its close parallel to the National Gallery scene in *The Wings of the Dove*, for which it was undoubtedly the prototype.[16] Milly Theale overhears an American woman commenting to her daughters on what Milly first assumes to be a painting: " 'Handsome? Well, if you choose to say so.' It was the mother who had spoken, who herself added, after a pause during which Milly took the reference as to a picture: 'In the English style.' "[17] Turning, finding herself "in fact among small Dutch pictures" and not, as the overheard remark had led her to think, in the midst of English works, Milly soon spots a gentleman who had clearly in-

16. J. A. Ward also compares these two scenes; see his *The Imagination of Disaster: Evil in the Fiction of Henry James* (Lincoln, 1961), 133.

17. Henry James, *The Wings of the Dove* (2 vols.; New York, 1909), Vols. XIX–XX of the New York Edition of Henry James (26 vols.; New York, 1907–17), XIX, 291; hereinafter cited in footnotes and parenthetically in the text as *WDI* and *WDII* respectively.

spired her compatriot's comment. In a sequence of gradual realizations, Milly first makes out that the gentleman is Merton Densher, then that someone is noticing her in turn—though Densher still has not done so—then that the one watching her is Kate Croy, that Kate is Densher's companion, and that, when mutual recognitions are at last exchanged, there is a "monstrous oddity" in their encounter that must be covered by a superlative effort on Kate's part to make Milly "provisionally take everything as natural" (*WDI*, 292–94).

The parallel in *The Ambassadors* is nearly exact. Having all day treated his sensuous apprehension of a rural excursion primarily as aesthetic data, as the very reproduction in nature of a Lambinet landscape he had wanted to buy many years ago, Strether observes Madame de Vionnet and Chad floating into the frame as wanted compositional elements, as "exactly the right thing" supplied as if "on purpose to fill up the measure." He notices then, in succession, their particular persons—"a young man in shirtsleeves, a young woman easy and fair," a couple "expert, familiar, frequent"—then that he has been noticed by the woman, the boat at the same time drifting "wide, the oarsman letting go," next that the woman is Madame de Vionnet, then that her companion is Chad, and at last that there is some question about acknowledging their mutual recognition, which Strether resolves by "agitating his hat and his stick and loudly calling out." Afterwards, after the "sharp fantastic crisis" of the narrowly averted "violence of their having 'cut' him," Strether sees "that they had something to put a face upon, to carry off and make the best of, and that it was she who, admirably on the whole, was doing this." Milly and Strether are forced in these encounters to take in similar revelations: Milly glimpses the complicity of Kate and Densher that Kate had been at pains to keep from her; Strether sees at last what Chad and Madame de Vionnet have been intent on keeping from him, that theirs is a relationship of physical intimacy (*AM*, 307–310).

One reason why so many of the scenes of delayed recognition come about during moments of aesthetic contemplation is surely that James wants to intensify the responsiveness of the observers to the imminent revelation. Because they have been engaged with works of art, the revelations find them in states of heightened receptivity to the look of things. The reader is similarly affected. As Matthiessen points out in his discussion of Strether's discovery of the adultery, "the skill with which James has held our eyes within his frame has so heightened the significance of every slight detail that such a recognition scene leaps out with the force of the strongest drama."[18] That the scenes are prolonged, involving vision and revision, bespeaks James's intense interest in the process of consciousness and allows him to show how the realizations develop dialectically in ironic reversals of the onlookers' presuppositions and initial impressions. Aesthetic detachment collapses by degrees into wholly unexpected personal involvement. This is particularly true of the two incidents just examined. Their force derives in large measure from a dynamic opposition between art and life. Art establishes the frame within which artful, human subterfuges are laid bare. The intrusion of life into the frame destroys the perfect charm of art by revealing the deceptiveness of particular characters and also by inspiring them to embarrassing, if heroic, efforts to cover up (though in the National Gallery scene, to be sure, the cover-up succeeds, abetted by Milly's own willingness to be taken in). Strether, moreover, is brought to realize the duplicity of Madame de Vionnet, who has been so eminently the embodiment of European civilization and culture, the shining exemplar, like Gloriani, of an apparently successful European fusion of life and art.[19] Such a synthesis is clearly a Jamesian ideal, but the stress here lies on its highly problematic nature. In Strether's great recognition scene, art and life are juxtaposed in such a way that they expose each other, and what had seemed "exactly the right thing" at the moment when the lovers "had so remarkably swum into Strether's ken" turns out, in the course of a process of intense observation, to have been what Strether knows the conscience of Woollett would consider a very wrong one (*AM*, 312).

I should like to point out, in the remainder of the present chapter, the prevalence of polarities and their movement at critical moments toward resolution at various levels of organization in *The Ambassadors*, beginning with small compositional units and working toward a more detailed account than I have yet given of the transformation Strether undergoes throughout the entire course of the novel.

18. Matthiessen, *Henry James: The Major Phase*, 36.

19. Of course, what underlies the sculptor's fine surface is, however elegant, still merely appetite, whereas what underlies Madame de Vionnet's beautiful surface is an intense, passionate sincerity, both in her love for Chad and in her deep desire to have Strether's respect.

The novel is rich, first of all, in oxymoronic phrases, the most condensed expressions of James's polarities. Here are a few representative items from the long catalogue of such phrases that might be drawn from *The Ambassadors*: Strether's past had been "a dreadful cheerful sociable solitude, a solitude of life or choice, of community"; "strange and beautiful" to Strether is Madame de Vionnet's "soft acuteness"; as for Mrs. Newsome, "he had literally heard her silent"; Waymarsh turns a "sombre glow" upon Strether; and, at the very end of the novel, Miss Gostrey sighs "it at last all comically, all tragically, away" (*AM*, 61, 181, 208, 224, 271, 345). These phrases are closely related to one of James's favorite devices, recurrent in *The Ambassadors*, the proposal of antithetical descriptions, summaries, and interpretations, as in the following examples: "too stupid or too intelligent"; "he had either soared above or sunk below"; "it was too late—unless indeed it were possibly too early"; "they might take their choice of his doing it from humility or from pride" (*AM*, 132, 176, 223, 263).

Throughout the novel, sentences built upon antithesis are abundant. These are often, moreover, among the most telling and memorable descriptions of the characters and of their relations to each other. Strether, for instance, must confess to Miss Gostrey that "he was Lambert Strether because he was on the cover, whereas it should have been, for anything like glory, that he was on the cover because he was Lambert Strether." When Strether finds himself deeply impressed by Chad's grey hair, it becomes clear that "if Strether was to feel young . . . it would be because Chad was to feel old." Later, contrasting Marie de Vionnet's *objets* with those collected by Chad and Miss Gostrey, Strether reflects that the latter two persons "had rummaged and purchased and picked up and exchanged, sifting, selecting, comparing; whereas the mistress of the scene before him, beautifully passive under the spell of transmission—transmission from her father's line, he quite made up his mind—had only received, accepted and been quiet." Chad, Strether reports to Miss Gostrey, "was amazed to find the hand I had laid on him to pull him over suddenly converted into an engine for keeping him still." When Strether visits Madame de Vionnet in Book Ninth, chapter I, he is "divided in truth between the sense of having everything to tell her and the sense of having nothing at all" (*AM*, 62, 93, 146, 192, 228). When he visits her in Book Twelfth, Strether's complicated simultaneous impression of her wonderful, rare distinction and of her terrible, common suffering is expressed in the following sentence, in which each of the last two main clauses develops by a law of opposition to what has come before it: "She was older for him to-night, visibly less exempt from the touch of time; but she was as much as ever the finest and subtlest creature, the happiest apparition, it had been given him, in all his years, to meet; and yet he could see her there as vulgarly troubled, in very truth, as a maidservant crying for her young man" (*AM*, 323).

Similar laws of opposition govern the form of the ideas entertained by the characters. Thus, Madame de Vionnet's final wisdom is "that it's not, that it's never, a happiness, any happiness at all, to take. The only safe thing is to give." Both Strether and Miss Gostrey think of polar extremes as establishing fields within which one may swing, rapidly, violently, from one pole to the other. Thus, Strether thinks that "it was the advantage of his having let his fancy lose itself for a little in the gloom that, as by reaction, the prospect began really to brighten from the moment the deputation from Woollett alighted on the platform." He sees Chad as in pendular alternation between the pull of Woollett and the attractions of Paris, and he takes comfort "in the swing of Chad's pendulum back from that other swing, the sharp jerk towards Woollett, so stayed by his own hand." Miss Gostrey has seen Strether himself as in an analogous predicament, and Strether realizes in the end that she has known all along the nature of Chad and Madame de Vionnet's friendship but that she has concealed her knowledge from him to prevent "a revulsion in favour of the principles of Woollett. She had really prefigured the possibility of a shock that would send him swinging back to Mrs. Newsome." Strether has the same idea in mind when he warns Little Bilham, in the midst of his famous declaration for life in Book Fifth, that he is "a case of reaction" and that "the voice of reaction should, no doubt, always be taken with an allowance." Strether's version of naturalistic determinism, as he delivers it to Little Bilham in the same speech, is a dialectical affair, a question of the relation of "a helpless jelly, one's consciousness," to the "mould, either fluted and embossed, with ornamental excrescences, or else smooth and dreadfully plain," into which it is poured. Rather than wholly support either of the two opposed ideas of determinism and freedom, however, Strether finds a *via media*: he affirms determinism, but then dodges the apparently logical consequence of denying free will by endorsing an existential commitment to "the illusion of freedom" as a moral imperative—"Do what you like so long as you don't make *my* mistake. For it was a mistake. Live!" Strether's idea that one ought consciously to act as if one were free is a synthesis of the two conceivable absolutist positions in the philosophical contest of necessity and freedom. His position, in short, constitutes a moderation of extremes (*AM*, 132, 200, 202, 321, 328).

The dialectical structure of the ideas considered by the characters in *The Ambassadors* is reiterated in the dialogues in which they engage. Repeatedly, James's highly stylized dialogues turn upon exchanges of opposing terms. Consider, for example, the following conversation between Strether and Miss Gostrey:

> "What—by failure—do you stand to lose?"
>
> He still, however, wouldn't have it. "Nothing!" he exclaimed, and on the messenger's at this instant reappearing he was able to sink the subject in their responsive advance. When, a few steps up the street, under a lamp, he had put her into her four-wheeler and she had asked him if the man had called for him no second conveyance, he replied before the door was closed. "You won't take me with you?"
>
> "Not for the world."
>
> "Then I shall walk."
>
> "In the rain?"
>
> "I like the rain," said Strether. "Goodnight!"
>
> She kept him a moment, while his hand was on the door, by not answering; after which she answered by repeating her question. "What do you stand to lose?"
>
> Why the question now affected him as other he couldn't have said; he could only this time meet it otherwise. "Everything." (*AM*, 56)

Immediately there is another reversal. Miss Gostrey, who has just melodramatically rebuffed Strether ("Not for the world"), now melodramatically pledges herself to him ("Till death!").

Similar instances abound, and I shall cite only a few in the interest of brevity. When Miss Gostrey tells Strether that "everything's impossible," he replies that "I see where you're coming out. Everything's possible." Since Strether and Miss Gostrey are among the Jamesian elect who are "able remorselessly to analyze," their discussions in particular are full of antitheses and, occasionally, of resolutions of them, as when she pronounces "mere battered indifference" to be the *tertium quid* between "exaltation" and "courage" and also as when Strether tells her, apropos of the Review he edits under Mrs. Newsome's patronage, "Oh we're not loved. We're not even hated. We're only just sweetly ignored." But characters other than Miss Gostrey have the same sorts of conversations with Strether. "You may," Madame de Vionnet tells him, "no doubt, often pull up when things become *too* ugly; or even, I'll say, to save you a protest, too beautiful." Jim Pocock's remarks about Mrs. Newsome and Sarah at the end of Book Eighth, chapter II (see p. 28 above), are of the same variety. And Chad, despite the abysmal lack of imagination that he has "in common with his mother," deals neatly with the turn and counterturn of the following exchange with Strether, in which he tries to meet the questions of his mother's ambassador about Madame de Vionnet:

> "But is this lady against your interests at home?" Strether went on.
> "Not directly, no doubt; but she's greatly in favour of them here."
> "And what—'here'—does she consider them to be?"
> "Well, good relations!"
> "With herself?"
> "With herself."
> "And what is it that makes them so good?"
> "What? Well, that's exactly what you'll make out if you'll only go, as I'm supplicating you, to see her."
> Strether stared at him with a little of the wanness, no doubt, that the vision of more to "make out" could scarce help producing. "I mean *how* good are they?"
> "Oh awfully good."
> Again Strether had faltered, but it was brief. It was all very well, but there was nothing now he wouldn't risk. "Excuse me, but I must really—as I began by telling you—know where I am. Is she bad?"
> " 'Bad'?" Chad echoed it, but without a shock. "Is that what's implied—?"
> "When relations are good?"

This, incidentally, is the same ironic play on the meanings of "good" and "bad" that occurs in *The Awkward Age* (see *AA*, 167 and, especially, 284) and also, by implication, in *The Wings of the Dove* (*AM*, 40, 47, 51, 136, 143–44, 298, 324).[20]

James's paragraphs in *The Ambassadors* characteristically move from initial statements to new, dialectically related propositions. In

20. See pp. 65–66, below.

the following example, Strether's sense of Mrs. Newsome during the period of awaiting the Pococks' arrival is explored:

> The increase of his darkness, however, and the quickening, as I have called it, of his tune, resided in the fact that he was hearing almost nothing. He had for some time been aware that he was hearing less than before, and he was now clearly following a process by which Mrs. Newsome's letters could but logically stop. He hadn't had a line for many days, and he needed no proof—though he was, in time, to have plenty—that she wouldn't have put pen to paper after receiving the hint that had determined her telegram. She wouldn't write till Sarah should have seen him and reported on him. It was strange, though it might well be less so than his own behaviour appeared at Woollett. It was at any rate significant, and what *was* remarkable was the way his friend's nature and manner put on for him, through this very drop of demonstration, a greater intensity. It struck him really that he had never so lived with her as during this period of her silence; the silence was a sacred hush, a finer clearer medium, in which her idiosyncracies showed. He walked about with her, sat with her, drove with her and dined face-to-face with her—a rare treat "in his life," as he could perhaps have scarce escaped phrasing it; and if he had never seen her so soundless he had never, on the other hand, felt her so highly, so almost austerely, herself: pure and by the vulgar estimate "cold," but deep devoted delicate sensitive noble. Her vividness in these respects became for him, in the special conditions, almost an obsession; and though the obsession sharpened his pulses, adding really to the excitement of life, there were hours at which, to be less on the stretch, he directly sought forgetfulness. He knew it for the queerest of adventures—a circumstance capable of playing such a part only for Lambert Strether—that in Paris itself, of all places, he should find this ghost of the lady of Woollett more importunate than any other presence. (*AM*, 195)

The wonderful paradox in the handling of Mrs. Newsome, whose absence intensifies her identity, is one of the signs "of artistic good faith" in which James particularly glories in the preface to the novel (*AN*, 319). In Book Second, feeling that Mrs. Newsome's "tone was even more in her style than in her voice," Strether had speculated that "he might almost, for the hour, have had to come this distance to get its full carrying quality" (*AM*, 60). Now, in Book Seventh, the paragraph just quoted fully develops the paradox, gradually reversing the idea in the opening sentences that Strether is "hearing almost nothing" from Mrs. Newsome—and that he is able to foresee an utter cessation of her letters—until, at the end of the concluding sentence, the absent woman's silence stands opposed by the climactic image of her "ghost" as "more importunate than any other presence."

Many of the books in *The Ambassadors* turn upon just such dramatized oppositions. Book Third, for example, opens with Strether's confession "that he had been captured" by Little Bilham, who, as he learns in Book Third, chapter I, is Chad's lieutenant, acting "on his daily instructions," and closes with Strether's resolution to take the offensive in his mission of getting Chad to return to Woollett, "to seize his chance" "by a night-attack, as might be." Book Fifth opens with Strether's periodic assurance to himself "that he shouldn't reach the truth of anything till he had at least got rid of" "his odious ascetic suspicion of any form of beauty" and closes with his taking from Chad, as testimony that Madame de Vionnet is "without reproach," the assertion that hers is indeed "a beautiful life." The first few paragraphs of Book Seventh present a Strether who sinks "his problem" and who is "trying to escape" from himself and from the necessity of judgment, and the last paragraph of the book finds him eager for confrontation with the Pococks, for a full accounting, "literally impatient to know the cost." The introduction to Book Ninth is Strether's complaint to Madame de Vionnet about the Pococks' failure, "as a policy," to acknowledge Chad's transformation; at the end of the book, after having learned that Madame de Vionnet and Chad have arranged a marriage for Jeanne—which greatly disconcerts Strether, disturbing his feelings about both Chad and the Countess—he discovers that indeed one of the Pococks, the remarkable Mamie, shares his perception of Chad and looks with a consciousness "disinterestedly tender" yet all-noting upon the relations of Chad, Madame de Vionnet, Jeanne, and Jeanne's fiancé, Monsieur de Montbron (*AM*, 70, 88, 93, 118, 144, 170–71, 198, 228, 253).

Not every book in the novel develops in this dramatic, ironic fashion, but the overall structure of the books, taken together, may be viewed as closely parallel to that of *The Awkward Age*, as a spiral dialectic in which the first and last books are critical for evaluation of the intervening ones and are opposed to the middle books, which present an extreme of opposition both to the original point of view and to the parallel, initiated, wider, wiser, final one. By the end of Book Seventh of *The Ambassadors*, Strether's attitude toward Chad Newsome's attachment has undergone a reversal: the proprieties of Woollett, under the banner of which Strether had been led to condemn Chad's life, have given way to his ever-enlarging sense of life's possibilities. The process of reversal—through which Strether comes to promise Madame de Vionnet that "I'll save you if I can," to assert that Chad "ought to be ashamed of himself" if he gives her up, and to assure her that he will see her through because "I can't in honour not see him [Chad]"—begins on the first page of the novel and is the cumulative effect of virtually every intervening passage, scenic or dramatic. Fluid medium that it is, Strether's consciousness is subject to minute and subtle gradations of discrimination and inference. One can, nevertheless, identify distinct stages in his progress. In Chester, for example, Strether is aware of enjoying, to a degree culpable to the moral sense of Woollett, the freedom and pleasure of a stroll with Miss Gostrey. He acknowledges that he is "always considering something else . . . than the thing of the moment," and he places himself in Miss Gostrey's hands with his admission of wanting ("Oh, unspeakably") to live more fully in the moment. He has thus, even in chapter I, moved some distance from Woollett. He has not yet gone far, but he is under way, and "it was already upon him even at that distance—Mr. Waymarsh was for *his* part joyless" (*AM*, 26–27, 152, 170, 181).

Books First and Second are as much dramatic as expository in that they depict the continual expansion of Strether's sensibility. The air of European civilization grows richer in London than it had been in Chester. Strether's imagination, inhaling deeply of it, casts the brilliant figure of Woollett's Mrs. Newsome as Queen Elizabeth to Miss Gostrey as Mary Stuart. The ironic opposition of the great Protestant queen to an image of her Catholic (symbolically Continental) rival is a measure of Strether's increasing alienation from Woollett, as had been his recognition, in the preceding chapter, that in Waymarsh's eyes Miss Gostrey might have been "a Jesuit in petticoats, a representative of the recruiting interests of the Catholic Church. The Catholic Church, for Waymarsh—that was to say the enemy, the monster of bulging eyes and far-reaching quivering groping tentacles—was exactly society, exactly the multiplication of shibboleths, exactly the discrimination of types and tones, exactly the wicked old Rows of Chester, rank with feudalism; exactly in short Europe" (*AM*, 38). The

Atlantic widens perceptibly in the middle of Book Second, when Strether arrives in Paris. He has a sense of freedom and possibility made poignant by his age and by his remorseful recollections of his young manhood. The measure of Strether's development in Books First and Second may be taken by comparing the remarks about Waymarsh with which each book opens and closes, remarks that delineate an increasingly sharp opposition between the two old friends.

Strether's superior reaction to Paris, his appreciation of the refinement of even the smallest details of European culture, makes "the difference" he feels in himself "so much greater than he had dreamed it would be." Yet the values of Woollett still command his intentions. In London, he practically gapes when Miss Gostrey suggests that Chad's supposed affair may be a refining rather than a brutalizing influence. In Paris, he rationalizes his sense of freedom as a gift from Mrs. Newsome, a further measure of his obligation to enforce her will on Chad. But his imagination is in ferment, however dimly he is aware of its undermining his old allegiance. More and more, throughout Book Third, Paris charms him. The discovery of Little Bilham is a delight to Strether. He is as much pleased by his having so quickly grasped the charm of his new friend as by the intrinsic appeal of "the little artist man." Waymarsh, embodying the "sacred rage" of the New England conscience, becomes an obstacle to Strether's enjoyment of Little Bilham, to whom Strether is drawn despite—or rather because of—Bilham's being "notoriously, as he puts it himself, not from Boston." Waymarsh reacts irritably to Strether's first intimations of the amenities of Chad's milieu.

> "Oh I don't want to meet him," Waymarsh impatiently growled. "Why don't he go home?"
>
> Strether hesitated. "Well, because he likes it over here."
>
> This appeared in particular more than Waymarsh could bear. "He ought then to be ashamed of himself, and, as you admit that you think so too, why drag him in?"

Strether does not "quite yet admit it." He is even perhaps a bit amused with Waymarsh, though he allows that "there's no doubt I want you to come down on me and squash me." Clearly, at any rate, he is far enough along in his transformation to be "so freely," as he says, taking "my chance of the possibility, the danger, of being influenced in a sense counter to Mrs. Newsome's own feelings." He has already "blindly, almost wildly" enjoyed the freedom of smoking with Miss Barrace when Chad enters at the climax of Book Third. Strether has now so far learned that he does not "know anything" as to take in, wide-eyed but unflinchingly, the made-over heir to Woollett's unnamed industry (*AM*, 60, 72–78).

Yet still Strether is of Woollett's party. In Book Fourth, chapter I, made nervous by his fresh apprehension of Chad, he hurriedly but clearly reports the purpose of his mission to the astoundingly "easy," "smooth" young man who will become, should his embassy succeed, his stepson. From this point on, the trend of Strether's initial reversal accelerates. Chad remonstrates with him for the prejudice his commission implies: "Do you think one's kept only by women?" Strether is more and more delighted with the charm of Chad's surroundings and with the interest of the society he frequents. But Chad, though he maintains he is free, exhibits alterations of a manner attainable only under the hand of a woman—a woman, moreover, of distinctly noble refinement. It does not lie within Strether's experience to make this out for himself, but the independence of his imagination allows him to take it from Miss Gostrey. If, however, the woman is "excellent," Strether infers that she may nevertheless be "of people who are *not* nice." Chad himself may not be, as Miss Gostrey says, "so good as you think." So Strether tries to brace himself, and so he is cautioned against the proven charm of Chad and the already guessed excellence of the unknown woman in Chad's life (*AM*, 96–97, 101, 106, 108).

Strether's conversation with Little Bilham in Book Fourth, chapter II, then, is of the utmost importance in persuading Strether to accept the goodness of Chad's relation, in making him see things the way Chad and Madame de Vionnet want him to see them, in a reversal of the suppositions and convictions of Woollett. Little Bilham, ever so winningly, turns an elegant trick for Chad. Despite careful qualifications, which are either ignored by Strether or taken by him as warrants of conscientious testimony, Little Bilham asserts how "awfully changed" Chad is and affirms the rarity of Chad's "case." And he assures Strether precisely on the issue with which Mrs. Newsome's ambassador has been concerned, for he tells him that Chad's "attachment" is "virtuous" (*AM*, 111–12). To see Chad's "excellent" woman as "virtuous," to take her virtue, moreover, as the explanation for Chad's not being, in fact, free, these things immensely complicate the situation for Strether. He sees perils ahead. He has yet to find out if the attachment is as Little Bilham states it. But he likes Little Bilham, so much so that even when he realizes, in Book Eleventh, that Bilham had intentionally misled him in Book Fourth, he characteristically and effortlessly forgives him. And Little Bilham's description of Chad's involvement as "virtuous" sets Strether up to fall as deeply under the spell of Madame de Vionnet as he does in Books Fifth, Sixth, and Seventh. Of course he does not, in Book Fourth, know the Countess, and he is even farther from settling on her as the woman in Chad's life, but her attraction for him, prepared for by Little Bilham's strategic dissembling in Book Fourth, will very shortly mark the greatest depth of Strether's seduction by Europe. After Book Seventh, his discriminating imagination, developed in the first half of the novel, carries him below the surface of the charms to which he has succumbed to a compassionate vision of good and evil, of passion and of human imperfection.

Book Fifth opens on the "wonderful day" on which Strether meets Madame de Vionnet, Jeanne, and Gloriani in the great artist's garden, a place that gives "him too, more than anything yet, the note of the range of the immeasurable town" and that sweeps "away, as by a last brave brush, his usual landmarks and terms." Several points in Book Fifth might be touched upon to indicate the new terms and landmarks—antitheses of Strether's usual ones—now emergent for the pilgrim of Woollett. He feels from the first Madame de Vionnet's "common humanity," and he is struck with the modesty she conveys to him and with her differing "scarcely at all—well, superficially speaking, from Mrs. Newsome or even from Mrs. Pocock." Although he had defined his mission to Miss Gostrey, in Book Second, as to protect Chad from life, he no sooner meets Madame de Vionnet than, strenuously and eloquently, he urges Little Bilham to "live all you can," for "it doesn't so much matter what you do in particular, so long as you have your life." Chad, who had been so much an object of Strether's disapprobation, has become "that rare youth he [Strether] should have enjoyed being 'like.'" Strether came to take Chad, for his own good, home from Europe as from a bad influence; now he has to take it from Chad that his reason for not returning to America with Strether is that Europe is "too visibly good for you." Indeed, Strether's earlier sense of the conceivably monstrous connotations of the Catholic church has been superseded here by his gratified impression of Gloriani's garden as "a great convent, a convent of missions, famous for he scarce knew what, a nursery of young priests." Finally, as mentioned a short time ago, Book Fifth opens with Strether's reflections on "his odious ascetic suspicion of any form of beauty" and closes with his taking it as a guarantee of Madame de Vionnet's virtue that Chad can call her life "beautiful" (*AM*, 118–20, 129, 132–33, 142, 144).

Books Sixth and Seventh complete the reversal thus dramatized in Book Fifth. In Book Sixth, chapter I, in "the air of supreme respectability" in which Madame de Vionnet receives him, Strether makes his promise to her that "I'll save you if I can." In Book Sixth, chapter III, by taking the privilege Madame de Vionnet offers of giving her binding advice about Jeanne, he implicates himself further in her affairs, and he sees that with her "thank you" "she had driven in by a single word a little golden nail, the sharp intention of which he signally felt." At the end of the book, Strether makes his opposition to his own original intention explicit by telling Little Bilham that Chad "ought to be ashamed of himself" if he gives up Madame de Vionnet. In Book Seventh, chapter I, Strether's "happy meeting" with Madame de Vionnet is "more lovely" than any other incident of his European excursion, and, at lunch with her, "for an hour, in the matter of letting himself go, of diving deep, Strether was to feel he had touched bottom." Never is Madame de Vionnet so romantically sublime for Strether as when, in a hilariously Protestant misreading of appearances, he is convinced that her relation with Chad must be "unassailably innocent" since "if it wasn't innocent why did she haunt the churches?" So he commits himself to "do his best to *be*" "a firm object" at which she will be "free to clutch," and so, promising to see Chad and her through, he feels the "golden nail she had then [in Book Sixth, chapter III] driven in" pierce "a good inch deeper." In the very next chapter, Strether's about-face, and Chad's too, become absolute, for Chad announces that he, for his part, is ready to return to Woollett, and Strether must implore him to "stay on with me" in Paris. The reason for his own transformation, as Strether explains to Miss Gostrey in Book Seventh, chapter III, is his perception of Chad's excellence, which determines him to resist giving Chad up to "the plan of which I was the mouthpiece," the plan of fetching the young man home to take up the advertising end of the family's manufacturing concern (*AM*, 146, 152, 164, 170, 174–76, 180–81, 188, 192).

All this time, to be sure, Strether is thoroughly in the dark about the true motives and feelings of Madame de Vionnet and Chad. He does not yet see that Chad is only Chad after all. He has no idea whatsoever of the cruelly high-handed treatment Chad has all the while been giving Madame de Vionnet nor of the desperate, brilliant, doomed campaign she has been waging to keep her lover. Whereas Books Fifth through Seventh show Strether at the antithesis of his original position, Books Eighth through Twelfth modify the extremity of his position in the middle books. The modification may first strike the reader as all taking place instantly, at the moment when Strether sees that his friends' friendship is a case of adultery. Yet, in the books following Book Seventh, though he never retracts an ounce of the appreciation that Madame de Vionnet and Chad have kindled in him, Strether sees their limitations—and his own as well—with ever greater accuracy, fullness, and complexity.

The process of vision now becomes more intricate than ever. From Book Eighth until the climactic revelation in Book Eleventh, chapter IV, Strether is subject to two countervailing currents. On the one hand, he feels himself more and more committed to the lovers and more and more inevitably opposed to Mrs. Newsome and to her extraordinary ambassador, Sarah. On the other hand, he has a rapprochement of sorts with another representative of Woollett, Mamie, and new information forces him to qualify his idealizations of Madame de Vionnet and Chad. The sudden, albeit momentary, inflation of Woollett's attraction for Strether at the time of the Pococks' arrival in Book Eighth, when he "gasped at what he might have lost," and the "quaint community of shipwreck" that he shares with Mamie in Book Ninth undermine his allegiance to the European party and help to prepare for his decision, despite his having permanently fallen out with Mrs. Newsome, to return to Woollett. When Madame de Vionnet tells him that she and Chad are marrying Jeanne, in Book Ninth, Strether feels immediately "that that wasn't the way Jeanne should be married," and he suffers indeed "a sensible shock," discovering in the matter "something ancient and cold" that has not hitherto figured in his sense of the Countess. Soon Chad gives Strether additional cause for concern. Although he persuades himself, in Book Ninth, chapter III, to interpret Chad's part in Jeanne's marriage as "his definite and final acknowledgment to Madame de Vionnet that he has ceased squirming," Strether learns from Chad in Book Eleventh, chapter I, that he does not want to care for her and that he is actively trying to succumb to the Pocock delegation (*AM*, 209, 237–38, 244, 251).

Since Book Eighth, then, James has been leading Strether around toward the position into which he is precipitated by his discovery of Chad and Madame de Vionnet on the river in the last chapter of Book Eleventh. Most critics have stressed the negative implications of the end of the novel. One commentator congratulates Strether for ceasing "to make the automatic equation between sex and sin, at least for others," but charges that "for himself the two sides of the dialectic remain unsynthesized, and the real end result of his adventures is to render America and Europe both unfit abodes for his soul." "The burden of *The Ambassadors*," Matthiessen complains, "is that Strether has awakened to a wholly new sense of life. Yet he does nothing at all to fulfill that sense." The implication of such remarks is that Strether, to validate his new knowledge, ought to remain in Europe—rather than return to America—and that he should act upon his discovery of all that he has missed by marrying Miss Gostrey, or, alternatively, by continuing, on the scene, in his devotion to Madame de Vionnet. But it is, after all, part of James's *donnée* for the novel, as Sears points out, that Strether's knowledge comes, for himself, too late. Furthermore, as one of these critics of Strether concedes, that Strether "does not fulfill himself is not a lapse on James's part but is, on the contrary, deliberate" since what Strether gains, as James says in the preface, is that "he now at all events *sees*" (*AN*, 308).[21]

Of course the objections of Matthiessen and others to what becomes of Strether at the end of the novel make good sense from certain moral perspectives prevalent in our own time. But those perspectives are at best irregularly coincident with James's. James may be humanely lenient with the adulterous women in his novels, sparing them the fates of their counterparts in, for example, Tolstoy and Flaubert, but he does not condone adultery and neither, ever, does Strether, so that even the suggestion that Strether does not see sin in the sexual relation of Chad and Madame de Vionnet is highly problematic and, in my

21. See Sears, *The Negative Imagination* 123, 145, and Matthiessen, *Henry James: The Major Phase*, 39.

opinion, probably anachronistic. When James contrasts "hot" morality and "icy" art (in "The Art of Fiction"), he means that the artist per se is not a moralist, but a cool-headed practitioner of his craft who may well delight, as Keats has it, as much in the creation of an Iago as of an Imogen; he does not mean that a work of art—whether an *Othello*, a *Cymbeline*, or one of his own fictions—does not finally have moral bearings and implications.

There is a great deal that disagrees with our hero's "spiritual stomach" as a consequence of his discovery in Book Eleventh, chapter IV. What consoles him about Madame de Vionnet's attempts to smooth over his discovery of the adultery is that he is not called upon openly to condone it, "that he hadn't been reduced to giving them his blessing for an idyllic retreat down the river." The quantity of what he is unwilling to condone—a refusal that I believe James affirms—underlies his explanation to Miss Gostrey that he will leave Paris precisely because Madame de Vionnet and he "might at any rate have been friends." James assumes, in fact, a community of values with his audience sufficient to make any special emphasis on the wrongness of adultery quite unnecessary. For this reason, he stresses, in Book Twelfth, the generosity of Strether's response to the lovers. The way of Woollett, as demonstrated by Sarah Pocock, is to withhold approval of any sort in the face of impropriety. Strether, by contrast, does not cease to value Madame de Vionnet's sublimity or Chad's attainments merely because he discovers their sin. The insight he has into Madame de Vionnet's anguish indeed strengthens the force of his appeal to Chad not to desert her, for he sees now that Chad's obligations to her go far beyond his fine manner (*AM*, 313, 332).

Strether's final position may be described as combining the best in his American background and in his European education. His scrupulousness comes out not only in his eschewing personal profit in his relations with Miss Gostrey and Madame de Vionnet (and also, of course, with Mrs. Newsome), but also in his continuing insistence, in Book Twelfth, on Chad's responsibility to his mistress. He no longer thinks Chad too good for Woollett, only that it would be too bad of him to abandon the Countess to the suffering to which we feel she is in any case doomed. Although some readers will inevitably feel that Strether should be condemned for a denial of Miss Gostrey's needs and for a retreat into what may appear to be a narrow, overly simple rectitude, he has the broader, more generous scruple that he is really in love with Madame de Vionnet, a scruple, of course, that he cannot spell out for Miss Gostrey. He does not decline her offer of marriage merely upon the grounds he articulates—indeed, the quantity of what delicacy suggests should remain unsaid between them accounts for a certain archness of tone in their last encounter. Strether's humanistic scrupulousness, above all, justifies Austin Warren's description of his development as "one of the latest refinements of the New England conscience," not as a rejection of it.[22] From Europe, Strether has learned to see. He comes, in the end, to *see* Mrs. Newsome, Madame de Vionnet, and himself as well. And he has developed, under the spell of Europe and under the constant steadying influence of his native moral sense, a capacity for disinterested appreciation, which is, for James, the highest form of love, and which is so far disinterested, in Strether's case, as to allow him to cherish what is fine in Madame de Vionnet even though her behavior—not only the adultery, of course, but even more her willingness to use him (and Chad as well)—clashes with his own moral scheme. Strether is, no doubt, as Miss Gostrey says, "dreadfully right," with a "horrible sharp eye for what makes" him so. Thus, however much he has been changed by the terrific education his sensibility has undergone, his journey has moved steadily toward the return: "He found on the spot the image of his recent history; he was like one of the figures of the old clock at Berne. *They* came out, on one side, at their hour, jigged along their little course in the public eye, and went in on the other side. He too had jigged his little course—him too a modest retreat awaited." His planned return is on one level literal, but it is also, as I have tried to suggest, metaphoric. Strether knows that he is going back "to a great difference," but he is not despondent about his future; at least he knows that "there will always be something" and says that "I shall see what I can make of it" (*AM*, 342–45). He returns, says Robert Durr, to "materially diminished but spiritually enlarged prospects in Woollett."[23] To deny that Strether is immensely improved by his experience seems to me to deny James his essential premise—the intrinsic value of the process of vision. If, finally, one concedes that Strether

22. Austin Warren, "The New England Conscience: Henry James and Ambassador Strether," *Minnesota Review*, II (1962), 160.
23. Durr, "The Night Journey in *The Ambassadors*," 25.

is better for all that he has been through, especially for the growth of his discriminating imagination, then his repatriation need not be seen as a "permanent exile" but as a return, on a higher level, to his point of origin, and thus as a nearly perfect enactment of the Romantic dialectic of spiral return.[24]

24. Sears, *The Negative Imagination*, 147.

CHAPTER TWO

The Sea-Change in *The Wings of the Dove*

I have chosen to focus my study of the dialectic of Henry James on his later novels because I believe that the mature prose is a more sensitive and revealing register of his distinctive character as a writer than the prose of his early and middle periods. Some readers, as Henry James said of his brother William, are "constitutionally unable" to enjoy the late novels. The style of the major phase is far more complex than James's earlier style. Its syntax is more elaborate. Periodic sentences with an enormous capacity for qualification abound. There is an amazing density of figurative language. Metaphors tend, increasingly, to serve where similes would once have sufficed, and they also tend, especially in *The Wings of the Dove* and *The Golden Bowl*, by rich accretion, to become symbols. The diction, especially because of experiments with translated French and modified English and American idioms, is highly eccentric. The technique of James's late novels, moreover—the author's quest for a key that will fit "both the dramatic and the narrative lock"—is for many readers a source of further mystification because of the confinement of point of view to selected, shifting reflectors, the dramatic suppression of crucial scenes, the strategic withholding of information, the alternation of picture and scene, and the habitually foreshortened endings.[1]

Published before *The Ambassadors*, *The Wings of the Dove* was

1. Henry James to William James, October 22, 1905, in Percy Lubbock (ed.), *The Letters of Henry James* (2 vols.; New York, 1920), II, 43; Matthiessen and Murdock (eds.), *The Notebooks of Henry James*, 188.

nevertheless written after it, the second of the completed novels of the major phase in order of composition. Critics have often drawn illuminating contrasts and comparisons between *The Wings of the Dove* and James's first indisputably great novel, *The Portrait of a Lady*.[2] Before turning to *The Wings of the Dove*, I should like to point out some of the polarities and syntheses operative in James's revision of 1906–1908 of *The Portrait of a Lady*, first published in book form in 1881. Consider, for instance, the following description of Ralph Touchett, striking because of the way James shifts, by fine gradations, from calling Ralph's attitude toward his fatal illness "indifference" in the first sentence of the paragraph to calling it "serenity" in the last sentence:

> A secret hoard of indifference—like a thick cake a fond old nurse might have slipped into his first school outfit—came to his aid and helped to reconcile him to sacrifice; since at the best he was too ill for aught but that arduous game. As he said to himself, there was really nothing he had wanted very much to do, so that he had at least not renounced the field of valour. At present, however, the fragrance of forbidden fruit seemed occasionally to float past him and remind him that the finest of pleasures is the rush of action. Living as he now lived was like reading a good book in a poor translation—a meagre entertainment for a young man who felt that he might have been an excellent linguist. He had good winters and poor winters, and while the former lasted he was sometimes the sport of a vision of virtual recovery. But this vision was dispelled some three years before the occurrence of the incidents with which this history opens: he had on that occasion remained later than usual in England and had been overtaken by bad weather before reaching Algiers. He arrived more dead than alive and lay there for several weeks between life and death. His convalescence was a miracle, but the first use he made of it was to assure himself that such miracles happen but once. He said to himself that his hour was in sight and that it behoved him to keep his eyes upon it, yet that it was also open to him to spend the interval as agreeably as might be consistent with such a preoccupation. With the prospect of losing them the simple use of his faculties became an exquisite pleasure; it seemed to him the joys of contemplation had never been sounded. He was far from the time when he had found it hard that he should be obliged to give up the idea of distinguishing himself; an idea

2. The *locus classicus* of comparative studies of these novels is Ernest Sandeen's "*The Wings of the Dove* and *The Portrait of a Lady*: A Study of Henry James's Later Phase," *PMLA*, LXIX (1954), 1060–75. See also Lotus Snow's "The Disconcerting Poetry of Mary Temple: A Comparison of the Imagery of *The Portrait of a Lady* and *The Wings of the Dove*," *New England Quarterly*, XXXI (1958), 312–39.

> none the less importunate for being vague and none the less delightful for having had to struggle in the same breast with bursts of inspiring self-criticism. His friends at present judged him more cheerful, and attributed it to a theory, over which they shook their heads knowingly, that he would recover his health. His serenity was but the array of wild flowers niched in his ruin.[3]

The changes James made from the original version of this paragraph work to raise Ralph's preoccupations from a primarily material plane to a spiritual one. In the first version, for example, Ralph had discovered "the delights of observation," not "the joys of contemplation." James's revision also clarifies a meaning that was latent but obscure in the original, that Ralph has undergone a spiritual evolution, that his "serenity" is a higher form of the first term in the paragraph, "indifference," representing the incorporation into his awareness of the painful experience of nearly dying in Algiers. This spiral development in Ralph's consciousness is not clearly brought out in the text of 1881 because there James had spoken, at the beginning of the paragraph, of "indolence," not of "indifference"; toward the end of the paragraph, of "native indifference," not of "inspiring self-criticism"; and in the last sentence, of Ralph's having "simply accepted the situation," not of "serenity."[4] The gradual process of qualification through which Ralph's indifference becomes serenity, finally, is a synthesis of an opposition in which "indifference" is the explicit antithesis and "involvement" the implicit thesis. This sort of transformation occurs throughout *The Portrait of a Lady* and, as we shall see shortly, throughout *The Wings of the Dove*.

In view of my examination later in the present chapter of transformations enacted in the marine imagery of *The Wings of the Dove*, James's use of marine imagery to dramatize changes in Isabel Archer's consciousness in *The Portrait of a Lady* is of particular interest. At the close of the first major section of the novel, Isabel envisions Caspar Goodwood as a possible future protector, "a clear and quiet harbour enclosed by a brave granite breakwater" (*PLI*, 323). In the end, she comes face to face with a chance to yield to that protection. In the

3. Henry James, *The Portrait of a Lady* (2 vols.; New York, 1908), Vols. III–IV of the New York Edition of Henry James (26 vols.; New York, 1907–1917), III, 53–54; hereinafter cited in footnotes and parenthetically in the text as *PLI* and *PLII* respectively.

4. Henry James, *The Portrait of a Lady* (Boston, 1882), 32–33. In this edition, the paragraph is the last half of a longer one.

following passage (again James's late revision, but this time without significant departures from the original text), the sea operates as a vast symbolic repository: upon it floats the whole of Isabel's history as felt in the particular moment; in it are contained Caspar's presence and the possibilities he offers her; through it the nearly overwhelming tide of her immediate emotions is metaphorically stated:

> Isabel gave a long murmur, like a creature in pain; it was as if he were pressing something that hurt her. "The world's very small," she said at random; she had an immense desire to appear to resist. She said it at random, to hear herself say something; but it was not what she meant. The world, in truth, had never seemed so large; it seemed to open out, all round her, to take the form of a mighty sea, where she floated in fathomless waters. She had wanted help, and here was help; it had come in a rushing torrent. I know not whether she believed everything he said; but she believed just then that to let him take her in his arms would be the next best thing to her dying. This belief, for a moment, was a kind of rapture, in which she felt herself sink and sink. In the movement she seemed to beat with her feet, in order to catch herself, to feel something to rest on. (*PLII*, 435)

The paragraph works out a transformation from pain and self-defense against Caspar to rapture and a vision of refuge in him. And the two are linked by the image of the sea, which is at first her hurt, her "immense desire to appear to resist," then her confusion, and finally her impulse to let Caspar take her in his arms, the "rapture" in which she sinks and sinks.

The metaphorical eccentricity here may at first puzzle the reader. Overtly, the sea is equated with "the world." How, then, can Caspar be at once a rushing torrent and, retrospectively, a harbor enclosed by a breakwater on the shores of this sea while Isabel's emotions are a tide upon it? James turns the trick of this near-impossibility by his characteristically Romantic habit of mixing up the external and the internal world. The world as Isabel experiences it is made up, among other things, of Caspar's readiness to encircle her in his embrace and of all the emotions flowing in her consciousness. The possible problem of a lack of consistent relation between the vehicle of the sea and the tenor of James's figure is resolved when one understands that Isabel's experience of the world is the sea and that Caspar's act and her emotions are particulars of it. James makes it clear, moreover, that his procedure in figuring Isabel imitates her own mode of consciousness, for "the confusion, the noise of waters, all the rest of it, were in her own swimming head" (*PLII*, 436).

Isabel's beating of her feet ("in order to catch herself, to feel something to rest on") is a dimly sensed, perhaps partly subconscious resistance to her enraptured sinking. The resistance prepares for the next transformation, which occurs a few sentences later, after Caspar's lightning kiss. Isabel had "heard of those wrecked and under water following a train of images before they sink. But when darkness returned she was free . . . There was a very straight path" (*PLII*, 436). Isabel's path, her withdrawal from Caspar to Osmond, from whom she is decisively alienated, is a synthesis that many readers will feel as negative, for though James intends an affirmation of Isabel's choice of awareness and suffering with Osmond over safety and nullity with Caspar, to have none but these alternatives may seem the essence of Isabel's doom. The effect of her refusal of Caspar is nevertheless as of a synthesis because it removes her from the immediate, sensational interplay of rapture and pain.

Similarly, whole chapters may turn on dialectical pivots. Chapter XLVI, in which the Osmonds battle about Lord Warburton's half-hearted courtship of Pansy, presents, in the pattern of dialogue, the disintegration of the already ambivalent sympathy of Isabel for Osmond. When Osmond suffers the disappointment of Warburton's failure to propose to his daughter, Isabel has "a perfect consciousness of Osmond's emotion" and, while wishing "Lord Warburton to triumph before her husband . . . at the same time she wished her husband to be very superior before Lord Warburton." But her response is finer when Osmond, repeating an earlier charge, accuses her of working against him:

> "Are you going back to Lord Warburton?" Isabel asked. "I'm very tired of his name."
>
> "You shall hear it again before we've done with it."

Here the bond between them snaps: "He was going down—down; the vision of such a fall made her almost giddy: that was the only pain. He was too strange, too different; he didn't touch her." When he falsely charges her with having intercepted a letter to him from Lord Warburton, Isabel slowly gets up: "standing there in her white cloak, which covered her to her feet, she might have represented the angel of disdain, first cousin to that of pity." So the chapter achieves a synthesis in which the community of marriage (love) is the implicit thesis, hatred (a community of antagonism) the explicit antithesis, and disdain (and pity) the resolution (*PLII*, 268, 275–76).

The whole pattern of *The Portrait of a Lady*, finally, is bipolar: Isabel, poor, free, happy, and ignorant, ends up wealthy, confined, unhappy, but aware. Yet, despite the negative aspect we have already noted of the resolution she achieves, she develops—like Strether in *The Ambassadors* and like Milly Theale and Merton Densher in *The Wings of the Dove*—according to the Romantic dialectic of spiral return. Her return to Gilbert Osmond, in this view, is a return on a higher level to her original idealism, purged of egoism by suffering and by the concomitant growth of her awareness. Isabel had started out seeing the world as a place for the "free expansion" of her selfhood (*PLI*, 68). By the time she decides to marry Osmond, the transformation of her idealism has already begun, for "the desire for unlimited expansion had been succeeded in her soul by the sense that life was vacant without some private duty that might gather one's energies to a point" (*PLII*, 82). In this phase of her development, her transformed, concentrated idealism ironically contributes to her playing into the disaster of marriage to Osmond, for her egoism still operates in the vanity of her desire to make a superior appearance. The vanity of appearances is a veil that she does not pierce until actuated by suffering in her great meditation in chapter XLII. Only in Isabel's return to Rome, not for her own sake primarily (though she does affirm for herself the value of full awareness, of—in Keats's phrase—"the wakeful anguish of the soul") but for Pansy's, is the transformation to a higher idealism fully realized, and that is why her decision to return was the right place to close her story, even though James was consciously running the risk of being charged with having left his heroine "*en l'air*."[5]

The Wings of the Dove is similarly governed, stylistically, structurally, and thematically, by dialectical transformations. Masterfully working "*both* the dramatic and the narrative lock," James arrays his themes in

5. Matthiessen and Murdock (eds.), *The Notebooks of Henry James*, 18. For further discussion of the Romantic form of affirmation in *The Portrait of a Lady*, see the concluding chapter of the present study.

oppositions: America and Europe, wealth and poverty, mortal affliction and brutal vitality, ideas and goods, renunciation and possession, openness and concealment, transcendental desire and actual limitation, innocence and initiation, the requirements of the heart and social requirements, spiritual and carnal love, and so on. Shakespeare works with such reiterated pairings of ideas, and, like Shakespeare, James mirrors his thematic oppositions over and over in his dramatic materials, most of all in his characters and their relationships. For example, Kate is dialectically opposed to Milly, to Densher (the psychology of their love is based on their opposition), and, especially in the first third of the novel, to Aunt Maud; Densher is opposed to Lord Mark, to Aunt Maud, and to Kate in turn; Kate's relation to Lord Mark and Densher's relations to Kate and Milly are all opposed to each other, and of course the contrast between Densher's relations with the two women is central to the meaning of *The Wings of the Dove*.

The imagery of the novel, furthermore, changes in dialectical fashion and at times presents vivid images of the process of transformation itself. Thus, the meaning of the dove changes from innocence and vulnerability to transcendence and triumph, and Densher has consciously to recall "that doves have wings and wondrous flights, have them as well as tender tints and soft sounds."[6] The overarching dramatic movement of the novel, obfuscated in James's preface but quite clear in the novel and *Notebooks*, is Densher's partial transfer of allegiance from Kate to Milly, partial because the transfer does not include his physical desire, which remains fixed on Kate. Densher's final attitude includes, among other important elements, a grim synthesis in him of knowledge of evil, which is concomitant with the discovery of sexual pleasure, and guilt, concomitant with his resolve not to compromise the higher values he has come to appreciate because of Milly.

We are introduced to the dialectical pattern in the novel in the alternatives with which Kate struggles in Books First and Second. When she accepts residence with her Aunt Lowder, she is aware of the dangers and yet believes that she may somehow contrive things so as to come out in possession of everything and with her own values still intact, her faith in them unbetrayed. She has taken in superintendance two objectives that are raised, by her passionate attachment to them, to the very nearly sublime: retrieval of the honor of her

6. *WDII*, 218.

family and fidelity to Merton Densher. Her father's disgrace has produced in her an intensified sense of duty to behave nobly and unselfishly and a desire to escape the morally degrading consequences of poverty, made so vivid by Marian. Although her love for the inveterately poor Densher is wholly opposed to the demands her family makes on her, she undertakes at once to maintain her attachment to Densher and to satisfy their requirements. It would seem that she is set on the reconciliation of diametrically opposite claims on herself, yet she is so attractive and socially gifted that we are urged to believe in the resolutions that would, for her, constitute triumph. Touched, whether we believe or not, by her dream of perfection, we are not aware until much further on in the novel that her idealism, in the circumstances, is hubristic. Her belief in herself, her pride, is finally unequal to the conditions in which fate has placed her, and so her proud idealism becomes, in this sense, an essential ingredient of her tragedy.

For there is a third object, beyond honor and love, that her father and sister press upon Kate as her primary obligation to them—money: "Marian met her with a readiness that was practically pert. 'To *have* it, first. Not at any rate to go on not having it. Then we should see.'" (*WDI*, 39–40). Kate's devotion to her family, in spite of its shame, is admirable, not less so because her family calls upon her to seek material advancement. Fortune, in Kate Croy's society, as Milly Theale's case demonstrates, is the key very nearly to life itself, to freedom. Although her Aunt Lowder's establishment represents an opportunity for Kate, she might, were she acting for herself alone, refuse it because of Maud Lowder's opposition to Merton Densher. But Kate does not act selfishly. Although James carefully adulterates the purity of Kate's motives by letting us in on her discovery, early in her stay at Lancaster Gate, of "how material things spoke to her," Kate takes up residence with Mrs. Lowder primarily in submission to the use to which her father and sister wish to put her. They have as much as insisted that she do so. She would have been, otherwise, quite prepared to sacrifice her opportunity with her aunt, to give it all up for them and for Densher. Instead, acting for them according to their own lights, she goes to live at Lancaster Gate, enters "the cage of the lioness" with an awareness that her personal happiness and freedom will be the probable sacrifice (*WDI*, 28, 30).

If Kate seems to have placed herself in an impossible situation, her vital intelligence and passionate integrity make us feel that she may yet prevail. In her own mind, she has ventured onto a field in which the play of conflicting forces is such that they seem to cancel each other out. It is thus that she estimates her position after her interview with Marian at the end of Book First: "She had denied everything and every one, she reflected as she went away—and that was a relief; but it also made rather a clean sweep of the future" (*WDI*, 44). This is, however appealing, a self-deceiving analysis. To deny everything, as James's characters are fond of saying, is to deny nothing. What Kate has in fact when she goes to live with Mrs. Lowder is little more than her brave, Romantic, finally futile faith in the ability of her imagination to reconcile the antithetical requirements of her love for Densher, her desire to overcome her family's dishonor, and her damning lack of any chance for fortune beyond whatever may lie in Maud Lowder's conditional gift. In the last chapter of the novel, Kate is also faced with alternatives—Densher and poverty or riches without Densher—and, with her odd integrity and her perception, despite her not sharing in it, of Densher's spiritual transformation, she admits that she cannot reconcile the alternatives and is quicker than her indecisive lover—such, villain though she is, is her moral courage—to pronounce the end of their plan of marriage: "We shall never be again as we were" (*WDII*, 405).

Densher's spiritual transformation is the central dramatic action in *The Wings of the Dove*. He moves, in Blakean terms, from innocence to organized innocence, and his journey follows the Romantic paradigm of spiral return. For Densher begins in the refreshing but too-simple innocence of his first love for Kate Croy, passes through a period of complicity in Kate's plot against Milly Theale, and at last, under the spell of Milly's forgiveness, rises in a mood of blessedness and renunciation to a transcendent, informed innocence. When a transformation of the sort that Densher undergoes occupies the greater part of a novel of the length of *The Wings of the Dove*, the gradations through which the change is worked may be multifold. James's style, especially in the way he controls the timing of important disclosures and discoveries, practically guarantees a lengthy and complex process. There is always a point, however, at which the balance clearly shifts. In *The Wings of the Dove*, it is when Densher begins to tilt from Kate toward Milly, a movement initiated at "the whole actual centre" of the book, the "misplaced pivot" in Book Fifth.[7] Four distinct episodes (each of which contains several scenes) constitute Book Fifth. Chapters I and II present the party at Matcham; III and IV give us Milly's visit to Sir Luke Strett and her walk in Regent's Park; V and VI portray the "hot and stale" night on which Maud Lowder asks Milly to sound Kate on the possibility of Densher's having returned and also on which Kate warns Milly that "you may very well loathe me yet"; chapter VII, finally, contains Milly's encounter with Kate and Densher at the National Gallery and the subsequent luncheon at Milly's hotel. Each of these episodes is part of the "whole actual centre" of the novel, but the conclusion of Book Fifth—the first London meeting of Milly and Densher—is the effective pivot. It brings to a climax the preparatory work of the first half of the novel by providing the occasion that irrevocably alters the relations of the three young persons and steers them onto their tragic course. It provides, for the first time, the suggestion that Densher may constitute, for Milly, salvation from the abyss. At the same time, we get a stronger sense than we have hitherto had of Kate as the manipulator of Milly and Densher: "Miss Theale had meanwhile the sense that for him too, on Kate's part, something unspoken and wonderful was determinant" (*WDI*, 262, 282, 294).

Densher's attitude toward Milly, on the occasion of their renewal of acquaintance in London, is less complicated than her attitude toward him. Although chapter VII marks Densher's embarkation on the journey toward his transformation in the concluding chapters of the book, he is far more deeply in relation with Kate at the end of Volume I than with Milly. He is, in fact, so considerably subject to Kate's will as to be chafing under its pressure. To understand his initial response to Milly, in Book Fifth, we must place it against the impressions that loom largest for him, the fresh perception he has of Kate after rejoining her from his American assignment. We do not believe any the less in his love for Miss Croy, but we are made aware that their relationship has entered a new phase, the elements of which become clear very soon, in Book Sixth. Their separation has sharpened his "impatience" for full enjoyment of his love, and Kate's "expertness" in man-

7. Henry James, Preface to *The Wings of the Dove*, in *AN*, 306.

aging their secret life together has become an irritation. In the light of his central relationship with Kate, Densher sees Milly as a part of one of Kate's strategems:

> Her dear Milly, popping up in his absence, occupied—he couldn't have said quite why he felt it—more of the foreground than one would have expected her in advance to find clear. She took up room, and it was almost as if room had been made for her. Kate had appeared to take for granted he would know why it had been made; but that was just the point . . . Miss Theale was perhaps at the present juncture a possibility of the same sort as the softened, if not the squared, Aunt Maud. It might be true of her also that if she weren't a bore she'd be a convenience.

Densher, we recall, though handsome "in the English style," is only imperfectly cast in the English mold. Maud Lowder's "conclusively British" furnishings "represented for him a portentous negation of his own world of thought." His migratory upbringing makes it necessary for him to insist that he is a "Briton": "But brave enough though his descent to English earth, he had passed, by the way, through zones of air that had left their ruffle on his wings—he had been exposed to initiations indelible." He does not see Milly, then, as his compatriots do, as the dazzling, dazzlingly exploitable princess.[8] She is "little Miss Theale," an admittedly extraordinary American young person, of whose type he had seen, in America, "but too many." He is in the English mold only so far as he contemplates a comparatively minor exploitation of Milly, thinks of perhaps gaining through her occasions and opportunities to meet with Kate (*WDI*, 78–79, 93, 291; *WDII*, 5, 10, 13–14).

Milly, on the other hand, discovers in the course of the luncheon in chapter VII, "that she liked" Densher, "as she put it to herself, as much as ever." Portrayal of the degree of feeling signified by Milly's liking for Densher has been, up to this point, a matter of the utmost tact. Nevertheless, James gives us enough to make the following inferences. Milly has been in love with Densher, or on the verge of it, since their three brief meetings in New York. Although she herself does not call it love, though she is doubtless not conscious of it as

8. Sir Luke may seem an exception to the exploitative instincts of the English characters, though his attendance on Milly is "proof of a huge interest as well as of a huge fee" (*WDII*, 308).

such, clearly she would rise to love if only she were bidden to do so. Her tact and her instinct for renunciation—even before she is given "straightway the measure of the success she could have as a dove"—make for her reticence and reserve when Susan Stringham suggests that they might see in London the young man whom Susan was earlier made "rather sorry to have missed." "There had been," in Mrs. Stringham's view, "just enough in this relation to meet, to provoke, the free conception of a little more." Milly does indeed think of Densher, despite her assertion of indifference, so that, when Lord Mark appears to her as one of "those characteristic cases of people in England who concealed their play of mind so much more than they advertised it," she reflects that "even Mr. Densher a little did that." By the time a mystery has arisen for her about Kate and Densher, she has acknowledged her own feeling for him sufficiently to note that "we're not quarreling about it, Kate and I, *yet*." Quarrel, of course, Milly would never do, but she provokes Susan to ask her if she wants "to run away from" Densher. If Milly's reply ("I don't know *what* I want to run away from!") dispels for Susan "any ghost of any need of explaining," it should not do so for us (*WDI*, 136–37, 151, 198–99, 284, 299).

Many times before she meets Densher with Kate at the National Gallery, Milly has seen Kate undergo a transformation, has seen her, intensely if always momentarily, as through Densher's eyes. Although jealousy may be too coarse an identification of the phenomenon, it is clearly an operation of mediated desire, expressed according to the dialectical pattern with which I have been concerned. What Milly sees as other in Kate when Kate appears as Densher's beloved is precisely an effect of Kate's being rich where Milly is poor, in Kate's being loved by the man Milly loves. When Henry James was small, he tells us, the people in his circle were "so *other*—that was what I felt; and to *be* other, other almost anyhow, seemed as good as the probable taste of the bright compound wistfully watched in the confectioner's window."[9] Milly's perception of Kate's otherness is the expression of her irrepressible desire to be *other* herself, other in the exact sense in which Kate answers the term in being Densher's beloved.

Returning to Milly's conscious avowal to herself of "liking" Densher

9. Henry James, *A Small Boy and Others* (New York, 1913), 175.

"as much as ever" in chapter VII of Book Fifth, one should recall the extent to which others have prepared her to allow herself just such a recognition. She has been told that she may at least entertain compassion for Densher since his love of Kate is unrequited. When she fears that Kate may in fact love Densher (and she does positively fear it), she takes an active part in her own deception: "Merton Densher was in love and Kate couldn't help it—could only be sorry and kind: wouldn't that, without wild flurries, cover everything? Milly at all events tried it as a cover, tried it hard, for the time; pulled it over her, in the front, the larger room, drew it up to her chin with energy. If it didn't, so treated, do everything for her, it did so much that she could herself supply the rest." In addition, Sir Luke's insinuation that love may be the best medicine for her "condition" makes Milly's surfacing attraction to Densher all the more poignant when he appears in his increasingly accessible guise as Kate's rejected suitor. Milly is not only free to like him; she has the best of reasons for wanting an affectionate, intimate relation. For the moment, she must make do with the banal after-lunch conversation. Densher prattles to her—she hardly speaks at all—of his American experiences, and he goes away thinking that she is a bore. She, for her part, is sufficiently cautious to surmise that his view of her, at least partially, would have much "in common with—as she now sighed over it—*the* view." One notes that Milly never allows her expectations of Densher to rise except in response to the false appearances with which others attack her. She has hopes, of course, but unlike the other characters, she will not wage campaigns for their realization. Her hopes—as distinguished from her expectations—arise from "the only thing she did know," "that she liked" Densher. With Susan's "feverish glitter" reminding Milly that she lives on the edge of the abyss, Densher becomes a likely handhold, and "it was therefore on the whole because Densher's young hostess was divided from it by so thin a partition that she continued to cling to the Rockies." Densher, then, so weighed upon, starts to tilt toward Milly, though he does not even begin to suspect it until much later (*WDI*, 298–302).

The novel has a tripartite structure, recalling, as many readers have observed, the three-act structure of the well-made play. Books First and Second constitute Act I. They show us how Kate and Densher, "all unconsciously and with the best faith in the world . . . are laying a trap for the great innocence to come." They are, James continues in his preface, "forces unwittingly waiting to close round my eager heroine." Act II, comprising Books Third through Seventh, introduces Milly into the trap, dramatizing the way "the possibilities shining out of" her are met (*AN*, 303–304). Act III, from Book Eighth on, completes the action prepared unintentionally by Kate and Densher in Act I: the trap closes on the dove, who yet, by transcendent love and forgiveness, triumphs in death, changing forever the lives of her entrappers. The National Gallery episode with which Book Fifth concludes (discussed in detail as a scene of delayed recognition in my chapter on *The Ambassadors*) occurs roughly two-thirds of the way into Act II, and it is actually somewhat short of the midpoint of the novel. I cannot agree with James that it is really in fact "a misplaced pivot." It seems rather a well-placed one in view of the dialectic of the three-act form (complication, peripety, denouement). The latter half of the novel, what James thought "the false and deformed half," strikes me, furthermore, as a great success precisely because of its foreshortening. The imagery, in Act III especially, thins out, and the pace, accelerated by an increasing proportion of dialogue, picks up. Dramatically, psychologically, and stylistically, much of the effectiveness of *The Wings of the Dove* depends on the luxuriance of the build-up and the rapidity of the crash.

I will return shortly to the major dialectical transformations in *The Wings of the Dove*. I want first to point out the prevalence of polar tensions and the intermittent movement toward resolution of them in increasingly smaller compositional units of the book: first in a representative book, Book Eighth, then in a chapter, chapter III of Book Eighth, next in a paragraph describing Lord Mark early in Book Fourth, and finally in brief oxymoronic descriptions of the characters drawn from throughout the novel. Afterward, I shall discuss the water images in *The Wings of the Dove* in order to show how they provide brilliant images not only for the predicaments of the characters but also for the dialectical process according to which all the elements of the novel evolve.

Book Eighth chronicles a complex phase in the changing relations of Densher and Kate and Milly. Three chapters—the first descriptive of Densher's situation shortly after his arrival in Venice, the last two scenic presentations, one of a colloquy between Kate and Densher in the Piazza San Marco, the other of Milly's soirée at Palazzo Leporelli—reflect the overall three-part design of the novel (about which more shortly). Book Eighth epitomizes the way in which Milly, though she is undoubtedly the heroine of *The Wings of the Dove*, seems to stand outside the action. For the dramatized change in the book is all between Kate and Densher. To be sure, the changes in Kate's and Densher's positions are as if plotted by triangulation, with Milly providing the third point of reference. Kate must pay a price for maneuvering Densher into greater familiarity with Milly and at last consents to his demand that she come to him. Ironically, the promised passage in Densher's room, far from assuring him possession of Kate, will weigh in discriminations between her and Milly that prepare him for his final spiritual renewal, for his assumption, in the end, of an attitude amounting to renunciation of Kate. Early in the following book, Book Ninth, after passages emphasizing Densher's appreciation of Milly—of how she "practically purged" "his strange relation" to her and of how "something outside, beyond, above themselves, and doubtless ever so much better than" he and Kate "wrought for them"—Densher becomes upset by the idea of Milly's entering his apartment. His quarters have acquired, for his guilty devotion, the nearly supernatural aura of his lovemaking there with Kate. His reluctant permission to visit "when you like" elicits Milly's fine response, a reply exactly the opposite of the pledge given by Kate in Book Eighth. Milly declares that she will not visit if doing so will drive Densher from Venice:

> "I won't go."
> "Then *I* won't go!" she brightly declared.
> "You mean you won't come to me?"
> "No—never now. It's over."

Even in Book Eighth, where Kate and Densher are the principal actors, we receive, through them, a dramatic transformation in the imagery used for Milly. Densher sees how Milly looks to Kate, a figure of bright splendor and power, qualities associated with the magnificence of Milly's wealth. This vision of Milly, especially for Densher, is enhanced by her personal radiance, by her white dress, by her pearls, by the transcendent glow she achieves for Sir Luke. Almost at the same time, Densher makes Kate's dark design explicit—"Since she's to die I'm to marry her"—and Kate puts the seal on their illicit sexual compact. Here again, James's dialectical tendency operates; Milly's brightness, amidst "even more candles than their friend's large common allowance," which "lighted up the pervasive mystery of Style," is at its greatest luminosity just as Kate and Densher speak openly of their darkest intentions (*WDII*, 203, 225, 239, 247).

The three chapters of Book Eighth represent a gradually but insistently progressive transformation in Kate and Densher's understanding of each other. We learn, in the first sentence of the book, of Densher's dislike for his hotel, a dislike rapidly translated into his irritation with Kate. His feeling is multifaceted, but it is first and foremost his sexual irritation, a theme James has developed throughout the book, with special intensity from Book Sixth onwards. Kate, handsome brute, "thanks to her pure talent for life," has met every display of hesitation on Densher's part, as Cleopatra meets Antony's moments of indecision, with a display of sexual power, usually by an embrace, sometimes by holding his hands and sounding the depths of his eyes, and occasionally, as at a delicate moment in chapter II of Book Eighth, by dismissing him (*WDII*, 176; see also 20, 95, and 201). Densher cannot be so toyed with without at last being driven to press his demand. The dynamic of Densher's predicament and of his campaign to resolve it informs the tripartite structure of Book Eighth thus: his move out of his hotel in chapter I of Book Eighth heralds his urging Kate to come to him in chapter II and her assent at the end of chapter III. Crudely reduced, the dialectic of Book Eighth poses sexual frustration and satisfaction as antitheses, with an explicit promise of satisfaction as the synthesis. Simultaneously, the power of Kate's gift for intrigue and of her sexuality is contrasted with the power of Milly's wealth, grace, and style.

Chapter III of Book Eighth is the most intensely dramatic passage in the last third of the novel. It too repeats the tripartite design of the whole work. We have, first, a conversation between Densher and Mrs. Stringham, of which Milly is the foremost topic; second, an expository passage, which builds the current of Densher's perception of Milly, "different, younger, fairer," and which climaxes in his meeting with Kate and in their mutual dazzlement before Milly's efflorescence, in the light of which the image of the dove undergoes a decisive transformation, its wings, to Densher's dim perception, spreading in "an inordinate reach" "for protection"; and third, immediately following, the long parley—with occasional glances across the room to Milly—between Kate and Densher. If Densher may be said to have tilted toward Milly earlier, one must allow that even in this chapter he can still put it to himself that his feelings "were all for Kate, without a feather's weight to spare." Yet he is, in chapter III of Book Eighth, profoundly affected by Milly, almost supersensitively responsive to her high grace. His appreciation of her is aesthetic and not, as it will be later, spiritual, but it is the kind of aesthetic appreciation available in James's fiction predominantly to those whose superior capacities qualify them for redemption. Densher takes in, for example, the way Milly acquits herself "as hostess . . . under some supreme idea, an inspiration which was half her nerves and half an inevitable harmony." His sense of Milly as "happily pervasive" accompanies his mounting anxiety about Kate's designs, which he only clearly makes out for the first time in the final third of the chapter (*WDII*, 204, 214, 218).

The chapter opens with a cryptic reference to Densher's having had a chance to ask Kate a question—we are not told what the question was until considerably further on—which he would have asked in their conversation in the Piazza San Marco had he not been so preoccupied with asking her to come to him. The first words repeat James's description, at the end of the preceding chapter, of Densher's relief that Kate had not met with "cheap reprobation" his plea that she come to his rooms. Here is the last sentence of chapter II of Book Eighth: "So far she was good." Here is the first sentence of chapter III: "She was good enough, as it proved, for him to put to her that evening, and with further ground for it, the next sharpest question that had been on his lips in the morning—which his other preoccupation had then, to his consciousness, crowded out" (*WDII*, 201–203).

Densher's growing need is to know exactly what Kate is up to in her handling of him and Milly. When his questions at last come out—How can it be that Maud Lowder is squared? Why has Mrs. Stringham failed to tell Aunt Maud about Kate's engagement to Densher? What, given everyone's falling in with Kate's ideas, is to be gained?—they suggest that he has never before had to specify Kate's objectives because his imagination has never encompassed even the possibility of so much silent complicity from so many interested parties. Now that he sees Kate's campaign making such smooth headway, he wants to know what she is driving at. Thus the plot is forced into open, ugly expression. And thus it is that Densher, who earlier in Book Eighth had seen himself "on a high ridge, steep down on either side, where the proprieties . . . reduced themselves to his keeping his head," takes the plunge, promising, in effect, to be so far bad as to stay in Venice with Milly after Kate and Aunt Maud depart, if Kate too will promise to be so far bad as to come to him (*WDII*, 175). The ironic, implied forecast of Kate's acquiescence is the echo, in the first sentence of the chapter, of the close of the last: "She was good enough." One notes, again, that the sharpness of Densher's need for a sexual validation of his relation to Kate rises with his estimation of Milly's value and with his acceptance of a continuing, increasingly intimate association with Milly.

The pattern of the movements toward synthesis in large structural units of *The Wings of the Dove* can be very intricate, especially when several transformations overlap, as they do in Book Eighth as a whole and in chapter III in detail. For example, the transformation beginning with Densher's dissatisfaction with his hotel and the one beginning with the allusion to Kate's being "good" converge on the same conclusion, Kate's "I'll come" (*WDII*, 231). In smaller divisions of the text, the dialectical pattern generally assumes a simpler, clearer outline. Thus, in Book Eighth, paragraph after paragraph develops along dialectical lines. The first paragraph in the book opens with Densher's dislike of his hotel and concludes with his gaze at the "little white papers" that advertise a vacancy in the lodgings to which he will shortly decide to move. The second paragraph passes from the idea of Densher's association with Milly as all at Kate's bidding to the image of Milly and Densher "blown together" in the "whirlwind of suggestion" with which Palazzo Leporelli surrounds Milly, thus shifting the explanation of Densher's behavior from one pole, that of Kate's influence, to another, that of Milly's aura. The third paragraph begins with Densher's possible boredom with Milly, a "cousin afflicted," and moves to what is, to Densher's consciousness, a more active condition, his irritation with Kate and with the way her "talent for life" stands out in her. The fourth paragraph shifts from Densher's feeling of passivity in Kate's hands to his acquisition of new rooms, an act that will enable him to have his will of her. The fifth paragraph begins with the information that Densher was "amusing" on the subject of his change of quarters and ends with the remark that his account "charmingly sounded" the note of "hollowness" for the first time.

The gradual stages by which James typically moves, in paragraphs, from an initial statement to a new, dialectically related proposition are easy to see in the passage cited below from chapter I of Book Fourth, the dinner party at Lancaster Gate—an occasion to which James thought chapter III of Book Eighth corresponded, squared "to the same synthetic firmness" (*AN*, 301):

> Lord Mark's intelligence meanwhile, however, had met her own quite sufficiently to enable him to tell her how little he could clear up her situation. He explained, for that matter—or at least he hinted—that there was no such thing to-day in London as saying where any one was. Every one was everywhere—nobody was anywhere. He should be put to it—yes, frankly—to give a name of any sort or kind to their hostess's "set." *Was* it a set at all, or wasn't it, and were there not really no such things as sets in the place any more?—was there anything but the groping and pawing, that of the vague billows of some great greasy sea in mid-Channel, of masses of bewildered people trying to "get" they didn't know what or where? He threw out the question, which seemed large; Milly felt that at the end of five minutes he had thrown out a great many, though he followed none more than a step or two; perhaps he would prove suggestive, but he helped her as yet to no discriminations: he spoke as if he had given them up from too much knowledge. He was thus at the opposite extreme from herself, but, as a consequence of it, also wandering and lost; and he was furthermore, for all his temporary incoherence, to which she guessed there would be some key, as packed a concretion as either Mrs. Lowder or Kate. The only light in which he placed the former of these ladies was that of an extraordinary woman—a most extraordinary woman, and "the more extraordinary the more one knows her," while of the latter he said nothing for the moment but that she was tremendously, yes, quite tremendously, good-looking. It was some time, she thought, before his talk showed his cleverness, and yet each minute she believed in that mystery more, quite apart from what her hostess had told her on first naming him. Perhaps he was one of the cases she had heard of at home—those characteristic cases of people in England who concealed their play of mind so much more than they advertised it. Even Mr. Densher a little did that. And what made Lord Mark, at any rate, so real either, when this was a trick he had apparently so mastered? His type somehow, as by a life, a need, an intention of its own, took all care for vividness off his hands; that was enough. It was difficult to guess his age—whether he were a young man who looked old or an old man who looked young; it seemed to prove

> nothing, as against other things, that he was bald and, as might have been said, slightly stale, or, more delicately perhaps, dry: there was such a fine little fidget of preoccupied life in him, and his eyes, at moments—though it was an appearance they could suddenly lose—were as candid and clear as those of a pleasant boy. Very neat, very light, and so fair that there was little other indication of his moustache than his constantly feeling it—which was again boyish—he would have affected her as the most intellectual person present if he had not affected her as the most frivolous. The latter quality was rather in his look than in anything else, though he constantly wore his double eyeglass, which was, much more, Bostonian and thoughtful. (*WDI*, 150–52)

From the first statement that "Lord Mark's intelligence" was sufficient to explain "how little he could clear up" Milly's situation to the concluding remarks that he "would have affected her as the most intellectual person present if he had not affected her as the most frivolous" and that he looked "Bostonian and thoughtful," the paragraph demonstrates considerably more insight on Milly's part than a recent critic seems to allow in arguing that "the game of treating Milly as if she were a fully initiated member of the circle" provides "a source of mild sadistic pleasure."[10] Surely, as this commentator says, Milly's ignorance of the society she has entered is "obvious and abysmal." But that several statements by Milly from chapter I of Book Fourth are taken by the same critic as accurate characterizations of Lord Mark suggests that Milly's perception, given her ignorance, is of extraordinary penetration. Although Milly believes more and more in Lord Mark's cleverness, of which Maud Lowder has given her notice, the paragraph offers her astute qualifications of what it means to speak of "Lord Mark's intelligence." What does his intelligence tell her? It tells her that he could explain little. He throws out "a great many" questions but follows "none more than a step or two." He might "prove suggestive" but yields "no discriminations." Perhaps from an excess of knowledge—"the opposite extreme from herself"—he too is "wandering and lost." His "temporary incoherence," his vapid comments on Maud Lowder and Kate, lead to Milly's observation that he must be of the notorious English type who "concealed their play of mind so much more than they advertised it." At last, after a glance at Lord Mark's physical appearance, Milly sees his frivolousness as compromising his intellect, "though he constantly wore his double eye-

10. Sears, *The Negative Imagination*, 78.

glass, which was, much more, Bostonian and thoughtful." The cumulative suggestion of the paragraph is that Lord Mark, clever in the way of European sophistication, is seriously flawed, "frivolous," no doubt, in having no moral basis and yet "Bostonian" in being most dreadfully unimaginative. For Boston, as we have learned earlier from Mrs. Stringham, is a "grave" place where one could expect nevertheless to hear "clever Boston things" (*WDI*, 105–106). Milly, at any rate, seems to be thinking chiefly of appearances when she takes Lord Mark as frivolous and Bostonian. But such observations underlie her great rejoinder to Lord Mark a few pages later: "You're blasé, but you're not enlightened. You're familiar with everything, but conscious, really of nothing. What I mean is that you've no imagination" (*WDI*, 162). There is no doubt that Lord Mark is judged, in the closing chapters of the novel, to have given this proposition certain proof. Milly, in short, is trenchant in her analysis of Lord Mark, though she fails fully to grasp the implications, for her, of living in the brave new world that has such men in it. For Henry James, imagination, vitally responsive and unremittingly moral, is the sine qua non of the highest intelligence. In the paragraph quoted above, Milly suggests that Lord Mark, if he is no fool, has yet an incapacity for the upper reaches of consciousness. In the dialectic of pure mind and stony insentience, he occupies a medial position; he is merely clever, "Bostonian and thoughful."

In the stylistic details of *The Wings of the Dove* one finds, quite as much as in *The Ambassadors*, virtually innumerable reflections of the overarching synthesis the book accomplishes. Each character, for example, is described in terms of polarities. Here is Kate's conception of herself early in Volume I: "she saw herself as handsome, no doubt, but as hard, and felt herself as clever but as cold; and as so much too imperfectly ambitious, furthermore, that it was a pity, for a quiet life, she couldn't decide to be either finely or stupidly indifferent. Her intelligence sometimes kept her still—too still—but her want of it was restless; so that she got the good, it seemed to her, of neither extreme" (*WDI*, 58). And here is part of Densher's mixture of contraries:

> He was in short visibly absent-minded, irregularly clever, liable to drop what was near and to take up what was far; he was more a prompt critic than a prompt follower of custom. He suggested above all, however, that wondrous state of youth in which the elements, the metals more or less

precious, are so in fusion and fermentation that the question of the final stamp, the pressure that fixes the value, must wait for comparative coolness. And it was a mark of his interesting mixture that if he was irritable it was by a law of considerable subtlety—a law that in intercourse with him it might be of profit, though not easy, to master. One of the effects of it was that he had for you surprises of tolerance as well as of temper. (*WDI*, 48–49)

And here, for a brief last example, is Milly: "She had arts and idiosyncracies of which no great account could have been given, but which were a daily grace if you lived with them; such as the art of being almost tragically impatient and yet making it as light as air; of being inexplicably sad and yet making it as clear as noon; of being unmistakably gay and yet making it as soft as dusk" (*WDI*, 115).

In comparison to that other late-Jamesian villain Charlotte Stant, Kate Croy has perhaps suffered from a lack of critical championship, but Sallie Sears makes about as good a case for Kate as one can imagine in *The Negative Imagination*, where she provides a provocative reading of the novel essentially from Kate's point of view. To be sure, James wanted to "make my medal hang free" so that "its obverse and its reverse, its face and its back, would beautifully become optional for the spectator." Yet, he adds, "it was none the less visibly my 'key,' as I have said, that though my regenerate young New Yorker, and what might depend on her, should form my centre, my circumference was every whit as treatable" (*AN*, 294). Sears treats the eminently treatable circumference, the back rather than the face of the medal. Explicitly, she denies that Milly's forgiveness is the source of an authentic spiritual regeneration in Densher, and while allowing that James intended to portray a Densher "morally reborn," she charges that "it is one of those cases where instead of being *shown*, as James would put it, we have to take the word of the 'poor author' for it."[11]

But Sears does not once allude to what I take to be the figural center of the novel, the complex series of marine images, both literal and figurative, that enacts the dialectic of the moral transformations of

11. *Ibid.*, 93–94. In her discussion of *The Wings of the Dove*, Sears remarks several times on the bipolar elements of its construction and of James's imagination in general (see *ibid.*, 73, 85). She argues, in fact, that "James's concern with formal balance and opposition" is behind what she considers his failure in portraying Densher's putative moral rebirth. James's preoccupation, says Sears, "with the mathematics of situation" misled him into ending the novel " 'neatly' " rather than with fidelity to the "emotional effect" of the "total work" (p. 96).

Milly and Densher.[12] The marine images are themselves subject to a transformation, the "great greasy sea" of the scenes in London in the first half of the novel becoming, in Venice, a magical medium, "where the sun on the stirred seawater, flickering up through open windows, played over the painted 'subjects' in the splendid ceilings" and where "the scattered pinks, yellows, blues, sea-greens, were like a hanging-out of vivid stuffs, a laying-down of fine carpets." There are well over one hundred images that participate in this transformation. The sea-change they represent stands for at least three major changes: first, the change that takes place in Milly between the time she turns her face to the wall and the last time she receives Densher, leaving him "forgiven, dedicated, blessed"; second, the subsequent change in Densher; and third, the overall governing dynamic of transformation in the novel itself (*WDII*, 132, 294, 343).

F. O. Matthiessen notes in passing, in *Henry James: The Major Phase*, what is clearly an allusion to Ariel's song in *The Tempest*:[13]

> Full fathom five thy father lies;
> Of his bones are coral made;
> Those are pearls that were his eyes;
> Nothing of him that doth fade
> But doth suffer a sea-change
> Into something rich and strange.
> Sea nymphs hourly ring his knell:
> *Burden*. Ding-dong
> Hark! now I hear them—Ding-dong bell.
> (*The Tempest*, I, ii, 397–405)

Just two pages before Lord Mark tells Milly that English society is like a "great greasy sea," she sees "how she was justified of her plea for people and her love of life": "it wasn't then, as the prospect

12. By "marine images" I mean not only water images but also images of ships, seafaring, shipwrecks, and aquatic life.

13. Matthiessen, *Henry James: The Major Phase*, 60. Matthiessen's discussion of *The Wings of the Dove* is suggestive of several of the arguments in the present chapter. I am especially indebted to Matthiessen for his compact remarks on the water imagery in the novel and on James's "Shakesperian use of storm and calm" (p. 73). But his remark that "the author of a long novel can scarcely depend on iterative imagery to produce atmosphere to the heightened degree that a poet can in the compressed length of a play" (p. 63) compels me to reply that when repetitions of a type of image are as frequent as the reiterations of marine images in *The Wings of the Dove* (slightly more frequent, on average, than one every seven pages) the atmospheric effect may indeed achieve a poetic intensity.

seemed to show, so difficult to get into the current, or to stand at any rate on the bank. It was easy to get near—if they *were* near; and yet the elements were different enough from any of her old elements, and positively rich and strange" (*WDI*, 145–48). Ariel's dirge for Alonso describes a physical sea-change, of which Northrop Frye comments, "it seems strange that a melancholy elegy over the dissolving of all things in time should be the emotional crux of the play."[14] But the elegy is over Alonso, who is not really dead, and it is not about the dissolving of things but about their transmutation. Alonso's eyes have not become pearls, nor his bones coral, but he is changed, ethically and spiritually, during the three hours between his shipwreck in the sea-storm that Prospero has raised and the end of the play. "Full fathom five," the sea-change, may be taken as an emblem of changes in the spiritual quality of the characters in the play, changes that Prospero presides over in a mood of benevolence and forgiveness.

In *The Wings of the Dove*, the sea-change similarly becomes an emblem of the change that Milly suffers during the sea-storm in Venice and of the later change in Densher because of Milly's benevolence and forgiveness. Thus, of the marine images I have noticed in the novel, forty-five refer to Milly and her situation and forty-nine to Densher and his predicaments. Both characters undergo recurrent metaphoric immersion. They are, moreover, the only characters significantly figured this way. Aunt Maud is only once associated with marine imagery, when she is said to steer among conversational subjects "as if they were islets in an archipelago" and then to resume, "with a splash of her screw, her cruise among the islands." Mrs. Stringham figures Milly in marine imagery, in some of which she herself, as Milly's associate, participates, but on her own she is only represented thus once, quite casually, when a remark by Milly leaves her "at sea." Kate is associated with marine imagery fifteen times, but of these, eight refer to her relation with Densher. The most significant of the remaining ones—when Densher exclaims to Kate, "It's rather good then for yourself too that you're as strong as the sea"—reminds us that the sea, more than being merely a symbol of society, stands for life itself, so that Kate, with her famous vitality, is quite appropriately associated with the creative-destructive element in which

14. Northrop Frye, Introduction to William Shakespeare, *The Tempest* (Baltimore, 1959), 22.

Milly and Densher undergo their transformations. For Kate, like her aunt, is "a grand natural force." It would seem odd indeed, if James were not using these images as a leit-motif, that they should not be distributed equally among the principal characters. That their application, rather, seems to conform to a coherent, complex symbolic interpretation of the experience of two particular characters suggests that we would do well to reconsider Matthiessen's conclusion that James's images do not operate as leit-motifs in *The Wings of the Dove* (*WDI*, 161–62, 216; *WDII*, 54, 105).[15]

Can one say that James probably intended to import, through marine imagery, the symbolic associations of the sea-change in *The Tempest* into *The Wings of the Dove*? The multiple resonances between James's imagery and *The Tempest* are strong evidence of intentional design. First, there are numerous verbal echoes of the play in James's novel. After the initial "rich and strange" in Book Fourth, the adjectives occur many times in association with Milly, as when she thinks of the Bronzino portrait that she resembles as "strange and fair" (*WDI*, 220).[16] Although the word *sea-storm* is a rarity—it is not even listed in the *OED*—it occurs in *The Tempest* (I, ii, 176–77) and in *The Wings of the Dove* (*WDII*, 257). Second, there are many figurative resonances between novel and play. On several occasions, James's characters are imaged as enisled, as the characters in *The Tempest* in fact are. Densher thinks of Kate and himself as on a "small floating island" (*WDI*, 66). Susan Stringham has a similar image for Milly's (and her own) situation: "The sense was constant for her that

15. See Matthiessen, *Henry James: The Major Phase,* 72. In his book on James's imagery, Alexander Holder-Barell discounts the importance of water imagery in *The Wings of the Dove,* arguing, incredibly to my mind, that only three of the water images are of any importance (see *The Development of Imagery and Its Functional Significance in Henry James's Novels* [Bern, 1959], 121). For other critics who hold, on the contrary, that water imagery is of major importance in the novel, see Matthiessen, *Henry James: The Major Phase*, 62–63; Crews, *The Tragedy of Manners*, 72; R. W. Short, "Henry James's World of Images," *PMLA*, LXVIII (1953), 957–58; Robert L. Gale, *The Caught Image: Figurative Language in the Fiction of Henry James* (Chapel Hill, 1964); and Gheorghita Dumitriu, "Henry James's Use of Imagery in 'The Wings of the Dove,' " *Analele Universitatii, Bucuresti, Limbi Germanice*, XXII (1973), 67–74.

16. In a notebook entry that antedates the composition of the novel by seven years, James wrote that Milly's yearning should be for "some act of generosity, of passionate beneficence," removing it "from the class of egotistic pleasures" and making it "something fine and strange" (Matthiessen and Murdock [eds.], *The Notebooks of Henry James*, 172).

their relation might have been afloat, like some island of the south, in a great warm sea that represented, for every conceivable chance, a margin, an outer sphere, of general emotion; and the effect of the occurrence of anything in particular was to make the sea submerge the island, the margin flood the text. The great wave now for a moment swept over" (*WDI*, 199). Long before the sea submerges the island in Venice, where the paving, "greasy . . . with the salt spray" (*WDII*, 261) during the sea-storm, recalls the "great greasy sea" of Book Fourth, James has provided many images of Milly as a ship (see *WDI*, 104 and 112–13) and also of her as one subject to shipwreck (see *WDI*, 24, and *WDII*, 53). When she goes down in "the ark of her deluge" (*WDII*, 143) in Venice, then, the idea of her possible shipwreck in a sea-storm has been well established. In addition, James's using Milly's pearls as the resplendent symbol of her value recalls the pearls in Ariel's dirge, especially in the light of Densher's image of the revelation that Milly has given him as "a priceless pearl cast before his eyes—his pledge given not to save it—into the fathomless sea" (*WDII*, 396).[17]

I hope it will be a sufficient demonstration of the coherent and continuous development of the marine imagery in *The Wings of the Dove* to select for comment the major instances involving Milly Theale, both for the sake of efficiency and because the experience of the sea-change is primarily Milly's and is only secondarily and associatively Densher's. My reading of this group of images in *The Wings of the Dove* supports the traditional interpretations of the novel by such critics as F. O. Matthiessen and Dorothea Krook and accords with James's explicit statements about his intentions in the novel, particularly about his intention that Milly should effect a genuine spiritual conversion of Densher. There are clearly other noteworthy strains of imagery in the novel—the animal imagery, the abyss imagery, and the imagery of disease and health are examples—but none of them, I believe, is so extensive, so dramatically emphasized, or so invested with notable verbal intensity as the marine imagery.[18]

17. There is also possibly an echo of *Othello* here. Densher's image of the pearl cast away specifically refers to Milly's last letter, which he has already seen Kate burn. But, though he feels the loss acutely, we know that he has taken, even without the letter, the revelation that the heiress of all the ages had for him.

18. Jean Kimball argues that the central metaphor in the novel is the abyss (in her "The Abyss and *The Wings of the Dove*: The Image as Revelation," in

Crucial to my interpretation, moreover, is the perception—beyond the density, emphasis, and intensity of the marine imagery—of a meaningful arrangement of the most important images in this group.[19] The reader is recommended to bear in mind the following summary description of this pattern when considering the subsequent survey of images associated with Milly.

In the early books of the novel, most importantly during the introductory survey of Milly through Mrs. Stringham's eyes, the current of marine images is primarily associated with the society that Milly has encountered in England, a perilous sea in which one may well, at maximum risk, run upon submerged motives. In later books, as the peril to Milly grows, the suggestions of shipwreck do not diminish, but at the same time the water imagery becomes increasingly associated with Milly herself, especially with her aura and with the enchanting environs of Palazzo Leporelli. The sea is now at once beautiful and perilous, and this dichotomy is dramatized in the descriptions of the Venetian water world before, during, and after the sea-storm. The key, finally, to this overarching movement from marine imagery that characterizes English society and that suggests peril to marine imagery that is involved chiefly with Milly and with beauty as well as with peril is the allusion to the sea-change in *The Tempest*, where the sea is both a destroyer and the element in which, metaphorically, profoundly beautiful moral change occurs.[20] It is only, the figures

Tony Tanner [ed.], *Modern Judgments: Henry James* [Nashville, 1970], 262–82). There are, in fact, surprisingly few repetitions of the image of the abyss after Milly's highly dramatic perching on the verge of a real abyss in chapter I of Book Third, and the most prominent of these repetitions is absorbed into the larger pattern of the water imagery. For when Milly follows her declaration that "I want abysses" with the wish that "we shall sound the depths—I'm prepared for the worst—of sorrow and sin," the abysses turn from alpine to submarine (*WDI*, 186–87).

19. Of course, James's novels, especially the later ones, are rich in marine imagery. But I do not find, in *The Ambassadors*, for example, or in *The Golden Bowl*, the sort of significant symbolic pattern in the overall development of the images of ships and of the sea that seems to me to operate in *The Wings of the Dove*. For this reason, and also because of the absence of any allusion to *The Tempest* in *The Ambassadors*, I find unconvincing Richard Chartier's argument that the water images in that novel enact a sea-change (see his "The River and the Whirlpool: Water Imagery in *The Ambassadors*," *Ball State University Forum*, XXII [Spring, 1971], 70–75).

20. This is not to say that the allusion to *The Tempest* will illuminate each individual marine image, but only that it casts light on the general arrangement of all of the marine imagery. It will not help—may well, in fact, hinder—one's

cumulatively suggest, as a shipwrecked creature that Milly can attain her apotheosis and inspire Densher's transformation.

The first applications of marine imagery to Milly's case appear in chapter I of Book Third, where there is a close connection between the literal and figurative sea images. Mrs. Stringham, having agreed to enlist with Milly on her transatlantic excursion, thinks that she "had accordingly placed herself, by her act, in a boat that she more and more estimated as, humanly speaking, of the biggest, though likewise, no doubt, in many ways, by reason of its size, of the safest." A few pages later, she expands on the conceit:

> It was her [Milly's] nature, once for all—a nature that reminded Mrs. Stringham of the term always used in the newspapers about the great new steamers, the inordinate number of "feet of water" they drew; so that if, in your little boat, you had chosen to hover and approach, you had but yourself to thank, when once motion was started, for the way the draught pulled you. Milly drew the feet of water, and odd though it might seem that a lonely girl, who was not robust and who hated sound and show, should stir the stream like a leviathan, her companion floated off with the sense of rocking violently at her side.

James is emphasizing—as Holder-Barell notes (see n. 15 above)—the extent of Milly's wealth and Mrs. Stringham's passive subservience to her. In the paragraph immediately following this passage, Mrs. Stringham's thoughts turn from figurative seafaring to "the voyage itself, by the happy southern course, to the succession of Mediterranean ports, with the dazzled wind-up at Naples" (*WDI*, 104, 112–14).

The next significant cluster of water images associated with Milly occurs in chapter I of Book Fourth, the first dinner party at Lancaster Gate. We have, initially, the previously quoted passage in which Matthiessen identified James's allusion to *The Tempest*, then Lord Mark's comparison of English society to "the vague billows of some great greasy sea in mid-Channel," and shortly thereafter Milly's assessment of what may lie beneath its surface: "she had, on the spot, with her first plunge into the obscure depths of a society constituted from far back, encountered the interesting phenomenon of complicated, of possibly sinister motive." Similarly, suspecting an affinity between

---

understanding, for example, of Aunt Maud's touring the archipelago and splashing her screw.

Kate and Lord Mark, Milly wonders if "the handsome girl" will duplicate "the relation into which she was sinking" with him. The entire dinner party, in fact, takes place in a liquid medium. Here Milly sees Mrs. Lowder as cruising her conversational archipelagoes, and here words reach James's heroine "like plashes of a slow thick tide." The "immediate lesson" of Milly's social success, for her and Mrs. Stringham, is stated in the first paragraph of the next chapter: "they just had been caught up by the incalculable strength of a wave that was actually holding them aloft and that would naturally dash them wherever it liked" (*WDI*, 150, 153–54, 159–60, 167).

The incidence of water imagery associated with Milly is high throughout the remainder of Volume I of the novel. The examples following are illustrative, not exhaustive. In chapter II of Book Fourth, Milly imagines that she and Kate are "thoroughly afloat together." Chapter III of Book Fourth contains Milly's wish to "sound the depths . . . of sorrow and sin," Mrs. Stringham's image of her relationship with Milly as an island over which a great wave sweeps, and also her reflection that "finally, too, weren't they braving the deeps? They got their amusement where they could." "Launched" by Lord Mark at the party at Matcham, where "they were all swimming together in the blue," Milly feels "all the freshness of response of her young life" as "a fuller flood" that "somehow kept bearing her up." Matcham "served to Milly, then and afterwards, as a high-water mark of the imagination." In chapter III of Book Fifth, the minutes of her consultation with Sir Luke affect Milly as "ebbing more swiftly than her little army of items could muster," and she is apprehensive that she has been "in fact launched in some current that would lose itself in the sea of science." In the interview with Sir Luke, Milly introduces shipwreck imagery into the novel: "I'm a survivor," she tells him, "of a general wreck." In chapter IV of Book Fifth, Milly is "borne up for the hour" of her walk in Regent's Park, where "grey immensity" becomes "her element," where revelations come "rolling over her" like waves, and where her realization of the meaning of Sir Luke's treatment of her is "a final and merciful wave, chilling rather, but washing clear." Here are three last examples from the closing chapters of Book Fifth. In chapter V, Mrs. Lowder's interest in her, like Sir Luke's, makes Milly feel "as if her doom so floated her on that she couldn't stop." In chapter VI,

> it pressed upon her then and there that she was still in a current determined, through her indifference, timidity, bravery, generosity—she scarce could say which—by others; that not she but the current acted, and that somebody else always was the keeper of the lock or the dam. Kate for example had but to open the flood-gate: the current moved in its mass—the current, as it had been, of her doing as Kate wanted . . . This fantasy indeed, while they sat together, dropped after a little; even if only because other fantasies multiplied and clustered, making fairly, for our young woman, the buoyant medium in which her friend talked and moved.

And in chapter VII, Milly positively covets "the case of escape, of living under water, of being at once impersonal and firm" (*WDI*, 172, 187, 201, 209, 210, 213–14, 230, 231, 241, 247, 251–52, 271, 274–75, 288).

In Volume II—the half of the novel that James thought was deformed by foreshortening—the frequency of marine images specifically associated with Milly declines, perhaps partly as a consequence of the pervasive literal water images that establish the Venetian background, but also as a result of the thinning out of imagery in general in the latter portion of the book. In Densher's eyes, significantly, Milly's element becomes more and more aqueous and, at the same time, more and more his own. Thus, in chapter III of Book Sixth, he thinks of Milly Theale's success as favored "by one of those common caprices of the numberless foolish flock, gregarious movements as inscrutable as ocean-currents. The huddled herd had drifted to her blindly—it might as blindly have drifted away." When Densher decides to go for a carriage ride with Milly, thereby "turning his corner," we read that "if he had been drifting it settled itself in the manner of a bump, of considerable violence, against a firm object in the stream." Later, during Milly's brilliant soirée at Palazzo Leporelli, he has a "sense of immersion in an element rather more strangely than agreeably warm." For he feels Milly "diffuse in wide warm waves the spell of a general, a beatific mildness. There was a deeper depth of it, doubtless, for some than for others; what he in particular knew of it was that he seemed to stand in it up to his neck. He moved about in it and it made no plash; he floated, he noiselessly swam in it, and they were all together, for that matter, like fishes in a crystal pool." On the next page, noting that Milly has been determined in her uncustomary choice of a white dress (as against her "inveterate black") by Sir Luke, Densher reflects that "he couldn't be invidious, even to profit by so high a tide," because "he felt himself too much 'in' it." Apprehensive, at the time of Sir Luke's second arrival in Venice, that the surgeon might make such an advance as to "prove for him somehow a pledge or a committal" to Milly, Densher is "afraid of it as a current that would draw him too far." And, again, Densher's image of casting the pearl of Milly's revelation "into the fathomless sea" reminds us that metaphoric as well as actual pearls ought, in a consistent figure, to be of submarine origin, the rich culmination of a sea-change (*WDII*, 43, 88, 212–14, 295, 396).

A more ominous strain of imagery in Volume II couples Milly with ships and shipwrecks. In chapter V of Book Sixth, in conversation with Densher, Milly places herself in a boat beyond her control and implicitly more frail than the great liner suggested by the imagery in Book Third:

> "However, everything's done and the wind's in our sails."
>
> "May you scud then happily before it! But when," he asked, "do you come back?"
>
> She looked ever so vague; then as if to correct it: "Oh, when the wind turns."

The idea of running helplessly before the wind takes a menacing coloring from the talk of shipwreck that Kate and Densher have just had in the preceding chapter. Densher, Kate tells him, may "console" Milly "for all that, if she's stricken, she must see swept away." "Do you mean," Densher asks a few moments later, "she has something past patching?"

> And before she could answer: "It's really as if her appearance put her outside of such things—being, in spite of her youth, that of a person who has been through all it's conceivable she should be exposed to. She affects one, I should say, as a creature saved from a shipwreck. Such a creature may surely, in these days, on the doctrine of chances, go to sea again with confidence. She has *had* her wreck—she has met her adventure."
>
> "Oh, I grant you her wreck!"—Kate was all response so far. "But do let her have still her adventure. There are wrecks that are not adventures."
>
> "Well—if there be also adventures that are not wrecks!"

Densher's "creature"—though the word itself is common in James—here seems to me affectingly resonant with the dove symbolism with which Milly is invested and also with the image of the deluge that occurs to Milly herself in Venice just before Lord Mark unexpectedly materializes to propose marriage. In Palazzo Leporelli, into which, in chapter III of Book Seventh, she had been said to "sink into possession . . . where the sun on the stirred sea-water, flickering up through open windows, played over the painted 'subjects' in the splendid ceilings," Milly's thoughts have swerved, with more than a hint of desperation, to images of drowning. To Eugenio, she has silently communicated this wish in regard to her entourage: "Yes, get me an hour alone; take them off—I don't care where; absorb, amuse, detain them; drown them, kill them, if you will: so that I may just a little, all by myself, see where I am." Then "she was conscious of the dire impatience of it, for she gave up Susie as well as the others to him [Eugenio]—Susie who would have drowned her very self for her."

> She made now, alone, the full circuit of the place, noble and peaceful while the summer sea, stirring here and there a curtain or an outer blind, breathed into its veiled spaces. She had a vision of clinging to it; that perhaps Eugenio could manage. She was *in* it, as in the ark of her deluge, and filled with such a tenderness for it that why shouldn't this, in common mercy, be warrant enough? She would never, never leave it—she would engage to that; would ask nothing more than to sit tight in it and float on and on.

Milly's clinging to the Palazzo here means, literally, her continuing to occupy it, but on the level of metaphor "clinging" has darker connotations, for the Palazzo is an ark and one does not usually think of clinging to a vessel unless it has been wrecked. The allusion to Noah's ark marks a transaction between the animal and marine imagery in the novel. One might note, in this connection, the appositeness of the association of Milly and the dove and Kate and the crow to the biblical narrative of Noah's use of a dove and a raven to reconnoiter for dry land (*WDII*, 52–53, 82, 132, 141–43).

In any case, Lord Mark appears, and Milly realizes that "she hadn't been so thoroughly alone with him since those moments of his showing her the great portrait of Matcham, the moments that had exactly made the high-water mark of her security, the moments during which her tears themselves, those she had been ashamed of, were the sign of her consciously rounding her protective promontory, quitting the blue gulf of comparative ignorance and reaching her view of the troubled sea." Pasquale, approaching to announce Densher, slips "in white shoes over the marble" and suggests to Milly's "perpetually charmed vision . . . a barefooted seaman on the deck of a ship." Never before so much as at this perilous crossing of Densher's path with Lord Mark's in Venice have we seen Milly so relentlessly floating on to her doom (*WDII*, 144, 167).

That doom engulfs her when Lord Mark returns to Venice and tells Milly about the plot that Kate and Densher have undertaken against her. The violence Milly feels in her abrupt disillusion about Densher—which is also a revelation of disorder in the moral universe—is impressed upon the reader by a dramatic change in the weather. The majority of the literal marine images in *The Wings of the Dove* describe the Venetian sea-storm, a phenomenon that is patently other than merely meteorological, not only because of the Shakespeare allusion, but also because the storm, in its coincidence with Milly's crisis, is clearly a part of James's symbolic machinery. Densher, moreover, interprets the storm symbolically, associating its onset and abatement with the second visits to Venice of Lord Mark and of Sir Luke respectively. As noted earlier, the "greasy" paving of the Piazza San Marco during the sea-storm recalls Lord Mark's description of society as a "greasy sea" (*WDI*, 150; *WDII*, 261). In view of the consistency and high frequency of marine imagery preceding the storm, it is hard not to view its outbreak as an eruption of symbolic imagery onto the literal plane of the novel. That is, one finds literal images that derive not—as Norman Friedman suggests is the case with some writers—from metaphors in previous works but from the dominant metaphors in earlier portions of the same work.[21] In any case, the sea-storm marks the figurative sea-change of Milly Theale and directly preludes the consequent transformation of Densher. Milly, who had "turned her face to the wall" in reaction to the disclosures of that "idiot of idiots," Lord Mark (as a drenched Susan Stringham reports to Densher at the height of the storm), emerges from it in the following "blest calm" as the transcendently beautiful being who summons Densher to a final interview and who thereby leaves him feeling "forgiven, dedicated, blessed" (*WDII*, 270, 285, 304, 343). In overcoming the despair that she feels at her discovery of evil and in winning her

21. Norman Friedman, "Imagery: From Sensation to Symbol," *Journal of Aesthetics and Art Criticism*, XII (1953), 31.

way to a higher innocence than that which she had previously possessed, Milly fulfills the pattern of spiral return and enables Densher to do so too.

Much more might be said about the marine imagery in *The Wings of the Dove*. There is a constant dualism about it. Water represents not only the life surrounding the characters but also, at times, the life within them. It is a destructive element but also a purifying one, connected not only with shipwrecks but also with the wave that washes clear and with the transforming process implied in the allusion to Ariel's dirge. The marine imagery recalls, in this respect, Friedman's characterization of the symbolism of water: "water is a grave and a womb, it floods and fertilizes, drowns and purifies, endangers and releases."[22] The water images represent English society and also, more generally, for both Milly and Densher, life in general, experience of the world—in fact, consciousness itself.

One of the most intriguing—and least commented upon—aspects of the novel is the question of why Milly does not die in mere bitterness. What goes on within her between the time she turns her face to the wall and her last, spiritually momentous interview with Densher? What, in fact, is the intimate process and content of the sea-change completed in Venice? Granted that this matter can never be resolved with certainty, I would suggest that there is only a single general line of interpretation that is at all consistent with the supernal portrait of Milly presented by James throughout the novel: in the undramatized, final days of her life, Milly comes to "read" Densher and Kate in much the same spirit as the most sympathetic commentators on them. She comes, that is, to understand many things, chiefmost among which are the ardor of Kate and Densher's love for each other, the extremity of Kate's predicament between the Scylla of affluent Aunt Maud and titled Lord Mark and the Charybdis of the never-to-be-well-off Densher, and the liability of Densher to be easily manipulated by Kate precisely because of his love for her and because of the intellectual disinterestedness that constitutes perhaps his strongest appeal. Empathizing thus with the other persons in the triangle, Milly feels her love for Densher as much as ever, and her forgiveness, dedication, blessing, and legacy are all monuments to her passion. That these

22. *Ibid.*, 37.

things—forgiveness, blessing, bequest, and all—come at last between Densher and Kate is a typically Jamesian turn of the screw, but the ironic outcome could not have been, in my view, Milly's purpose. The true note of Milly's intentions might well be taken from Christina Rossetti's poem "Everything That Is Born Must Die," a likely and, so far as I know, hitherto unnoticed source for James's title, here quoted in full:

> Everything that is born must die;
> Everything that can sigh may sing;
> Rocks in equal balance, low or high,
> Everything.
>
> Honeycomb is weighed against a sting;
> Hope and fear take turns to touch the sky;
> Height and depth respond alternating.
>
> O my soul, spread wings of love to fly,
> Wings of dove that soars on home-bound wing:
> Love trusts Love, till Love shall justify
> Everything.[23]

From Sallie Sears's point of view, the supposedly transformed Densher is, more than anything else, a prig. Priggish he may seem, to be sure, but only from the viewpoint of a contemporary morality prejudicial to the moral assumptions and expectations of Anglo-American culture in James's time. And one should add that he is also, in the closing chapters, resolute in a way he has not formerly been, renunciatory to a fabulous extent, changed in his feelings for Kate, and in general so different from the Densher we have known that to point out his priggishness is to direct attention to only a small part of the picture. One could argue that Densher has always been priggish in Sears's sense. But his acts of integrity, his refusal of Milly's fortune, his offer of marriage without money, and his admission that he is in love with the memory of Milly (denial of which Kate proposes, at the close of the novel, as the one way to keep her) must be weighed against the charges of smugness and superficiality that Sears brings against him. If there is something distasteful in the tests that he imposes on Kate, the reader should bear in mind that these are tactics

23. Rossetti's poem first appeared in her volume *Verses* (1893). Its probable connection with *The Wings of the Dove* was first pointed out to me by my graduate student James Frederick Smith.

in the one encounter he has with Kate in which he outmaneuvers her, that here, for the first time, he resists her manipulation. Sears's severest charge against Densher—and against James for ending the novel as he did—is that he minimizes his own guilt, shifting the burden of blame to Kate. I believe, on the contrary, that only a consciousness of the depth of his guilt makes him susceptible to the transformation wrought by Milly's forgiveness and blessing. Readers must decide for themselves if Densher's conversion is persuasive. There is ample evidence, in any case, that James worked on many levels to show it convincingly, most subtly and powerfully, to my mind, through the transformation that the marine images undergo, the sea-change of the imagery. The ugliness of the sea that Lord Mark describes to Milly in Book Fourth is recalled during the tempest in Venice, but it is in the fabulously changed water-world of chapter IV of Book Ninth, in the calm after the sea-storm, that Densher takes from Milly the gift of her sea-change, the pearl of spiritual wisdom, a gift that brings him up from "the deepest depth his predicament could sink him to" into the "sacred hush" of devotion to her memory (*WDII*, 301, 396).

CHAPTER THREE

Directions and Indirections: The Spiral Ascent in *The Golden Bowl*

The Golden Bowl, like *The Ambassadors*, has peculiarly lent itself to analysis in dialectical terms. No idea about the novel recurs so frequently in the commentaries as that James attempted in it a synthesis of the major thematic oppositions of his earlier work. This perception is almost the only common ground of those who have damned James for the failure of his intention and of those who have lauded him for high success. Sallie Sears, for instance, prosecutes her thesis that James's fictions render the conflict of irreconcilable oppositions—"the world as rent asunder, with half its goods on the left hand of God, half on the right, and no passage in between"—by arguing that Maggie Verver represents "the fusion of the negative attributes, not the positive, of James's polar vision of human nature, as if only the darker parts of man could finally cross the barrier, the white curtain, that divides him from himself." J. A. Ward's view in his first book on James was less hostile to Maggie, who, he wrote, achieves a "synthesis of her own innocence and Amerigo's experience (each a blend of good and evil)." Because Maggie's reconciliation of "American idealism and British practicality, combining, as it were, the spiritual love of Milly Theale and the practical genius of Kate Croy," seemed highly equivocal to Ward, his first version of the synthesis of *The Golden Bowl*, like Sears's, was negative: "In *The Golden Bowl* James achieves a resolution of the Europe-America antithesis principally because he is hesitant to place the burden of evil on the Europeans . . . he reveals that the common denominator of the two is their mutual participation in human sin." In his second book on James, Ward's view of the novelist's achievement is more positive, but the terms remain dialectical, for now Maggie, "the ideal Jamesian artist," discovers that "form is preserved only as it is strained," and so there is an "artistic synthesis between classical order and free organic growth."[1]

In general, defenders of the novel have argued that its resolution is affirmative. Quentin Anderson, though his allegorical reading of *The Golden Bowl* is unnecessarily complicated and finally unpersuasive, expresses the view most widespread among admirers of the novel, that it achieves a "reconciliation of 'Europe' (appearance) with 'America' (reality)." Treating the completed novels of James's major phase as a trilogy, Christof Wegelin says that they "picture in the first place, not Europe and America, but the American experience of Europe, the European experience of America. They are novels of initiation and conversion and, in *The Golden Bowl*, finally, of fusion." For Wegelin, the "social beauty in Madame de Vionnet" and the "high spiritual beauty in Milly Theale" come to "fusion in the marriage of Maggie Verver and the Roman Prince." Edwin T. Bowden remarks that "the American-European contrast and the moral-esthetic relationship . . . meet in climactic interfusion in *The Ambassadors* and *The Golden Bowl*." Leo B. Levy asserts that "James finally resolved the conflict between the two traditions in *The Golden Bowl*, where the intention (sometimes discernible in earlier works) of bringing the American sensibility into a living, significant union with Europe is fulfilled" in such a way that the novel "escapes melodrama." Donald L. Mull sees "Maggie's consciousness" as extending "to embrace antitheses for the attainment of a love which refuses to exclude." Because Mull takes the Prince to fall "totally short of Maggie's empathic imaginative inclusion," he believes that Amerigo's dependence on her "tragically illuminates the final sentence," producing "the tragedy which informs James's divine comedy—the ultimate synthesis of antitheses which the imaginative vision achieves." Dorothea Krook, whose book on James contains two distinct interpretations of *The Golden Bowl*, presented in separate chapters, says in the first, an argument

1. Sears, *The Negative Imagination*, 145, 210; Ward, *The Imagination of Disaster*, 139, 150, 153; Ward, *The Search for Form*, 216, 219.

for the redemptive function of Maggie Verver, that "the touchstone of taste is finally transcended by incorporation into the moral, where beauty and goodness are, at last and indissolubly, one." In her second chapter on the novel, Krook explores the grimness involved in Charlotte's development in Volume II, a note of pessimism at odds with the redemptive theme, and concludes that "in Henry James's total vision, the sense of the grimness and bitterness of human life is inseparably fused with the sense of its beauty and blessedness; that neither cancels out the other; and that the ambiguity is intended to express precisely this experience of their permanent, inseparable fusion."[2]

My purpose in the present chapter is not, however, to review the extraordinary critical controversies that *The Golden Bowl* has inspired. I have offered the foregoing citations, rather, to indicate the pervasiveness, in widely divergent readings of the novel, of dialectical terms—terms common, to cite further examples, to Stephen Spender and Ferner Nuhn, among the harshest critics of *The Golden Bowl*, and to John Bayley and Walter Wright, among its most eloquent defenders.[3] Most commentators have fallen into one of two camps: those who feel, as Wright puts it, that "Maggie Verver and her father Adam exemplify the evil which James identified with American puritanism and materialism" and those who believe that Maggie, at least, "is a virtual saint."[4] Many of the detractors, furthermore, level against James the charge of confusion, of lack of control of the ambiguities of the novel, and even of obliviousness to the existence of the ambiguities. A third camp might be said to be constituted by those recent critics who have tried to reconcile the two opposed readings; Dorothea Krook, Laurence Holland, Donald Mull, Walter Wright, and

2. Quentin Anderson, *The American Henry James* (New Brunswick, 1957), 346; Christof Wegelin, *The Image of Europe in Henry James* (Dallas, 1958), 88, 105; Edwin T. Bowden, *The Themes of Henry James: A System of Observation Through the Visual Arts* (New Haven, 1956), 97; Leo B. Levy, *Versions of Melodrama: A Study of the Fiction and Drama of Henry James, 1865–1897* (Berkeley, 1957), 28; Mull, *Henry James's "Sublime Economy,"* 157, 162–63; Krook, *The Ordeal of Consciousness*, 276, 324.

3. See Stephen Spender, *The Destructive Element: A Study of Modern Writers and Beliefs* (Philadelphia, 1953); Ferner Nuhn, *The Wind Blew From The East: A Study in the Orientation of American Culture* (New York, 1942); John Bayley, *The Characters of Love: A Study in the Literature of Personality* (New York, 1960); and Walter F. Wright, *The Madness of Art: A Study of Henry James* (Lincoln, 1962).

4. Wright, *The Madness of Art*, 242.

Philip Weinstein, despite many disagreements among themselves, all interpret *The Golden Bowl* in ways that attempt to mediate between the adversaries and the proponents of the novel. My own view, to put it as simply and as starkly as possible at the outset, is that the novel is a masterpiece of controlled ambiguity and that its resolution, while incorporating qualified tragic undertones, is above all affirmative and comic. I am particularly indebted to the pro-Verver critics, such as Bayley and Wegelin, and also to those whom I have described as in the third, mediating critical camp, especially to Krook and Mull, who both stress James's control of the tensions of the novel as well as the redemptive generosity of Maggie Verver.

Before proceeding with my discussion of the novel—an analysis of the principal characters in relation to the paradigm of the dialectic of spiral return—I want to make a further observation about previous commentaries on *The Golden Bowl.* All too often analyses of the novel become obsessive hunts for ambiguity, whether treated as an Empsonian criterion of value or as a measure of confusion and of artistic failure. Ambiguities, to be sure, are plentiful in this last and most richly complicated of James's completed novels. The critic ought, for this very reason, to proceed with special care and circumspection. The dangers of overinterpretation, ever-present in our post-Empsonian age, loom large indeed when one is in presence of a text like *The Golden Bowl.* Since vast numbers of English words will yield, to ingenious attention, multiple meanings, the significance of even a short lyric may be subject to virtually infinite permutations. The critic of a work of the scope of *The Golden Bowl* ought, perforce, to pay strict attention to the contextual control of the possible plurisignations in the text in order to arrive at a clear estimate of the most probable interpretation. Naturally, assessments of probable significance will vary from reader to reader, but the criterion of probability seems to me to be the one rational recourse if we are not to reduce complex works of literature to morasses of meaninglessness.

Because there can be no strict calculus of probability, such a standard allows for considerable interpretive latitude, but it will also rule out readings of *The Golden Bowl* like those set forth by Robert Marks and Jean Kimball, which so wrench the ostensible meanings of the text as to become what one can only call wildly improbable. Kimball's elevation of Charlotte Stant to the status of the heroine of the novel might deserve the sanction of anti-Verver critics were it not for the high improbability of her thesis that Charlotte and the Prince do not engage in an illicit affair but are only imagined to have done so by Maggie. Robert Marks carries a similar argument, incredibly, to a further extreme: not only has there been no adultery in Marks's reading, but Maggie Verver—despite many confirmations of Maggie's point of view in passages where other characters are the centers of consciousness, of none of which Marks takes account—is a wholly unreliable observer, whose baffled, incestuous passion for her father blinds her to the truth that Charlotte and Adam are all along deeply in love with each other. Kimball and Marks represent, to be sure, extremes of the liability to overinterpretation—if Marks's case may not perhaps more accurately be said to be one of drastic underinterpretation—but the fabulous intricacies of *The Golden Bowl* have drawn many readers into similar, if less glaring, improbabilities.[5] Consequently, though my primary effort in the following pages will be to demonstrate the dialectical organization of *The Golden Bowl* and to assess the implications of that organization for interpretation of the novel, I shall also be concerned with separating the most probable intendments of the ambiguities in the novel from those that seem to me at best merely possible.

The contrast between American and European values has been most frequently mentioned by critics as the central focus in *The Golden Bowl.* Such a view is not only understandable but to some degree justifiable; however, it should not keep us from taking seriously James's assertion that the international contrasts are secondary. Cargill, citing the relevant passage from James's preface to "Lady Barbarina," takes the novelist to mean that the national traits of the characters are less important than their cosmopolitanism.[6] His inference is no doubt true, but it seems to me that James was pointing not so much to the secondary nature of contrasts in general in *The Golden Bowl* as to the superseding of the international contrast by others

5. See Robert Marks, *James's Later Novels: An Interpretation* (New York, 1960), 111–30, and Jean Kimball, "Henry James's Last Portrait of a Lady: Charlotte Stant in *The Golden Bowl,*" *American Literature*, XXVIII (1957), 449–68. For an authoritative demolition of Kimball's argument, see Oscar Cargill, *The Novels of Henry James*, 397–400.

6. Cargill, *The Novels of Henry James*, 383.

more intrinsic to his conception of the novel. Here are James's remarks on the matter:

> The reader of these volumes will certainly see it [contrast] offered in no form so frequent or so salient as that of the opposition of aspects from country to country. Their author, I am quite aware, would seem struck with no possibility of contrast in the human lot so great as that encountered as we turn back and forth between the distinctively American and the distinctively European outlook . . . yet there are cases in which, however obvious and however contributive, its office for the particular demonstration, has been quite secondary, and in which the work is by no means merely addressed to the illustration of it. These things have had in the latter case their proper subject: as, for instance, the subject of "The Wings of the Dove," or that of "The Golden Bowl," has not been the exhibited behaviour of certain Americans as Americans, of certain English persons as English, of certain Romans as Roman. Americans, Englishmen, Romans are, in the whole matter, agents or victims; but this is in virtue of an association nowadays so developed, so easily to be taken for granted, as to have created a new scale of relations altogether, a state of things from which emphasized internationalism has either quite dropped or is well on its way to drop. The dramatic side of human situations subsists of course on contrast; and when we come to the two novels I have just named we shall see, for example, just how they positively provide themselves with that source of interest. We shall see nevertheless at the same time that the subject could in each case have been perfectly expressed had *all* the persons concerned been only American or only English or only Roman or whatever.[7]

There are, then, other contrasts, besides the important but allegedly secondary international one, upon which the dramatic side of *The Golden Bowl* may be said to subsist: reality and appearance, truth and falsehood, good faith and bad faith, material and spiritual goods, the moral sense and the aesthetic sense, innocence and initiation, conjugal and adulterous love, work and leisure, humility and pride, appreciation and exploitation, victim and agent, science and history. James reinforces these antitheses by fundamental oppositions among the major characters (Charlotte and Maggie, Maggie and the Prince, the Prince and Adam, Fanny Assingham and Bob) and by the use of minor characters as foils (the Lutches and Mrs. Rance to Charlotte, Lady Castledean and Mr. Blint to Charlotte and the Prince, the Jewish vendors to the central, Christian figures). In addition, the four

7. *AN*, 198–99.

principal settings of the novel, which have important symbolic bearings, fall into two contrasted pairs, the country houses, Matcham and Fawns, and the town houses at Eaton Square and Portland Place.

Thematic oppositions have clearly been the major cause of the widespread use of dialectical terms by commentators on *The Golden Bowl*, but the structural symmetry of the novel, as in the case of *The Ambassadors*, has also encouraged critics to see it as bipolar. J. A. Ward's very useful discussion of the novel in *The Search For Form* clarifies the way in which James based his drama on "duplication of incidents," such as the parallel conversations between Maggie and Adam Verver at Fawns in Books Second and Fifth. In general, Ward sees the overall form of *The Golden Bowl* as "dualistic."[8] The plot of the novel involves the characters in reversals similar to the reversals in *The Ambassadors*, giving rise to such comments as Tony Tanner's, who speaks of the "complete shift of positions" and suggests that "one might almost use the image of intersecting cones"—a figure strikingly reminiscent of Forster's hourglass paradigm for the structure of *The Ambassadors*. The division of the novel into two volumes, "The Prince" and "The Princess," has also been seen as expressive of the dualism of James's conception. Sallie Sears's observation, for example, that "the first half of the novel is (for the most part) a register of the Prince's consciousness of what is unfolding" and that "the second half is a register of the Princess's consciousness" comes directly on the heels of her remarks that "there are few events that are not susceptible of two interpretations," that "the duality is omnipresent and unrelenting," and that "two pairs of eyes see the events of this novel."[9]

James's comments in his preface to *The Golden Bowl* on the division of the novel into two volumes ought to have raised more questions than has apparently been the case. "The Prince," James says, "in the first half of the book, virtually sees and knows and makes out, virtually represents to himself everything that concerns us," and "the function of the Princess, in the remainder, matches exactly with his." A moment later, James allows "a possible objection":

8. Ward, *The Search for Form*, 204, 207. Ward does not, however, see the two volumes of the novel in polar opposition. For him, Volume II echoes rather than opposes Volume I. See *ibid.*, 203–206.

9. Tony Tanner, "*The Golden Bowl* and the Reassessment of Innocence," *London Magazine*, n.s., I (1961), 42; Sears, *The Negative Imagination*, 173–74.

> It may be noted, that is, that the Prince, in the volume over which he nominally presides, is represented as in comprehensive cognition only of those aspects as to which Mrs. Assingham doesn't functionally—perhaps all too officiously, as the reader may sometimes feel it—supersede him. This disparity in my plan is, however, but superficial; the thing abides rigidly by its law of showing Maggie Verver at first through her suitor's and her husband's exhibitory vision of her, and of then showing the Prince, with at least an equal intensity, through his wife's . . . It is the Prince who opens the door to half our light upon Maggie, just as it is she who opens it to half our light upon himself . . . We see Charlotte also at first, and we see Adam Verver, let alone our seeing Mrs. Assingham, and every one and every thing else, but as they are visible in the Prince's interest, so to speak—by which I mean of course in the interest of his being himself handed over to us. With a like consistency we see the same persons and things again but as Maggie's interest, *her* exhibitional charm, determines the view. (*AN*, 329–30)

J. A. Ward is alone in expressing perplexity at these ingenious Jamesian formulations. "In what sense," he asks, can "the 'things' in the two volumes" be " 'the same,' " given "the obvious difficulty with this idea . . . that there is a definite action, indeed a near-total alteration of the situation." Ward's response to this question is his investigation of the duplication in Volume II of incidents in Volume I. But other commentators have swallowed James's explanation whole. Dorothea Krook's observation on this matter typifies the usual critical response: "there are but two centres of consciousness, the Prince in the First Book, Maggie Verver in the Second, and they are used strictly in succession, without recourse to the relief of alternation."[10]

The question I would raise is different from Ward's and requires a different though perhaps complementary response. To my mind, the passage from the preface to the novel—Ward's understanding of the sameness of the two volumes notwithstanding—amounts to a most misleading description of *The Golden Bowl*. James seems to be engaging in special pleading, with which he probably deceived himself as well as many of his readers, with the motive of making the control of point of view in the novel conform to his cherished ideal of symmetry. Had he looked more deeply into what he had accomplished, he would, I believe, have discovered a more complex and meaningful pattern in the changing foci of consciousness in the novel, but a pattern which is

10. Ward, *The Search for Form*, 203; Krook, *The Ordeal of Consciousness*, 236.

also, finally, symmetrical. The inconsistency that James concedes and attempts to account for, the superseding of the Prince as central intelligence by Fanny Assingham in parts of Volume I, is only a minor portion of the deviation of the volume from James's description of it. In only twelve of the twenty-four chapters in the first half of the novel is Prince Amerigo the center of consciousness.[11] Of these, only two are devoted to any significant degree to opening doors to light on Maggie (chapters I and II of Book First); four others may be said to do so as a matter of decidedly subsidiary interest (chapters II, IV, V and VI of Book Third), for in them the Prince's attention is settled far more intensively on himself, on Charlotte, and on Fanny. The entirety of Book Second (seven consecutive chapters) is written predominantly from the point of view of Adam Verver. The most striking exception is a brief passage in chapter III of Book Second when we see Amerigo from Maggie's viewpoint (the relation that is supposed to obtain in Volume II, but not here in Volume I). One chapter (chapter I of Book Third) opens with Charlotte Stant as the central reflector and constitutes the only sustained passage in the novel from her point of view.[12] James's account in the preface, then, falls as soon as one looks closely at the development of point of view in Volume I. The novelist's description of Volume II, on the other hand, does not do such violence to his text; by and large, the second half of *The Golden Bowl* is a description of Maggie's changing perspectives with special emphasis on her relation to Amerigo.

The question, then, is whether there is some pattern, other than the one provided by James in the preface, capable of accounting for the structure of Volume I as well as for that of Volume II. If one bears in mind the dramatic opposition of the Ververs, father and daughter, on one side, and of the lovers, Charlotte and the Prince, on the other, an answer becomes, I think, possible: the focus of attention in the books of the two volumes alternates between the Ververs and the lovers. From the second half of chapter II on, Book First is about Charlotte and the Prince. Book Second belongs distinctly to Adam Verver, though the increasing focus on Charlotte as the question of

11. Each of the two volumes is divided into three books, which in turn are subdivided into chapters.

12. The only other passage from Charlotte's point of view is the single paragraph in chapter IV of Book Third in which we learn what Amerigo said in his telegram about Charlotte's engagement and what she made of his cryptic message.

his marriage to her approaches settlement prepares for Book Third, which is concerned chiefly with the relation of Charlotte and the Prince and which reaches a climax as the pair are about to take their adulterous excursion to Gloucester. The last two chapters of Book Third, during which Fanny speculates about Maggie's awakening to the situation, facilitate the transition to Book Fourth, in which the subject is the gradual conversion of Maggie's disquiet into suspicion and of her suspicion into certainty about her husband's infidelity with her stepmother. Books First and Third, then, belong to the lovers, Books Second and Fourth to the father and daughter.

Book Fifth clearly does not fit so well into my schema. As in Book Fourth, Maggie is the center of consciousness in Book Fifth, where we witness her subtlest and most complete triumphs over her adversaries. Nevertheless, there is an important sense in which this section of the novel may be assigned at least as much to the Prince and to Charlotte as to Maggie, for it can be fairly argued that, with the exception of chapter III (a conversation between father and daughter), Maggie's imagination throughout Book Fifth is involved, almost continuously and with increasing intensity, with the plight of the lovers. Thus, chapter I is largely given over to Maggie's divination of Amerigo's keeping Charlotte in the dark about Maggie's knowledge, to her speculation about his motives, and to her imagination of "the spacious but suspended cage, the home of eternal unrest," that figures Charlotte's delusion; in chapter II, stalked by Charlotte on the terrace at Fawns, Maggie gives her attention so thoroughly to her rival that the reader virtually experiences the two women as simultaneous centers of consciousness; and chapters IV and V are above all dramatizations of Maggie's intense sympathetic identification with Amerigo's abjection and Charlotte's anguish in the ordeal through which Maggie is all the while putting them.[13] That I am not drastically distorting this section of the novel to make it fit my analysis is suggested by the testimony of many sensitive readers (Sears, Mull, and Matthiessen among a host of others) that the most important impression they take from the final episodes at Fawns is not of any sensation proper to

13. Henry James, *The Golden Bowl* (2 vols.; New York, 1909), Vols. XXIII–XXIV of the New York Edition of Henry James (26 vols.; New York, 1907–17), XXIV, 229; hereinafter cited in footnotes and parenthetically in the text as *GBI* and *GBII*.

Maggie, even though hers is the central intelligence, but rather the mediated yet acutely poignant one of Charlotte's torment. Book Sixth, in any case, presents no such problem; stressing as it does the Ververs' final successful arrangement of their spouses, the closing section of the novel is dominated by Maggie and Adam.

The alternating dominance of the Ververs' spouses and of the Ververs themselves in the six books of *The Golden Bowl* is exemplary of the organic incorporation of the principle of opposition into the structure of the novel. The two sets of books, the first, third, and fifth, and the second, fourth, and sixth, are like two threads winding around each other, rising together in spiral fashion through the "duplication of incidents" outlined by Ward. In the first chapter of the novel, James shows us the Prince and Maggie together (in recollections by the Prince), and at the conclusion of the last chapter they are alone together too, but now, having passed through errors of vision and of grace unanticipated in their initial good fortune, they have emerged at a much higher level of awareness. Thus the novel can be described as an intricate but faithful enactment, like *The Ambassadors*, of the Romantic dialectic of spiral return.

Of particular significance for the interpretation of James's moral evaluation of Adam Verver is the explicit figure of a spiral ascent with which Verver's transformation from money-making tycoon to art-collecting aesthete is described. Even for critics sufficiently judicious *not* to assume, a priori, that Adam's fabulous wealth dooms him to serious moral imperfection, his character, more than that of any of the other principal persons in *The Golden Bowl*, has been shrouded in puzzlement and ambiguity. Is Adam's taste impeccable or is he inescapably a philistine? Does he respect the integrity of persons or does he treat them as things, as, primarily, objects for purchase? Does he become aware of whatever degree of culpability one ascribes to his innocence or is he oblivious to the end? Anti-Verver critics tend to see Adam as a philistine who reifies other people and who fails to grasp the moral implications of doing so. Even Donald Mull, who provides the most persuasive and comprehensive defense of Adam (at least among commentators who do not, like Caroline Gordon, simply ride roughshod over the genuine problems of interpretation surrounding this enigmatic figure), finds his character ambiguous, since "it is not so certain, in short, whether Adam Verver's attitude is the 'law of man' or the 'law of things'—whether his converting imagination allows him to enter, even with the objects of the world, into that right relationship which (as Henry James, Sr., had it) ought to characterize human dealings; or whether his aestheticism reifies human beings and renders them pawns for his manipulation."[14] But James's dialectical description of Adam's development prior to the action of the novel strongly suggests to me an affirmative valuation of him and provides, at the same time, a paradigm for his development after his marriage as well as for the maturation of Maggie and of the Prince, a paradigm, moreover, that Charlotte alone fails to fulfill. Consequently, in taking up the crucial questions of the moral responsibilities and liabilities of the four principal characters, I shall begin with Adam, move on to the Princess and the Prince, and conclude with Charlotte.

Adam Verver has the distinction of being by far the wealthiest person in James's unusually affluent fictional universe. Verver is one of the half dozen richest men on earth, a potentate of money. Adam's power, residing partly in his fortune and partly in his personal toughness, is brutally independent of his appearance, which is bland, unassuming, self-effacing: "he looked, at the top of his table, so nearly like a little boy shyly entertaining in virtue of some imposed rank, that he *could* only be one of the powers, the representative of a force—quite as an infant king is the representative of a dynasty" (*GBI*, 324). Adam is as much, indeed, a captive of his wealth as an infant king of his hereditary obligations. The rank is "imposed" willy-nilly; no matter how bland he is, he cannot escape deference, though he longs to do so. If, as Laurence Holland suggests, Adam's "money and the other values associated with the American character" create the "language of the new imperium," which "the others are induced to speak" but which "threatens to rule out, by its very power and fluency, the 'reciprocity' the Prince aspires to," Adam himself is irritated by the failure of communication.[15] For example, "with Mrs. Assingham he never felt quite sure of the ground anything covered; she disputed with him so little, agreed with him so much, surrounded

14. Mull, *Henry James's "Sublime Economy,"* 142. See also Caroline Gordon, "Mr. Verver, Our National Hero," *Sewanee Review*, LXIII (1955), 29–47.

15. Laurence Bedwell Holland, *The Expense of Vision: Essays on the Craft of Henry James* (Princeton, 1964), 352.

him with such systematic consideration, such predetermined tenderness, that it was almost—which he had once told her in irritation—as if she were nursing a sick baby." He wishes the Prince would "strike something" that he, Adam, had not "been brought up to," not that it would "ruffle the smoothness" but that it "might a little add to the interest." In general, "this attribution of power" presses "upon him hard and all round," and the dazzling white curtain of wealth through which the Prince cannot penetrate to a clear view of his father-in-law simultaneously cuts Adam off from the Prince. Adam's isolation from persons on the other side of the curtain must be seen in significant measure as the result of their interested (and in the Prince's case, to be sure, sincere) efforts to please him. The isolation accounts, in part, for his innocence and for his closeness to his daughter, who alone has long been familiar with him on his side of the "dazzling curtain of light" (*GBI*, 22, 131, 136–37, 158).

Adam is in his mid-forties when the novel, which covers a period of about five years, opens. At the time of his marriage to Charlotte Stant, he is forty-seven years old. He acquired his fortune early, in less than two decades, for we know that he began to do so when he was twenty and that he had given up business for his life as a collector of objets d'art when Maggie was ten years old, when he was thirty-seven or thirty-eight. Matthiessen complained that Adam's phenomenal success and his modesty of temperament are so incongruous as to undermine credibility. The combination is, to be sure, unusual, but one might reply to Matthiessen that the contrast appears so violent because of the stereotype of the robber baron: driving, flamboyant, brutally vital—a stereotype to which James himself never alludes. But I should think that Verver's oddity in this regard is an aspect of James's exploitation of the conventions of the fairy tale, a practice noticed by many readers, including, for example, Nuhn and Matthiessen himself. We do not learn how Adam's money was made, and only his "amiability" and the inscrutable monotony to which he subjected his imagination during his years in business are given as admittedly inadequate explanations of his oddity ("a dim exploration of phenomena once vivid" [*GBI*, 128]). His fortunate history is a given of the novel, and his romanticism is the faith of a man with every reason to be supremely easy that the goods of life are wont to deliver themselves into his hands.

The reasonableness of his aspirations confirmed for him by his magical success, Verver is in many ways the most Romantic character in James's fiction. James pointedly suggests the association of the Ververs with Romanticism when he has the Prince, in the opening pages of the novel, recall telling Maggie that "you Americans are almost incredibly romantic." What qualifies them for this description, in Amerigo's eyes, is their "extraordinary American good faith," the consequences of which can only be expressed in oppositions: they "see too much" when they " 'don't, at least,' he had amended with a further thought, 'see too little' " and "the funny thing, he had respectfully submitted, was that her father, though older and wiser, and a man into the bargain, was as bad—that is as good—as herself." Even more essentially Romantic than Adam's good faith is his belief in the power of the imagination to resolve contradictions. Just before he makes his decision to propose to Charlotte, for example, in a lone midnight vigil, he consciously pursues a resolution of his difficulties by an imaginative synthesis: "He had as to so many of the matters in hand a divided view, and this was exactly what made him reach out, in his unrest, for some idea, lurking in the vast freshness of the night, at the breath of which disparities would submit to fusion and so, spreading beneath him, make him feel he floated." The passage not only is reminiscent of the Coleridgean ideal of the God-like power of the mind to unify but also suggests that the childlike Adam has the Wordsworthian susceptibility that Coleridge called "freshness of sensation" (*GBI*, 10–11, 205–206).

Verver's subsequent moment of illumination is only one of several instances of his having sudden, vivid insights that create fundamental alterations in his views. Here is how James describes Adam's discovery of the way his marriage to Charlotte might be rationalized as being undertaken "for his child" (*GBI*, 209):

> As at a turn of his labyrinth he saw his issue, which opened out so wide, for the minute, that he held his breath with wonder. He was afterwards to recall how just then the autumn night seemed to clear to a view in which the whole place, everything round him, the wide terrace where he stood, the others, with their steps, below, the gardens, the park, the lake, the circling woods, lay there as under some strange midnight sun. It all met him during these instants as a vast expanse of *discovery*, a world that looked, so lighted, extraordinarily new, and in which familiar objects had taken on a distinctness that, as if it had been a loud, a

spoken pretension to beauty, interest, importance, to he scarce knew what, gave them an inordinate quantity of character and verily an inordinate size. The hallucination, or whatever he might have called it, was brief, but it lasted long enough to leave him gasping. (*GBI*, 207)

Susceptibility to such visions is perhaps the most markedly Romantic trait of Adam Verver. One might think of Adam's visions as analogous to Joycean epiphanies or perhaps, especially since the visions are related as past perfect retrospection, as similar to Wordsworth's "spots of time."[16]

James alludes not to Wordsworth, however, but to another Romantic poet, Keats. The "vast expanse of *discovery*" in the passage just quoted is clearly an allusion to the following, earlier description, an allusion for the purpose of linking the two moments in Adam's development as instances of the same mode of vision:

> He had never spoken of himself as infallible—it wasn't his way; but apart from the natural affections he had acquainted himself with no greater joy, of the intimately personal type than the joy of his originally coming to feel, and all so unexpectedly, that he had in him the spirit of the connoisseur. He had, like many other persons, in the course of his reading, been struck with Keats's sonnet about stout Cortez in the presence of the Pacific; but it was probable that few persons had so devoutly fitted the poet's grand image to a fact of experience. It consorted so with Mr. Verver's consciousness of the way in which at a given moment he had stared at *his* Pacific that a couple of perusals of the immortal lines had sufficed to stamp them in his memory. His "peak in Darien" was the sudden hour that had transformed his life, the hour of his perceiving with a mute inward gasp akin to the low moan of apprehensive passion that a world was left him to conquer and that he might conquer it if he tried. It had been a turning of the page of the book of life—as if a leaf long inert had moved at a touch and, eagerly reversed, had made such a stir of the air as sent up into his face the very breath of the Golden Isles. To rifle the Golden Isles had become on the spot the business of his future, and with the sweetness of it—what was most wondrous of all—still more even in the thought than in the act. The thought was that of the affinity of Genius, or at least of Taste, with something in himself—with the dormant intelligence of which he had thus almost violently become aware and that affected him as changing by a mere revolution of the screw his whole intellectual plane. (*GBI*, 140–41)

This account of Adam's vision accords well with the idea of the dia-

16. See Hisayoshi Watanabe, "Past Perfect Retrospection in the Style of Henry James," *American Literature*, XXXIV (1962), 165–81.

lectic of spiral ascent. The reference to the "revolution of the screw" emphasizes that Adam's transformation is formally circular, and the change in "his whole intellectual plane" is clearly the ascent, through that revolution, to the summit of "his 'peak in Darien'." James has in fact prepared one to make such an analysis by having Adam represent his career specifically as a spiral ascent. Earlier in the same chapter, he is said to see himself as having "come out; quite at the top of his hill of difficulty, the tall sharp spiral round which he had begun to wind his ascent at the age of twenty, and the apex of which was a platform looking down, if one would, on the kingdoms of the earth and with standing-room for but half a dozen others" (*GBI*, 131).

There is no doubt, moreover, that the spiral of Adam's career has been a process of reversal, circling to the position in which we find him in Book Second by way of its antitheses. Thus the new leaf of Adam's Keatsian revelation has not merely been turned but "eagerly reversed." The opposition between the old Adam and the new is insistently diametric:

> It was the strange scheme of things again: the years of darkness had been needed to render possible the years of light. A wiser hand than he at first knew had kept him hard at acquisition of one sort as a perfect preliminary to acquisition of another, and the preliminary would have been weak and wanting if the good faith of it had been less. His comparative blindness had made the good faith, which in its turn had made the soil propitious for the flower of the supreme idea. He had had to *like* forging and sweating, he had had to like polishing and piling up his arms. They were things at least he had had to believe he liked, just as he had believed he liked transcendent calculation and imaginative gambling all for themselves, the creation of "interests" that were the extinction of other interests, the livid vulgarity even of getting in, or getting out, first. That had of course been so far from really the case—with the supreme idea all the while growing and striking deep, under everything, in the warm rich earth. He had stood unknowing, he had walked and worked where it was buried, and the fact itself, the fact of his fortune, would have been a barren fact enough if the first sharp tender shoot had never struggled into day. There on one side was the ugliness his middle time had been spared; there on the other, from all portents, was the beauty with which his age might still be crowned. He was happier doubtless than he deserved; but *that*, when one was happy at all, it was easy to be. He had wrought by devious ways, but he had reached the place, and what would ever have been straighter in any man's life than his way henceforth of occupying it? (*GBI*, 144–45)

Many critics have attacked the credibility of Adam's conversion and have accused him of an immoral complacency about his personal history. Donald Mull's comment on Adam's thoughts about his having "wrought by devious ways" seems to me an apt response to the billionaire's critical detractors. "Recognition of the early deviousness," Mull writes, "is what critics seem unwilling to grant Adam Verver, not to mention the justice of his observation on happiness, or the possibility of a happiness untainted by the tone of the old deviousness. Such a recognition is hardly justification of a new deviousness, unsensed by Verver; but the intervening conversion must be acknowledged, and critics loath to admit the power for conversion of the human imagination are better off not reading Henry James." Even more to the point for my argument is that Adam's *via negativa*, the dependence of the "years of light" on the preceding "years of darkness," is the basic form of the spiral dialectic. That "devious ways" should lead to an eminently straight way of occupying one's place is resonant, moreover, not only with the "sharp spiral" "hill of difficulty" of Adam's career but also with the important Romantic notion of the generative power of polarities—with, for example, the great creative contraries of William Blake. In particular, the straight outcome of Adam's deviousness recalls Blake's maxim that "Improvement makes straight roads, but the crooked roads without Improvement, are roads of Genius."[17]

The spiral dialectic is the form of Adam's development in the course of the novel as well as of his life prior to its action. His recognition that "he had wrought by devious ways" is by no means the only indication of his capacity to grasp the essential structure of his experience and to use his understanding of it as an instrument of personal growth. In Blakean terms, his story is a criticism of innocence in favor of a higher, organized innocence. His two major conversations with Maggie in Volume II, in Regent's Park in chapter V of Book Fourth and on the lawn at Fawns in chapter III of Book Fifth, contain several clear indications that Adam has been unfairly charged by anti-Verver critics with unshakeable complacency about the self-involved simplicity he and Maggie have enjoyed before their marriages and up through the first two years of Adam's. In chapter V of Book Fourth,

17. Mull, *Henry James's "Sublime Economy,"* 136; Erdman (ed.), *Poetry and Prose of William Blake*, 37.

he suggests to Maggie that they suffer from "a kind of wicked selfish prosperity" that has "made us perhaps lazy, a wee bit languid—lying like gods together, all careless of mankind." When he remarks that they "haven't no doubt enough the sense of difficulty" and Maggie asks "enough for what?" Adam's reply is "enough not to be selfish":

> "I don't think *you* are selfish," she had returned—and had managed not to wail it.
>
> "I don't say that it's me particularly—or that it's you or Charlotte or Amerigo. But we're selfish together—we move as a selfish mass. You see we want always the same thing," he had gone on—"and that holds us, that binds us, together. We want each other," he had further explained; "only wanting it, each time, *for* each other. That's what I call the happy spell; but it's also a little—possibly—the immorality."
>
> " 'The immorality'?" she had pleasantly echoed.
>
> "Well, we're tremendously moral for ourselves—that is for each other; and I won't pretend that I know exactly at whose particular personal expense you and I for instance are happy. What it comes to, I dare say, is that there's something haunting—as if it were a bit uncanny—in such a consciousness of our general comfort and privilege. Unless indeed," he had rambled on, "it's only I to whom, fantastically, it says so much. That's all I mean at any rate—that it's 'sort of' soothing; as if we were sitting about on divans, with pigtails, smoking opium and seeing visions. 'Let us then be up and doing'—what is it Longfellow says? That seems sometimes to ring out; like the police breaking in—into our opium den—to give us a shake." (*GBII*, 90–92)

In chapter III of Book Fifth, on an occasion reminiscent of their first long conversation at Fawns (chapter IV, Book Second)—"the whirligig of time had thus brought round for them again . . . the same odd impulse quietly to 'slope' " (*GBII*, 253)—their positions of chapter V of Book Fourth are to some extent reversed.[18] Now Maggie speaks of their selfishness and Adam protests. James, however, has taken care to show us that both Maggie and her father recognize the possible immorality of their original, careless self-satisfaction, and Adam's objection to the imputation here in Book Fifth expresses his desire to reassure Maggie of his innocence and not a real failure of recognition on his part.[19] The reversal in their positions from those of Book

18. One notes, incidentally, the consonance of the whirligig image (an allusion to *Twelfth Night*, V, i, 363) with the spiral form of the novel.

19. Donald Mull speaks well to this point: "Whether or not the Ververs ever achieve knowledge of their own culpability has been hotly contested; but those muted, elliptical conversations between Adam and Maggie in Book Second [*i. e.*,

Fourth may be said to be merely superficial, for at this point they have, implicitly, a joint consciousness of their responsibility. The reversal of their attitude of Book Second, by contrast, is fundamental and thoroughgoing. They have, by chapter III of Book Fifth, attained to so much lucidity as to make their earlier discussion "purblind" ("incapable of clear mental, moral, or spiritual vision," says the *OED*), so that Adam now looks back on their state at the outset as "benighted innocence" (*GBII*, 253, 260).

The reader is never certain of the precise extent of Adam's knowledge about the adultery. But that Adam does recognize that something is wrong is clear not only from his remarks to Maggie in the episodes I have just cited but also from her conviction of his knowledge and from his generally tacit collaboration, throughout Volume II, with his daughter's campaign to save both their marriages. In their conversation in chapter III of Book Fifth, for example, Maggie "knew by his eyes, the light at the heart of which he couldn't blind, that he was, by his intention, making sure—sure whether or no her certainty was like his" (*GBII*, 267–68). The proof of his certainty is in his taking up of Maggie's hints that they should give up their project for a summer excursion together without their spouses and, later, that he should return with Charlotte to American City.[20] More generally, he conforms to Maggie's policy of silence, of concealment of knowledge, in order to sustain the conditions of ostensible domestic harmony under cover of which the four marriage partners may realign themselves, correcting their false equilibrium, with the least possible violence to the personal integrity of each. For Adam, as for Maggie, the creation of the new equilibrium is an assumption of responsibility at no small cost in individual ease and equanimity, as the heavily emphasized, peripatetic meditations preceding his decision to return to America suggest. Having undertaken marriage to Charlotte in a state of "benighted innocence," having come to see "a little, possibly, the immorality" of a happiness requiring the "personal expense" of others, and having suffered through his discovery of betrayal by his wife, and worse, of

---

in Volume II] point toward a recognition of guilt, coexisting with an attempt by each to conceal from the other the wounding fact of knowledge" (Mull, *Henry James's "Sublime Economy,"* 153).

20. For a view of these acts of Adam's as indecisive as to whether or not he knows about the affair between Charlotte and the Prince, see Krook, *The Ordeal of Consciousness*, 313–14.

the betrayal of Maggie by Amerigo, Adam decides to return to America as the culmination of the part he plays in Volume II in the establishment of a much higher rightness than that which he had, earlier and too complacently, believed himself to enjoy.

It must be said, before going on to the other characters, that there are difficulties about Adam, ambiguities that are inevitably adduced in arguments less sympathetic to him than mine. Most significant is the disturbing group of passages that may, arguably, imply a view of Adam as a cold and calculating manipulator who buys the Prince and Charlotte without regard for their distinctive humanity. Much of the answer to that view of Adam must wait upon discussion of Charlotte and the Prince. Suffice it for the moment to point out that none of the evidence for this condemnation of Adam is unambiguous. For instance, in the final chapter, there is a reference to the Prince and Charlotte as "human furniture," a phrase invariably cited by critics who convict Adam of an unconscionable reification of others. Because, however, Adam Verver is one of the foremost exemplars in James's fiction of the converting imagination, and because, moreover, an earlier reference to his own "spiritual furniture" (*GBI*, 197) at a point at which he is the center of consciousness shows, as Mull puts it, "how inextricably the worlds of *objet* and spiritual principle are mixed in Adam's mind," the words "human furniture" have a wide range of possible implications and ought not to be taken as the bald indictment of Adam that they often seem to be in the context of anti-Verver tracts. Perhaps, after all, the use of the phrase is casual, for the same words appear in the Prince's reminiscence of Charlotte's account of her childhood, and there they do not seem capable of bearing the weight that some readers have placed on their occurrence near the end of the novel.[21]

Another aspect of Adam that many readers have understandably found disturbing is the apparent cruelty of his handling of Charlotte in the final chapters, focused through Maggie's eyes in her image of the "long silken halter looped round" Charlotte's neck by which Adam leads his wife. Aside from Maggie's resources of empathy, about which more shortly, what James seems to me to be emphasizing is

21. Mull, *Henry James's "Sublime Economy,"* 144. For Charlotte's remarks about "the rather shabby but still ever so pretty human furniture of her early time," see *GBI*, 55.

not so much the cruelty of Adam as the tragic necessity of subjecting a creature as unregenerate as Charlotte to the discipline symbolized by the leash. Surprisingly, no one has commented on the connection between Charlotte's tether and the major symbol of value in the novel, the golden bowl. Just as "the golden bowl—as it *was* to have been," unflawed and therefore practically unbreakable, is the image of the ideal condition to which Maggie aspires as she struggles to restore her marriage, so the silken halter is the image for the restoration of Charlotte's union with Adam. It is silken, not silver, but it does "gleam," exhibiting a "perfect durability," and surely it is meant to put one in mind of the silver cord in *Ecclesiastes*, broken therein, like the golden bowl, and now, like the metaphoric bowl in the novel, repaired (*GBII*, 216, 287, 331). James's figure is also resonant with Blake's variation on the biblical imagery in Thel's motto (a possible source for the title of James's novel):

> Does the Eagle know what is in the pit?
> Or wilt thou go ask the Mole?
> Can Wisdom be put in a silver rod?
> Or Love in a golden bowl?[22]

If Adam's relation with Charlotte seems finally harsher than Maggie's with the Prince, it is because his is the way of Wisdom, his daughter's the way of Love, and the course of each is determined in large measure by the differing capacities of their spouses to respond to different kinds of treatment. I would not argue that the probable allusions to *Ecclesiastes* and *The Book of Thel* and the appropriateness of Adam's conduct to Charlotte's character completely exonerate him from the charge of cruelty, but only that James must have intended these things to minimize, mitigate, and mediate the grim appearance of Verver's solution to his wife's infidelity.

As mentioned earlier, by far the most persuasive defense of Adam Verver to date—and the most judicious in weighing the arguments of anti-Verver critics—is Donald Mull's, whose reply to readers who have seen Adam's aestheticism as fundamentally philistine is thoroughly convincing. But Mull balks at Stephen L. Mooney's argument

22. Erdman (ed.), *Poetry and Prose of William Blake*, 3 (and see also Harold Bloom's brief comment on Thel's motto, p. 808). F. O. Matthiessen was the first to suggest that James may have drawn on Blake's "cryptic verse"; see his *Henry James: The Major Phase*, 83.

that James's association of Adam with "Upon First Looking Into Chapman's Homer"—a poem that, Mooney says, "centers on the sublimation of the idea of conquest, translating the literal 'realms of gold' into a metaphor for states of intense consciousness"—"gives Adam the right to be rich, for his wealth is of the spirit."[23] "His wealth," replies Mull, "is just as thoroughly of the billfold." Mull goes on to assert the ambiguity that clings to Adam even in his sympathetic reading, "the suggestion that throughout the 'law of man' which obtains for him is diffused a refinement of the 'law of things' (and the converse suggestion that the 'law of things' has been subtilized in him to a near-humanistic level)." Mooney's case for Adam, based on the single Keats allusion, and oblivious, as Mull argues, "that metaphor is a relation between tenor and vehicle which qualifies both terms," is perhaps slight, but Mooney's initial insight, that the reference to the sonnet places Adam in a sympathetic light, is of value. Mooney helps one to see, at least, that the ambiguities in the passage containing the Keats allusion (*e.g.*, that "the business of" Adam's "future" is "to rifle the Golden Isles") are not directed against Adam but are emphatic, by ironic incongruity, of the completeness of the revolution entailed in his conversion—a preferable reading, I would argue, because in it the ironies are seen to support the apparent meaning of the passage. Indeed, the idea that Adam is genuinely rapacious is undercut immediately, in the same passage, by the information that "the sweetness of" the figurative conquest was, for him, "still more even in the thought than in the act."

Adam of course possesses "a rare power of purchase" (*GBII*, 360). His situation represents an important, omnipresent principle of James's imagination. Like many modern poets—and like, among his near-contemporaries, Browning, Meredith, and Hardy—James felt strongly the vital necessity of the Romantic secularization of the doctrine of incarnation. One thinks, for instance, of Dr. Williams' dictum "No ideas but in things" and of Wallace Stevens' lovely lines

> Beauty is momentary in the mind—
> The fitful tracing of a portal;
> But in the flesh it is immortal.

23. Mull, *Henry James's "Sublime Economy,"* 139–42; Stephen L. Mooney, "James, Keats, and the Religion of Consciousness," *Modern Language Quarterly*, XXII (1961), 399, 401.

The doctrine, in brief, is that spiritual values must be embodied—in things, in people's bodies, in specific actions. There is a real, ironic sense in which Adam (and Maggie) suffer from unachieved spiritual values—for all their talk of them—at the start. But what Adam does know is that love, like the collector's insight, is real only when embodied in objects. When he ends by telling Maggie that she has "got some good things" (*GBII*, 360), including the Prince, there is irony all right, perhaps even consciously directed against his own earlier buyer's attitude toward Amerigo. But it is a wonderfully complicated irony. Adam knows that the Prince and Charlotte must be possessed as physical objects if they are to be enjoyed spiritually, just as paintings must be. It may be sad, this fate of fallen man, that one must possess to love (and love in order truly to possess), but that is surely what James expresses through his account of Adam.

Readings such as Mooney's, in any case, seem to me to gain substance and credibility when placed in the context of James's use of the spiral dialectic as the pattern of Adam's development. The motif of spiral return, though it serves James as a formal model, is no simple aesthetic compulsion. It incorporates a range of values, all of which are positive, including the notions of progress and improvement, of transcendence, and of the reconciliation of oppositions, as well as an undertone of redemption attributable to the correspondence between the dialectic and the traditional Christian paradigm of salvation. That Adam's career is depicted by James in terms of the spiral dialectic strongly suggests to me that, in the admittedly numerous instances where a passage about Adam is susceptible of several contradictory interpretations, the weight of probability must fall on the ones most favorable to Adam—the more so since even most anti-Verver critics agree that James's intention to treat Adam sympathetically is clear. The ambiguities, nevertheless, have an appreciable function. They alert us to Adam's complexity and encourage us to take stock of his shortcomings, as James has and as Adam himself does to a significant if limited extent. The ambiguities are so widespread as to make the idea that James was unaware of them untenable. They occur, in large measure, because James's protagonists, the characters he means us to admire most, always have faults that lead them into error—for instance, Milly Theale's and Lambert Strether's almost eager willingness to be duped. It is perplexing, indeed, that objections are so often raised to the multiplicity of interpretations that James's work invites, whereas the variety of possible responses to the works of other authors—to, for instance, *Hamlet* and *King Lear*—is frequently cited as evidence of their depth, maturity, universality, and inexhaustibility and as an index of intellectual, imaginative, and poetic opulence. Though James may well have developed the radical ambiguities of *The Sacred Fount* in order to call into question the very concept of meaning itself, the ambiguities in *The Golden Bowl*, as in the great majority of his fictions, deepen significance without undermining it, at once bespeaking the rich complications of this novel and constituting an important element of its greatness.

If Adam Verver is, as the wealthiest and, perhaps, as the most Romantic of James's characters, an extravagant figure, so is his daughter, Maggie, as one of the most highly intelligent. Moreover, unlike the intelligences of other extremely bright James characters—unlike, for example, Nanda Brookenham's, Lambert Strether's, and Milly Theale's—Maggie's mature intelligence is not a given of her character, predating her experience in the novel, but is dramatically portrayed as developing under the stimulus of that experience. Before Book Fourth (the first section of Volume II), the simplicity of Maggie's American good faith and innocence keeps the acuity she later displays dormant, in marked contrast to the vital, knowing resourcefulness of Charlotte Stant. Unintelligent yet probably innocent—the innocence indicated especially by the tone of her conversation with the Prince, as Mull observes—is her telling her fiancé that he is a "*morceau de musée*" in Adam Verver's collection.[24] The remark plays straight into Amerigo's primarily economic sense of his marriage, and Maggie's prelapsarian innocence is such that she does not grasp the implications when he replies that he "cost a lot of money," though her answer—"'I haven't the least idea,' she had gravely answered, 'what you cost'"—makes him feel "for the moment vulgar" and indicates, further, her naïveté (*GBI*, 12). Ignorant, in general, are her misunderstanding of her husband's character, her passivity about her relation with him, her neglect of him in favor of her father, and her anxiety about Adam, which causes that neglect. Obtuse too, though one can-

24. See Mull, *Henry James's "Sublime Economy,"* 120–22.

not say that Maggie should have known better at the time, is the role she plays as matchmaker for her father and Charlotte.

Fanny Assingham is correct in her analysis of the dangerous deficiency in Maggie's intelligence in the first half of the novel: "It was as if her imagination had been closed to it, her sense altogether sealed" "to what's called Evil—with a very big E." At the end of Book Third, Fanny tells her husband that she has observed Maggie begin to take notice, that, as she had seen, "Maggie's awake." Book Fourth dramatizes Maggie's process of vision as she becomes more and more "awake" to her situation. Now she begins to recognize the stupidity of her attitudes in Volume I. For example, she asks herself if she has "accepted too passively the funny form of our life." When she feels "the whole weight of their case drop afresh upon her shoulders," she knows that "the prime source of her haunted state" was "her not having been able not to mind—not to mind what became of him [Adam]; not having been able, without anxiety, to let him go his way and take his risk and lead his life. She had made anxiety her stupid little idol."[25] Simultaneous with such insights about her past behavior is a growing tide of light about the oddities of the behavior of the Prince and Charlotte, about the ironically telltale "bath of benevolence," the "gilded cage" in which they seem to place her, about their being "arranged together" and she "apart." Most impressively, as Maggie's suspicions, sharpening, approach confirmation, she develops the fine arts of intrigue, she learns "almost from minute to minute to be a mistress of shades," and she does so almost as if by instinct, from the very start of Volume II, when Amerigo meets on his return from Matcham the brilliant gambit of Maggie's awaiting him where he least expects her, in their own home at Portland Place. Maggie's sudden and dramatic growth in intelligence, incidentally, is

25. Late in the novel, Maggie complains to Fanny that the separation of the two couples will be harder on her and Adam than on Charlotte and the Prince "since for them it's just, it's right, it's deserved, while for us it's only sad and strange and not caused by our fault" (*GBII*, 333). Some critics have cited the statement against Maggie, as though it negated her earlier recognitions of responsibility. It does not. At worst it shows that, perhaps with a tinge of self-pity, Maggie views the lovers' sins of commission, understandably I should think, as much graver than her own sins of omission. More likely, however, she means that the separation is necessary primarily for the sake of the Prince and Charlotte, since they have the task of putting their love affair behind them.

matched by an equal and opposite exposure of Charlotte's failures of vision, so that *she* comes to be figured as in a gilded cage of delusion and Amerigo, in the end, declares her "stupid" (*GBI*, 384–85, 401; *GBII*, 25, 44–45, 81, 142, 229, 348).

Early in the novel, Fanny Assingham poses a rhetorical question to her husband: "what is morality but high intelligence?" (*GBI*, 88). For some readers, Fanny's question has seemed a key to the system of value implied in the novel. S. Gorley Putt, for example, uses Fanny's question as the epigraph to his discussion of *The Golden Bowl* and comments that the "morality of the chosen objects of James's mature admiration has no religious sanction."[26] This is of course literally true, but it seems to me to be a gross misreading of James to think that he would have one regard a simple equation of morality with high intelligence in any but an ironic light. Intelligence, to be sure, is a necessary element of Jamesian high morality, but it is by no means the whole of it, for James's fictions present many very intelligent characters who are either immoral or amoral: Paul Muniment, Madame Merle, Mrs. Brookenham, Gloriana, Kate Croy, Maud Lowder, and Fanny herself, to name only a few. In fact, what qualifies Maggie Verver's intelligence as superlative is an essential moral component independent of mere intellectual power. Her intelligence, that is, is moral as well as worldly. For the most part, this aspect of Maggie's character is beyond Fanny's ken, but her stress on her young friend's awakening to "Evil" does point up that the blossoming of Maggie's intelligence takes its principal impetus from her discovery of a new element in the *moral* universe.

Maggie, of course, has always been concerned, in the artless American way, with moral straightness. The Ververs, as we learn just before their first long talk at Fawns, in Volume I, "each knew that both were full of the superstition of not 'hurting,' but might precisely have been asking themselves, asking in fact each other, at this moment, whether that was to be after all the last word of their conscientious development" (*GBI*, 160). We have already glanced at Adam's subsequent conscientious development. Maggie's, in Volume II, is multifaceted, and is certainly an extensive advance beyond, even a transcendence of, the dangerous superficiality and the negative content of a

26. Putt, *Henry James: A Reader's Guide*, 363.

moral code based on "not 'hurting.'" The growth of her capacity for self-criticism is a significant part of this development. So is her conscious shouldering of responsibility for correction of the violated moral order and of the false equilibrium among the Ververs and their spouses. If her vision of herself as "the scapegoat of old" shows that Maggie is not entirely above self-pity, it even more strongly indicates the heroism and self-denial of her taking on the "burden" of "the sins of the people." Her policy of silence about the potential scandal, of concealing her knowledge of the adultery, of peopling the scenes of her life with "serenities and dignities and decencies" rather than with "terrors and shames and ruins" follows from her sense that to give vent to "the straight vindictive view, the rights of resentment, the rages of jealousy, the protests of passion" "would have been to give them [Charlotte and the Prince] up," which "was, marvellously, not to be thought of" (*GBII*, 234, 236–37). Giving up the others means here not merely relinquishing their persons but more especially, as the scapegoat image suggests, leaving them in a state of moral abandonment. This is not to say, however, that Maggie's care for the others does not go beyond what might be thought of as a prissy concern for their salvation. On the contrary, the consistency of her esteem for the Prince's integrity and self-respect as a *galantuomo* is as scrupulous in Volume II as it was unwittingly deficient in Volume I, and her empathy with Charlotte in her suffering as well as her admiration for the endowments that make her rival magnificent shows a generous response to the feelings and individuality of others. Each of these aspects of Maggie's moral development in the second half of the novel, finally, sharply distinguishes her, as we shall see shortly, from Charlotte. Charlotte's stupidity, her lack of understanding of Maggie, is based on a fundamental moral obtuseness, whereas Maggie's developed intelligence, her full understanding of Charlotte, is based on a fundamental and passionately sympathetic moral insight, extended, complicated, organized, and strengthened by her experience of evil.

One of the paradoxes of Volume II of the novel is that Maggie's deep personal involvement in the situations depicted in it goes hand in hand with her detachment from them, a detachment that shows both in her ability to manage appearances with increasingly cool, theatrical skill and in her ability to hold those who have wronged her in high esteem. The paradox comes into being because Maggie feels three distinct and powerful kinds of love. Detachment is most difficult for her with the Prince, for whom her love is a blend of carnal and romantic elements. She must resist him as a "munificent lover," must resist his "unfailing magic" (sexual power) though it costs her "tears of suffered pain" to do so, in order to preserve her autonomy so that she can work to reclaim him for herself and to restore Charlotte to her father. She must, too, learn to look beyond her affection for him, utterly secure in its own intensity, which is what she is speaking of when she tells Adam that when "you love in the most abysmal and unutterable way of all—why then you're beyond everything, and nothing can pull you down." Adam, in response to this speech, sees Maggie in a way that epitomizes the sensuality and lyricism of her love for Prince Amerigo, taking from "the mere fine pulse of passion in it [her remark], the suggestion as of a creature consciously floating and shining in a warm summer sea, some element of dazzling sapphire and silver, a creature cradled upon depths, buoyant among dangers, in which fear or folly or sinking otherwise than in play was impossible" (*GBII*, 56–57, 262–63). Maggie's love for her father, extraordinary as it is, is decidedly subordinate to her love for her husband, as her decision to "sacrifice" Adam, considered as early as chapter IV of Book Fourth, indicates (see *GBII*, 82–83). The tenderness of the Ververs' care for each other and the deep sympathy between them that makes for their many moments of wordless communion is not the perversion that many anti-Verver critics hint (and that Robert Marks blatantly terms incest), but is rather a natural intimacy fostered by Adam's having raised Maggie on his own since her mother's death, when Maggie was ten, by their years of travel together in strange lands, and by their enormous wealth, which, as I suggested earlier, isolates them, setting them in a class apart from the other, merely wealthy people among whom they move.

Quite remarkable and of a different order from these first two types of love—the one romantic and sexual, the other filial—is the sentiment that, as Maggie assures Fanny Assingham, sustains her in her strategems of manipulation in Volume II. Hearing from Maggie how she makes the others "do what I like," Fanny pronounces Maggie "terrible" (reminding one, as if to highlight the reversal of roles, that the Prince, in Volume I, calls Charlotte "terrible" [*GBI*, 362] out of admiration for her genius for arrangement):

> Maggie thoughtfully shook her head. "No; I'm not terrible, and you don't think me so. I do strike you as surprising, no doubt—but surprisingly mild. Because—don't you see?—I *am* mild. I can bear anything."
> "Oh, 'bear'!" Mrs. Assingham fluted.
> "For love," said the Princess.
> Fanny hesitated. "Of your father?"
> "For love," Maggie repeated.
> It kept her friend watching. "Of your husband?"
> "For love," Maggie said again. (*GBII*, 115–16)

This is the "wide-open declaration of being in love" that F. O. Matthiessen found "slightly sickening," despite what he allowed to be James's intention of conveying "thus the rare inclusiveness of her generosity."[27] That is part of the intention, to be sure, but of equal importance is that Maggie does here precisely what Matthiessen thinks she fails to do: she discriminates between kinds of love. Maggie's reiterated "for love" makes it obvious that she sees herself as acting with a motive different from the feelings specifically appropriate toward one's father and husband, acting in the interest of a higher love, which transcends questions about one's particular relations with given persons. When Fanny asks, "Of your father?" Maggie, as it were, assents, making her first "For love" mean "for love of my father." In the same way, her second "For love" is made to mean "for love of Amerigo." Thus the third "For love" insists on a love that transcends both these first two. This, in my view, is the same capacity for disinterested appreciation that distinguishes Strether and that is, for James, the highest form of love. Its analogy in the religious symbolism of the novel is divine love, but the implicit comparison is by no means an identity and is probably intended to enlarge, as Frederick C. Crews would have it, our sense of the value of this faculty of James's most admirable characters, itself essentially secular and humanistic.[28] The religious symbolism, at any rate, is only latent in the passage, obliquely suggested by the polar opposition of terribleness and mildness, traditionally divine attributes, as in Blake's iconography of the tiger and the lamb (*vide* the beast and lamb imagery recurrent in *The Golden Bowl*). If, therefore, one takes this third kind of love to which Maggie is subject as a humanistic genius for disinterested

27. Matthiessen, *Henry James: The Major Phase*, 97.
28. See Crews, *The Tragedy of Manners*, 106.

appreciation, then the source of her conduct on several crucial occasions becomes clear, for this principle underlies at once her mature grasp of "the precious uniqueness of each of the three beloved persons," her care that their uniqueness "shall be unimpaired" by her "task of restoration," and her empathic relation with each of them.[29] Maggie is trying to make it clear to Fanny, in other words, that the ideal of such loving appreciation sustains her as she takes on, in Volume II, the burdens of shame, deception, and manipulation. The ideal is manifested most directly by her in acts of sympathetic identification; in them are concentrated the full powers of the heart and of the mind, conjunctive in a love that is at once impartial, comprehensive, and discriminating. Accordingly, for example, Maggie is at last far more able than the Prince to appreciate Charlotte's greatness, to understand her anguish, and to judge her fairly and generously—a contrast by means of which, furthermore, James makes us see that the way the Prince has loved Charlotte is far inferior to Maggie's way of loving everyone concerned.

Two related aspects of Maggie's conduct in Volume II have particularly disturbed many critics, including some who in general approve of Maggie as well as most of those who do not. One is that her strategy for saving the two marriages is manipulative and depends upon her mastery of deception and insincerity. The other is that her actions cause Charlotte considerable suffering, in which Maggie seems, at moments at least, cruelly to exult. Christof Wegelin, a reader most sympathetic to Maggie, calls her humbugging a "shocking inversion of values," though he immediately makes the more important point that "her means are determined by the web of deceit in which her life is caught."[30] I would suggest that there are two complementary ways in which James means one to take Maggie's falsehoods. Wegelin's disclaimer of her responsibility in the matter perhaps goes too far, but it seems to me to point in the right direction. Maggie's predicament may be compared to Hamlet's: each of them suspects wrongdoing close to home but is forced for a long time to conceal suspicion for want of trustworthy evidence. Hamlet is in a dilemma in which he must resort to feigning madness and to arranging "The Mousetrap,"

29. Krook, *The Ordeal of Consciousness*, 259.
30. Wegelin, *The Image of Europe*, 136.

the play-within-the-play. Maggie also must feign and stage scenes. One understands perfectly that Hamlet's deceptions are not the lies of a dishonorable man but the expedients of a true prince who is bereft of straightforward options. It is as though he follows Polonius' advice to Reynaldo that one should "by indirections find directions out," but with the replacement of the spy's sordid motives by more creditable ones compounded of nobility and pressing personal necessity. Maggie, like Hamlet, is a "good Machiavel." Her chief motives for choosing the course of falsehood are the noble desire to spare all the persons involved "terrors and shames and ruins" and the pressing personal need to win her husband from Charlotte. Her tactic is akin to the *salutaire hypocrisie* at least partially affirmed by James in *The Awkward Age* and *The Ambassadors.* It is the "modesty of convention" that Brada said "provokes and develops nevertheless real virtues" (see p. 19, above).

But though Wegelin is right that Maggie's "means are determined by the web of deceit" in which she is caught, she does choose, devise, refine, and pursue them. The element of choice is crucial for the second way in which Maggie's deceptions may be understood, in terms of the dialectic of spiral return, which governs her moral evolution as it does that of her father. In order to move out of her original state of simple innocence with its superficial sense of rightness into an organized innocence and a higher order of rightness, Maggie must pass through the antitheses of her point of origin, must know evil and participate in it, which she does by her use of the standard strategems of malevolence. Her indirections on the way to direction are parallel to the devious ways that bring her father out straight. It is in the nature of such a *via negativa*, moreover, that she must succumb temporarily to the corruption of the antitheses through which she passes, that she must rejoice, for brief moments, in the triumph of her will and the suffering of her adversary. In the end, largely by virtue of the intervening "inversion of values," she is far indeed from such mean exultations. To fasten on Maggie's momentary attitudes as she is in mid-passage is thus practically to turn upside down the true order and meaning of her experience.

As has been widely noted by Maggie's critical defenders, the depth of our sense of Charlotte's suffering is, by and large, a direct result of Maggie's empathy with her. In only a very few passages, of which the following is the most prominent, is there any evidence that Maggie may take pleasure in her stepmother's predicament:

> He [Amerigo] had given her [Maggie] something to conform to [the policy of concealment from Charlotte that Maggie knows about the adultery], and she hadn't unintelligently turned on him, "gone back on" him, as he would have said, by not conforming. They were together thus, he and she, close, close together—whereas Charlotte, though rising there radiantly before her, was really off in some darkness of space that would steep her in solitude and harass her with care. The heart of the Princess swelled accordingly even in her abasement; she had kept in tune with the right, and something certainly, something that might resemble a rare flower snatched from an impossible ledge, would, and possibly soon, come of it for her. The right, the right—yes, it took this extraordinary form of her humbugging, as she had called it, to the end. It was only a question of not by a hair's breadth deflecting into the truth. (*GBII*, 250–51)

Even here, the evidence that Maggie enjoys her rival's pain is ambiguous. To me it seems equally possible that Maggie's heart swells not at the idea of Charlotte's being "off in some darkness" but at the thought that she and Amerigo are "close, close together." If so, she is not delighting in Charlotte's suffering but in her own happiness. One notes, incidentally, that Maggie's lie to Charlotte is a cue she has taken from the Prince. The passage marks, in any case, the extreme of Maggie's mastery of and implication in the Machiavellian arts of managed appearances that James associates throughout the novel with Europe in general and with the Italianate Charlotte and the Roman Prince in particular. The "conscious perjury" of Maggie's acceptance of Charlotte's kiss of false reconciliation follows immediately. For the most part, the subsequent passages that highlight Charlotte's anguish convey not Maggie's pleasure in the part she plays in inflicting Charlotte's pain but her sympathetic participation in it. It is "for our young woman" (that is, for Maggie) that Charlotte's voice speaking of Adam's collection at Fawns sounds "like the shriek of a soul in pain," so that tears come to Maggie's eyes, "the lighted square" of the window at which she is standing "all blurred and dim." When Maggie imagines the wall that Amerigo has erected between Charlotte and himself, "it was positive in the Princess that for this she breathed Charlotte's cold air—turned away from him in it with her, turned with her, in growing compassion, this way and that," and "there were moments while she watched with her, thus unseen, when the mere effect of being near her was to feel her own heart in her throat, was to be almost moved to saying to her: 'Hold on tight, my dear—without *too much* terror—and it will all come out somehow.'" Maggie's "growing compassion" for Charlotte, moreover, has practical consequences, first in the lengths she goes to, in chapter V of Book Fifth, to preserve for Charlotte the appearance of triumph, of Charlotte's having chosen the return to America for herself, and, second, in her opposition to the Prince's relatively harsh view of Charlotte in Book Sixth, culminating in her remark that "I see it's always terrible for women" (*GBII*, 251, 282, 284, 292, 349). To whatever extent, finally, that Maggie's sympathy for Charlotte is not seen as mitigating the supposed cruelty of the Ververs' solution for Charlotte, the cruelty seems utterly unavoidable, for an outcome free of suffering for Charlotte is inconceivable. "The only other alternative for Maggie and Adam," says Donald Mull, "is renunciation—and renunciation can at this stage mean only to turn over to Charlotte a fortune and a Prince for whom she is little more than a cipher."[31]

Maggie's power, like Milly Theale's, is above all the power of forgiveness—the principal effects of which are felt by the Prince. Maggie is initially outraged, not so much by the adultery, as by what she believes to have been the bad faith of both the Prince and Charlotte when they married (and here is a clear parallel to Strether's main objection to the conduct of Madame de Vionnet: not the adultery so much as "the quantity of make-believe involved"). But Maggie is able to forgive the lovers because of her discovery, chiefly through Fanny Assingham, that they had meant to behave.

Turning now to the Prince and Charlotte, we shall see that the forgiveness works an authentic revolution in Amerigo, whose development follows the same spiral dialectic as do the personal histories of Adam and Maggie, but does not do so in Charlotte. Amerigo's initial good faith, genuine but subject to the severe limitations of his simplicity and his inability to grasp the nature and implications of the Anglo-Saxon moral sense, evolves by way of its own antitheses—the period of betrayal and adultery—into the better faith of his love for

31. Mull, *Henry James's "Sublime Economy,"* 160.

Maggie, inspired by his appreciation of her command of the worldly arts she displays in Volume II and even more by his acknowledgment of the power of her love and forgiveness, a power far superior to any force at Charlotte's command. Charlotte's good faith, though she does want to do right at the time of her marriage to Adam, is considerably more problematic than his, and she proves incapable of moral regeneration, so that the benefit she gets from Maggie's forgiveness is aesthetic, not moral: she is allowed to preserve her worldly magnificence with dignity and self-possession.

The best measure, perhaps, of the Prince's good faith at the outset of the novel, and of its limitations, is his anxiety in Book First. Figuratively, his perturbation is stressed by the opposition of the marine images with which he is associated to those associated with Maggie. Metaphors of travel by water dominate the opening chapters of *The Golden Bowl*. Maggie appears to generate them, for "she had images, like that, that were drawn from steamers and trains, from a familiarity with 'lines,' a command of 'own' cars, from an experience of continents and seas . . . from vast modern machineries and facilities whose acquaintance he [Prince Amerigo] had still to make." The stream of imagery introduced when Maggie says that she has "divided my faith into water-tight compartments" is taken up in quite another way by the Prince. We find him, in chapter I, a man at sea, "actually unsteadied," deeply agitated not only because his fate and his obligations have just "practically been sealed" but also because he does not and perhaps cannot yet know of what fate and obligation in his case will consist. It is a fine Jamesian irony that the Prince, so apparently cosmopolitan as to be "no more sharply 'foreign' to an English view" than, say, a " 'refined' Irishman," is at the same time so quintessentially defined by class and nationality as to be at a loss to understand the American father and daughter with whom he is about to join bloodlines and fortunes—predominantly his and theirs respectively. Although their language has "no note of strangeness" for him, "either for lip or for ear," he does not understand their values, their ways of seeing and feeling. He becomes a devotee of explanations "almost as if he collected them, in the manner of book-plates or postage-stamps, for themselves"—a nice parallel in the Prince to Adam's vocation as a collector. To the extent that the Ververs do not understand the Prince, they too are at sea. But while Maggie gives us the imagery of great transatlantic liners, the Prince sees himself in the plight of Gordon Pym, "drifting in a small boat further toward the North Pole . . . before him a thickness of white air that was like a dazzling curtain of light, concealing as darkness conceals" (*GBI*, 4–5, 14, 15, 22, 160–61). The composition of the curtain of light is in part the difference in tradition and national culture between the Ververs and the Prince: particularly, to his own mind, with respect to his lack of the moral sense "always," as he tells Fanny, "as you others consider it":

> "I've of course something that in our poor dear backward old Rome sufficiently passes for it. But it's no more like yours than the tortuous stone staircase—half-ruined into the bargain!—in some castle of our *quattrocento* is like the 'lightning elevator' in one of Mr. Verver's fifteen-storey buildings. Your moral sense works by steam—it sends you up like a rocket. Ours is slow and steep and unlighted, with so many of the steps missing that—well, that it's as short in almost any case to turn round and come down again."
>
> "Trusting," Mrs. Assingham smiled, "to get up some other way?"
>
> "Yes—or not to have to get up at all." (*GBI*, 31)

The Prince's figure brilliantly points up the fundamental opposition of the moral codes of the New and Old Worlds, and it also has a wonderful ironic dimension, both as applied to himself, since despite his preference for not having "to get up at all" he will ascend in the course of the novel a winding ("tortuous," spiral) moral staircase, and as applied to Maggie and Adam, since the "lightning elevator" morality will soon enough fail them and they too will find that the way up is tortuous, "slow and steep and unlighted." Even more than the foreignness of the Ververs' moral sense, finally, what gives Amerigo the apprehension of uncharted waters quite as much as his ancestral namesake would literally have had it is Adam's wealth. The collector's fortune, above all, irradiates and intensifies the impenetrable mist toward which the Prince feels the current steadily drawing him.

The note of grave agitation in the Prince, the positive implication of terror (the allusion to Poe is not at all gratuitous), gains urgency from the threat that his approaching marriage poses to his capacity to understand what Maggie wants of him and to provide it in quantities sufficient to compensate a billionaire. It is a natural fear of the unknown, a dread of losing oneself in that "white mist," and it is indeed well founded, for the Prince will eventually find himself in a "grey medium in which he helplessly groped." His perplexity is at once general and specific. The general anxiety attaches to his sense that "he was to constitute a possession, yet was to escape being reduced to his component parts," and this leads in turn to a very particular anxiety about what the Ververs see in him. He imagines that he may never be "tried or tested," and so may never know "how many pounds, shillings and pence he had to give." He sees that he is taken "seriously" in some way that he has not yet fathomed. He fears that he will not be able to justify the Ververs' investment in him precisely because he does not know what they could possibly consider a fair return. "Who but a billionaire," he wonders, "could say what was fair exchange for a billion?" He knows, at any rate, that he is "not, honestly, the man to calculate" (*GBI*, 23–24; *GBII*, 281).

In Book First, then, the Prince's good faith is genuine but is also genuinely imperiled. He wants to act rightly, but he cannot do so unless he knows how the right is defined. So he calls on Fanny Assingham, declaring himself about to start "on the great voyage—across the unknown sea." He is now more than ever in need of her explanations and help. Without them, he may some day be "wrong, *without* knowing it." *Galantuomo* that he is, he is steadfast for the voyage, but he needs to keep at least Fanny's "sail in sight for orientation." He is aware, most of all, that he must satisfy the Ververs' personal requirements as they have contracted to satisfy his financial ones, and he is afraid that they will remain in the "white mist," will not put what they want of him in a light where he can see it and respond (*GBI*, 26, 30).

The Prince is among James's greatest creations, not least because he has the novelist's admiration and respect—and wins the reader's—while displaying the many characteristics, necessarily problematic for James, that make him a striking antithesis to the men whose value is affirmed in the earlier novels, the good-hearted, scrupulous figures of the Ralph Touchett-Longdon-Strether line, all disqualified, by illness or by age, from active engagement in the main activities of life. Amerigo is sensuous, young, virile, expert in the sexual sense of the word of which James is so fond. Catholic in fact, he is pagan in sensibility. His aestheticism is a high form of materialism. His general idea of marriage is the European one; he naturally assumes that the functions of wife and lover are not only separable but almost incompatible. In Volume I, he thinks of Maggie as approximating "finally—

for it was analogy somehow more than identity—to the transmitted images of rather neutral and negative propriety that made up, in his long line, the average of wifehood and motherhood" (*GBI*, 322). Maggie has at first no glimmering of how alien the Prince's idea of marriage is from her own, and she scarcely begins to guess it until she feels in his protestation that "you've never been more sacred to me than you were at that hour [of his secret shopping trip with Charlotte]—unless perhaps you've become so at this one [of Maggie's confronting him with her discovery]" "as if something cold and momentarily unimaginable breathed upon her, from afar off, out of his strange consistency" (*GBII*, 199).[32]

The Prince's view of his marriage to Maggie, moreover, is first and foremost financial. In the beginning, Maggie's love is girlish, greatly inferior to the mature passion with which she will eventually deeply impress him. But he does not in any case recognize it, as his perplexity about his value for Maggie shows. He finds her only "charming," and what "mainly constituted our young man's 'romance' " is his view of the "furniture," the "vast modern machineries and facilities" at the Ververs' command, and the "money" and "power, the power of the rich peoples." The Prince muses whimsically and winningly on how his acquisition, by marriage, of a "scientific" modernity may be an "antidote to superstition, which was in its turn too much the consequence, or at least the exhalation, of archives," though the "presence in him" of his "race" "was like the consciousness of some inexpugnable scent in which his clothes, his whole person, his hands and the hair of his head, might have been steeped as in some chemical bath." His very recent family history includes, we are immediately informed, the marriage of a younger brother to a woman "of Hebrew race, with a

32. The meaning of Maggie's sensation as of "something cold and unimaginable" breathing upon her has been much disputed. See Dorothea Krook's explanation (in *The Ordeal of Consciousness*, 313) and Donald Mull's rejoinder (in *Henry James's "Sublime Economy,"* 185). My idea that Maggie's response is to the strangeness of the Prince's social traditions, which would seem to be the basis of "his strange consistency," is based in part on the parallel of her feeling with Strether's response to learning that Madame de Vionnet and Chad have arranged a marriage for Jeanne, that "it was—through something ancient and cold in it—what he would have called the real thing" (*AM*, 238). Similarly, when Isabel Archer foresees that Pansy Osmond will "in some odd way" need her help (a contingency that arises when Pansy is threatened with being married off by her father without regard for the girl's own affections), it is "with the effect of a chill" (*PLII*, 86).

portion that had gilded the pill" (*GBI*, 15–18). These details of the first chapter of *The Golden Bowl* merit attention because one cannot, as so many critics have attempted to do, fairly judge the Ververs' alleged guilt in purchasing the Prince unless one takes into account that Amerigo himself takes an unabashedly financial view of his marriage and that most of the monetary images cited in indictments of the Ververs are the Prince's images. He fancies Adam's looking at him as being "much of the same order as any glance directed, for due attention, from the same quarter, to the figure of a cheque received in the course of business and about to be enclosed to a banker," but whether this fancy gives us a reliable insight into Adam is debatable, the more so because the Prince consciously and immensely enjoys Adam's relieving him "of all anxiety about his married life [by occupying Maggie while Amerigo is preoccupied with Charlotte] in the same manner in which he relieved him on the score of his bank account" and also because, from the very first, when he looks at Adam and Maggie, his eyes are full of money. Even her "extraordinary American good faith," "her innocence, and yet at the same time her imagination" seem to him the color of the bath of money in which he imagines he sits "up to his neck" (*GBI*, 10, 292, 325). That he does not even begin to guess that the answer to his questions about his value are not to be found in Adam's balance sheets but in Maggie's emotional economy is half to be laid, no doubt, at the Ververs' door, but half the blame, surely, belongs to Amerigo. This is not, finally, to question Amerigo's good faith in asking Fanny to help him to avoid mistakes, but it is to insist that there are more reasons why he might be apprehensive about falling into error than he himself is aware of, reasons concerning the adequacy of his conception of marriage as well as the mysteriousness of the Americans.

In his simplicity, of course, Amerigo is not in fact conscious of the utter foreignness of the *mariage de convenance* to Maggie's way of thinking. Such a social institution has a predatory aspect of which the Prince is innocent, in the way that a natural predator is innocent. He enters into it virtually by instinct. Indeed, there is abundant evidence that, in general, his relations with women are unaffectedly exploitative. As Dorothea Krook argues, there is much to be said for Fanny Assingham's conclusion that Amerigo never really cared for Charlotte.[33] Critics appalled by Maggie's intervention in the resumed affair of Charlotte and the Prince tend to give the impression that their love is of great intrinsic beauty and value, as one feels was for a time true of Kate Croy and Merton Densher's love for each other. There is no question but that Charlotte is desperately in love with the Prince, but for him, the man who "liked in these days to mark them off, the women to whom he hadn't made love," "she was the twentieth woman, she was possessed by her doom." For the Prince, until he comes under Maggie's sway in the course of Volume II, is always one up on the women with whom he is involved:

> He had done nothing he oughtn't—he had in fact done nothing at all. Once more, as a man conscious of having known many women, he could assist, as he would have called it, at the recurrent, the predestined phenomenon, the thing always as certain as sunrise or the coming round of Saints' days, the doing by the woman of the thing that gave her away. She did it ever, inevitably, infallibly—she couldn't possibly not do it. It was her nature, it was her life, and the man could always expect it without lifting a finger. This was *his*, the man's, any man's, position and strength—that he had necessarily the advantage, that he had only to wait with a decent patience to be placed, in spite of himself, it might really be said, in the right. Just so the punctuality of performance on the part of the other creature was her weakness and her deep misfortune—not less, no doubt, than her beauty. It produced for the man that extraordinary mixture of pity and profit in which his relation with her, when he was not a mere brute, mainly consisted.

No wonder that in his sexually charged survey of Charlotte when she first appears before him at Fanny Assingham's in chapter III he compares her to a purse that he can weigh "in his open palm," hearing even "a little the chink of the metal"! When he and Charlotte become lovers after their marriages, he deeply and actively appreciates her personal magnificence, her sensuousness and passion and skill, but he does not love her, certainly not for herself, for his own diabolically persuasive rationale for the adultery is based on his need to show that—if Maggie is determined to emasculate him psychologically (however innocently)—he is still a powerful sexual conqueror: he will have Charlotte in order to assert his identity as *galantuomo*, in order to keep from being published "as idiotic or incapable." So, at the

33. See *GBI*, 391, 399, and Krook, *The Ordeal of Consciousness*, 291–94.

height of their passion, in the first paragraph of the very chapter in which the lovers prepare to leave Matcham, with its call to "impunities of pleasure," for Gloucester, where they will become lovers "in act and in fact," Amerigo reflects upon his profit in the same vein as in his first encounter in the novel with Charlotte: "he had after all gained more from women than he had ever lost by them; there appeared so, more and more, on those mystic books that are kept, in connexion with such commerce, even by men of the loosest business habits, a balance in his favour that he could pretty well as a rule take for granted." The Prince's attitude toward Charlotte in Book Sixth, which has disturbed several commentators because of his apparent lack of feeling for her after all that has passed between them, is not surprising if one credits the implication in passages such as those just cited that much less passes in the Prince's heart than may appear. On the face of the evidence, indeed, the Prince's absence of genuine loving feeling for Charlotte, his failure of reciprocity with her, makes a hash of the view that Charlotte's anguish is mostly Maggie's fault. She is the Prince's victim, more than anyone else's, unless of course she is more completely her own (*GBI*, 22, 47, 49–50, 332, 335, 350; *GBII*, 116).

Had volume II of *The Golden Bowl* belonged not to Maggie, as central intelligence, but to the Prince, we should have been treated to the intimate details of Amerigo's choice of Maggie over Charlotte. The Prince's transformation, which makes him no longer Charlotte's lover but incontestably Maggie's (as she will become, for the first time, incontestably his), comes to us only in oblique glimpses, and, coming to us as it does from Maggie, it is nearly as undisclosed as the transformation that Hamlet undergoes, offstage, during his sea voyage. We watch Amerigo take in Maggie's measured, aesthetic, exquisitely considerate replacement on the mantle of the fragments of the golden bowl. We grasp, through his wife's intuition, his subsequent deception of Charlotte, his failure to share with her his knowledge of Maggie's discovery. We learn of his unrest at Fawns and of his frequent trips to London, where Maggie sees him, in her mind's eye, "wander in the closed dusky rooms from place to place or else for long periods recline on deep sofas and stare before him through the smoke of ceaseless cigarettes" (*GBII*, 293). But though we know enough to appreciate the Prince's predicament, we are never privy to the moral and intellectual struggles that Maggie tactfully leaves him to wage on his own. Nevertheless, the Prince's character and situation are sufficiently clear for us to reconstruct the process of his turn from illicit worldly passion to conjugal love.

Prince Amerigo's sensibility is first of all aesthetic. His imagination is sensuous, responsive to exhibited beauty, to the beauty of style and manners as much as to that of *objets*. He is, in the second place, like Merton Densher, a man who likes to take his cues from others. He always places himself under someone else's guidance: first Fanny Assingham's, then Charlotte's, finally Maggie's. Initially he tries to behave as he believes the Ververs want him to behave. Later, in the adultery, he lets Charlotte take the lead, as he does, for example, in awaiting her approach to him in chapter IV of Book Third and, afterwards, in following her arrangements for the trip to Gloucester. He has, in addition, the intellectual capacity to understand the motives of others with one key exception: he does not, in Book First, understand the Ververs. That they are a mystery to him, "a dazzling curtain of light," arises, again, partly from their wealth and partly from his not possessing one sense, "the moral" (*GBI*, 22, 31). Maggie's conquest of the Prince in Volume II depends on her giving him precisely that, the moral sense, on her showing it to him in a light in which he can take it in, and also on her making it clear to him that she loves him passionately and that she can manage life better than Charlotte. She succeeds on every count because her conduct, her method of personal and moral demonstration, is aesthetically impeccable. Acting with restraint, forgoing what she imagines are the conventional responses to a husband's infidelity (recriminations, jealousy, tears: in short, scenes), she leaves from early on—in her slow arrangement, for instance, of the shattered bowl—room into which his imagination can expand. She has sufficient faith in him and love for him to believe that, left to make his own discoveries, he will rise to an adequate apprehension of her love and its meaning. It is to these things—to Maggie's tasteful restraint, her faith, and her love—that Amerigo responds when, "alone with his thoughts" at Portland Place, he is "thereby a good deal as if he were alone with *her*" (*GBII*, 294).

But the Prince's final preference for Maggie is a result at least in part of his changing view of Charlotte. The example of Maggie's conduct, which combines style with a profound, if narrowly focused, moral consciousness, encourages him to redefine his relation to Charlotte. If we accept it that the Prince "had already forgot about Charlotte" when his relation with Maggie began, then his resumption of his affair with her is best understood as an instinctive response to the unwitting wrong Adam and Maggie do him by giving him nothing to do.[34] He asserts his selfhood, as *galantuomo*, through the adultery. In a sense he does not even abandon his wife, for, as Fanny might say, to give her up he must have first possessed her. In consequence, Amerigo's illegitimate relation with Charlotte is negatively defined, the product of his nonrelation with his wife. In Volume II, when Maggie, awakening to evil, begins "to live," the relation between her and the Prince, and the possibilities for their marriage, begin to assert themselves in the Prince's imagination. He is himself painfully awakening, unable to ignore the distinctions between Charlotte and Maggie that become increasingly evident to him, coming above all to appreciate Maggie's peculiar sort of high intelligence, in the light of which he calls Charlotte "stupid" (*GBI*, 77, 383; *GBII*, 348).

The Prince, furthermore, comes to feel that Maggie's ideas leave "taste in him as a touchstone . . . all at sea," for he infers from them that "taste by itself, the taste he had always conformed to, had no importance whatever." Something else, then, is required, and that must be the moral sense for which the Prince has learned to look to Maggie. Her moral sense is the basis of the consideration and assurance of her way of dealing with the situation. Thus she earns Amerigo's respect, a respect that Charlotte, in corresponding measures, must forfeit. Charlotte is still, indeed, great, but Maggie has shown herself, in her own quiet way, ever so much more so. Because Maggie puts Amerigo in a position to realize the love underlying her forgiveness and to appreciate her moral superiority through his own intellectual and aesthetic responses, she inspires in him love as well as respect. In the end, his need of her equals hers of him. At last he is in a relation with a woman that is more reciprocal than predatory. At last, for him, lover and wife are conjoined in one woman. Maggie's con-

34. Colonel Assingham asks his wife if the Prince had not "already forgot about Charlotte." Her reply is something short of fully affirmative ("He wanted to. . . . He was capable of the effort"), but if the Prince's feelings toward Charlotte are as I have described them, then one must conclude that Charlotte was not on his mind when he met Maggie in Rome, as she clearly is not in the period immediately preceding his marriage—until, of course, she appears on the scene.

quest is complete when, seeing him struggle to take in "what she so wonderfully gave," after heroic ordeals of self-restraint, she is ready at last to surrender herself to him. Amerigo, like Adam and Maggie, has ascended a sharp spiral hill of difficulty; and, though his way up has been different from hers, he has issued, out of his progress from a too-simple good faith, through bad faith, to a better one yet, in much the same place as his wife (*GBII*, 345, 368).

Charlotte Stant alone among the four principal characters does not go through a circular, upward moral development. Her character is static where their characters are dynamic. Although the others all contribute to the false equilibrium, Charlotte is clearly the chief author of the sin in their lives, is, in fact, virtually the avatar of the "evil seated all at its ease where she [Maggie] had only dreamed of good; the horror of the thing hideously *behind*, behind so much trusted, so much pretended, nobleness, cleverness, tenderness" (*GBII*, 237). But she never admits error, guilt, or the slightest remorse, and of course she is unique among the four in this too. The Prince and Maggie are the main centers of consciousness. Adam's point of view is rendered in one of the most dense of the six books of the novel. But Charlotte's viewpoint is restricted to a single chapter and to a few subsequent, very brief passages. Gabriel Pearson observes that it is an "important fact about Charlotte that she cannot be dramatized. She is already dramatic—she loses her self in her performance," for, since she is "always driven upon the current of her instinctual life," "consciousness in her is a matter of superb performance."[35] One knows her chiefly by her appearances, by what she does, and the effect is to give her far less internal (psychological and spiritual) substance than the other main characters. When we first meet her, she is involved in deception for a purely selfish purpose. Having come to London supposedly to attend her best friend Maggie's wedding, having enlisted the groom's aid ostensibly to buy the bride a suitable present—of course it should be a surprise, which gives Charlotte her pretext for insisting on secrecy—she reveals that her motive really is to impress him, almost on the eve of his marriage, with the survival of the passion he aroused in her in an affair he has certainly put behind him, even if he has not

35. Gabriel Pearson, "The novel to end all novels: *The Golden Bowl*," in *The Air of Reality: New Essays on Henry James*, ed. John Goode (London, 1972), 319–20.

forgotten her absolutely (he does, after all, keep "those mystic books"): "To see you once and be with you, to be as we are now and as we used to be . . . What I want is that it shall always be with you—so that you'll never be able quite to get rid of it—that I *did*" (*GBI*, 96–97). This episode of initial self-serving intrigue by Charlotte does not, to be sure, discredit her protestations of good faith in later, more ambiguous circumstances, but it does cast a long shadow over her subsequent conduct.

Comparison of Kate Croy and Charlotte is devastating to Charlotte's character in at least two important respects. First, James's initial portrayal of Kate is calculated to impress the reader deeply with those springs of Kate's conduct that amount to extenuating circumstances: the poverty of her family, made concrete in the drab, depressing grind of the Condrip household and in Mr. Croy's failure and disgrace. Charlotte too is poor, and she is, in addition, alone, without close family, only "distant relations who are so afraid she'll make use of *them* that they seldom let her look at them" (*GBI*, 181). But these circumstances are not fictionally realized for the reader, as they are in Kate's case. What is dramatized at the outset, to repeat, is her questionable design on the affianced Prince. We are less likely to be moved by her poverty, in any case, than to marvel at her success in managing in spite of it, her ability to travel far and wide, for instance, and her familiarity with and easy access to the society of the very, very rich. For though James makes it clear that Charlotte is marvelously skilled in making herself wanted by the rich, he also stresses that she does so with great facility. We do not see her involved in demeaning tasks or in gross violations of her personal ideals, as is so often the case, for instance, with Lily Bart, Edith Wharton's protagonist in *The House of Mirth*.

Second, whereas Kate's thoughts (in the one section of *The Wings of the Dove* where she is the central intelligence) focus upon the possibilities for honorable conduct that may somehow redeem her extremely limiting circumstances, Charlotte's (in the one major instance where James lets us in on them, in chapter I of Book Third) are consumed with self-display and self-justification, with perhaps as brazen an indulgence in vanity as is ever allowed a major James character, along with a positive relish in the circumstances that allow her close association with the Prince—in, that is, the false equilibrium that Charlotte ought not to enjoy but to deplore:

> She was herself in truth crowned, and it all hung together, melted together, in light and colour and sound: the unsurpassed diamonds that her head so happily carried, the other jewels, the other perfections of aspect and arrangement that made her personal scheme a success, the *proved* private theory that materials to work with had been all she required and that there were none too precious for her to understand and use—to which might be added lastly, as the strong-scented flower of the total sweetness, an easy command, a high enjoyment, of her crisis.

Charlotte's immediate crisis is her opportunity to enlarge her liberty, her freedom to appear in public with Amerigo and without Adam or Maggie. In working this opportunity for all it is worth, she puts forward what will be her main justification for the imminent adultery, that the Ververs care for each other more than for their *sposi*. There is justice, as noted earlier, in Charlotte's observation. Although, as I have argued, Maggie in fact values the Prince more than she does Adam, Charlotte has had reason enough to conclude that "Maggie thinks more on the whole of fathers than of husbands." But Dorothea Krook is right nonetheless in saying that Charlotte "suggests vividly a modern allegorical figure of the deadly sin of Pride placed against a symbolic background of the modern world at its worldliest" and in taking Charlotte's "sense of power and pride" as the keynote of the episode.[36] Charlotte seems to exult in the way the Ververs' failures as spouses put justifications for the exercise of her power into her grasp. By the end of the chapter, she is unable to make out a remark addressed to her, so rapt is she in "the golden glow in which her intelligence was temporarily bathed" and in the reflection of "her success," "her exceptional radiance," in the faces of her interlocutors (*GBI*, 246, 257, 264).

Much has been made by anti-Verver critics of Charlotte's straightness in dealing with Adam's marriage proposal. She certainly goes to exceptional lengths to make her circumspection appear candid. She questions, for instance, whether there is room in his life for "another young woman" and also whether his notion of relieving Maggie's anxiety is "quite enough to marry me for." Later, when they have re-

36. Krook, *The Ordeal of Consciousness*, 302.

ceived Maggie's blessing—upon which Charlotte insists—she wonders if the blessing is fully to be credited, since it comes in a telegram addressed only to Adam, not to her too. Only on receipt of the Prince's telegram, the contents of which we do not learn until much later, does she accept Adam's proposal, in Paris, days after he had "spoken" in Brighton (*GBI*, 215, 222, 224). Especially in view of her poverty and Adam's wealth, not to mention her own confessed desire to marry, her scruples appear magnificent. For a number of reasons, one may wonder if she is not rather acting upon magnificent calculation. The largest item that makes the question pertinent is her withholding from Adam knowledge of her old, Roman relation with the Prince. As Donald Mull argues, though Adam's proposal "lacks the passion which some feel essential to the idea of marriage," "it has the virtue of complete honesty about its terms," an honesty that it seems to me contrasts sharply with Charlotte's failure to be open about her love for his son-in-law.[37]

This is a matter on which Charlotte's capacity for self-deception seems to have taken in many of her critical defenders as well as herself. She feels "inattackably straight" because she has offered, in Paris, to show Adam the Prince's telegram, which "would in all probability at once have dished her marriage," since it would have given away what had been between her and Amerigo. Just before the telegram arrived, however, she had extracted from Adam an outright statement that he would not look at such a message from the Prince.

> "I see what's the matter with you. You won't be quiet till you've heard from the Prince himself. I think," the happy man added, "that I'll go and secretly wire to him that you'd like, reply paid, a few words for yourself."
>
> It could apparently but encourage her further to smile. "Reply paid for him, you mean—or for me?"
>
> "Oh I'll pay with pleasure anything back for you—as many words as you like." And he went on, to keep it up. "Not requiring either to see your message."
>
> She could take it, visibly, as he meant it. "Should you require to see the Prince's?"
>
> "Not a bit. You can keep that also to yourself."

Her conscientious risk of pressing him to read the telegram, which

37. Mull, *Henry James's "Sublime Economy,"* 145.

arrives practically immediately, is really scarcely any risk at all, though she later appears to have forgotten that she had assured herself of her security in the matter beforehand. One notes, moreover, that the other obstacles she raises to the marriage proposal are really straw men, incapable of frustrating Adam's suit, effective only in saving her from the possible appearance of leaping too eagerly at her opportunity. For example, Charlotte's insistence on getting Maggie's blessing cannot be considered as a genuine risk of "dishing" the marriage, for it is all rather obvious that Maggie has been responsible for bringing Charlotte in for her father's sake. Charlotte's culpability is increased by the subsequent revelation that the Prince's telegram did not really, by her own reading of it, give her carte blanche for the acceptance she gives Adam on the spot. For Amerigo's message has always been ambiguous for her, meaning either that "he was happy enough . . . really seasoned and secure" or that "even without her his career was up-hill work for him" and that "the event would compel him to live still more under arms." She accepts Adam's proposal, then, quite in the teeth of the latter possibility, a fact that makes her deception of Adam and her factitious risk of betraying it all the more reprehensible (*GBI*, 235, 290–91).

Charlotte depends a good deal on the delicacy of others to cover her tracks—not just on Adam's delicacy in not looking (as she had got him to say that he would not look) at Amerigo's telegram, but also on the delicacy of Amerigo himself, which keeps him from outright expression of the skepticism he nevertheless betrays about "their having plotted so very hard against their destiny" as she insists when she presents them as victims forced "against their will into a relation of mutual close contact that they had done everything to avoid." Yet her own predilections, tactics, and responses are indelicate, crude, bold-faced. Crude indeed (and a far more shocking inversion of values than any that occurs through Maggie's conduct in Volume II) is Charlotte's insistence on the sanctity of consideration that she and Amerigo owe their spouses—an insistence that triggers, as it were, the climax of her seduction of him into the first stage of their infidelity, the violently erotic kiss with which they "sealed their pledge." It is unclear whether Charlotte really believes, as she avows in the same chapter, that she is "the best stepmother, after all, that really ever was," and in any case, her attitude, whether self-deception or high-handed hypocrisy, is no less crude than her questionable charge to the Prince that Adam is to blame for her childlessness is indelicate (*GBI*, 289–90, 305, 312).

The information Charlotte confides to the Prince that she will never have children and that it is "not, at any rate . . . my fault" (*GBI*, 307) has generally been taken at face value and interpreted as an indication of a major defect in Adam, which practically disqualifies him as a husband, since Charlotte's implication is that he is sterile or, perhaps, impotent. Sallie Sears, for example, suggests that Adam's supposed sexual inadequacy is an important aspect of Charlotte's cruel and unusual punishment of banishment to America.[38] I find it difficult, however, to take Charlotte's assertion, though she may well believe it herself, with anything but skepticism. Since, according to her, both she and Adam had "hoped and . . . believed" they could have a child, the failing she attributes to Adam is probably sterility, not impotence. How, one wonders, can she be sure, in the absence of modern clinical tests, that the problem is Adam's and not her own? Maggie, of course, is material evidence that Adam has at least not always been incapable of paternity. Charlotte, on the other hand, so far as we know, has never become pregnant, either by Adam or by the certifiably virile Prince. The cause, then, may well be in herself, and not her spouse, that she is childless. Even were the charge just, it seems to me that one should have to take it less as an indictment of Adam than as an exposure of Charlotte in a glaring breach of confidence. I admit, however, that I could go much further toward crediting Charlotte's denial that the fault is at all hers if I could find a single point in the novel at which, in any matter, however slight, Charlotte takes the least bit of blame. But because she never assumes personal responsibility—in her own eyes she is always "perfectly passive" (*GBI*, 289)—her statement, though it is of course possibly true, can only be evaluated in the context of an unbroken, compulsive string of self-justifications.

In Volume II, as she begins to lose her poise, this aspect of Charlotte's character, the paradox that her Florentine refinement overlies an essential coarseness, grows more pronounced. Her querulous demands on the Prince—the illustrative detail is Maggie's vision of her asking him "what tone, in God's name—since her bravery didn't suit

38. See Sears, *The Negative Imagination*, 170.

him—she *was* then to adopt"—contrast with Maggie's difficult, dignified, moral self-reliance. Charlotte's melodramatic anguish is played close to the surface; that she cannot keep from sounding "like the shriek of a soul in pain" contrasts with Maggie's stoic, modest suppression of agonies no less intense, her ability to "stuff my pocket-handkerchief in my mouth" and to "keep it there, for the most part, night and day, so as not to be heard too indecently moaning" (*GBII*, 110, 282, 292). Charlotte's utter lack of empathy is baldly exposed, for in her stepdaughter's imagination of Charlotte's final denunciation of her—a display, again, of Maggie's empathy with Charlotte—one feels a very important truth about Charlotte, her inability even to begin to imagine the torment we have seen Maggie suffer (see *GBII*, 329–30). Charlotte's extortion of a bill of innocence from Maggie in chapter II of Book Fifth and her eager seizing of the chance for apparent triumph that Maggie offers her in chapter V of the same book show that experience has altered her not at all or perhaps even for the worse. She shows no sign of repentance or remorse, not any tenderness or solicitude, except possibly for herself. When we first see her after her marriage to Adam, she is "a bit brazen" and brilliant with a "slightly hard radiance," but in Book Fifth, the long final stay at Fawns, she is harder than ever and rather more than a bit brazen (*GBI*, 247, 258). Her development over the period covered by the first five parts of *The Golden Bowl* might well be described as a reverse dialectic, a spiral descent: from the initial bad faith of her duplicitous shopping expedition with the Prince, she moves toward its antithesis in the period when she sincerely tries, so she says (we have only her word, since the narrative skips the years in question), to make Adam love her more than he loves Maggie, a phase from which she swerves back, during the adultery, into a villainy of betrayal far greater than that with which she began. In Book Sixth, however, there is a strong suggestion that Charlotte has undergone, offstage as it were, alone at Fawns with Adam, a conversion of some moral or spiritual efficacy, about which more in a moment.

Insofar as Charlotte seems to suffer more than Prince Amerigo, the difference is attributable to his capacity for moral improvement and even more to the naturalness of his participation in the illicit relation—less culpable than Charlotte's, James implies, because the tradition he has been brought up in sanctions his behavior, whereas Charlotte's American background makes her wholesale adoption of European values a sort of perversion. Like a long string of Jamesian characters, beginning with Winterbourne in "Daisy Miller" and Gilbert Osmond in *The Portrait of a Lady*, Charlotte has "lived too long in foreign parts." Charlotte, that is, flies in the face of a moral system that is her birthright, while the Prince flounders in the dazzling mist of his incomprehension of that system. Amerigo himself makes this distinction in explaining to Charlotte why he does not understand the Ververs as well as she does: "You're of the same race, at any rate—more or less; of the same general tradition and education, of the same moral paste. There are things you have in common with them. But I, on my side, as I've gone on trying to see if I haven't some of these things too—I, on my side, have more and more failed. There seem at last to be none worth mentioning. I can't help seeing it—I'm decidedly too different" (*GBI*, 310–11). James thus makes it clear that Amerigo's traditions, though they do not excuse his conduct, at least explain it.

I have argued that Charlotte alone of the four principal characters fails to grow in moral terms. This reading requires, however, a brief qualification, for in Book Sixth there are several indications that Charlotte's fate will not be one of such unmitigated suffering, and of such unredeemed villainy, as seemed likely in Book Fifth. Although Maggie says that Charlotte seems to be "dying for us," she and the Prince agree that Charlotte will live "for others," that she is "naturally so far, splendid as she is, from having done with life," and that "she's making her life . . . she'll make it." The rightness of their view is confirmed when Charlotte appears with her husband in the final chapter. Adam is still playing "out his long fine cord," but the image has lost its bite of punitiveness, for now Charlotte has visibly adopted as "her great opportunity" the "mission" "of representing the arts and graces to a people still languishing afar off and in ignorance." Now, furthermore, Adam and Charlotte give an unprecedented sense of harmony, seem so "conjoined for a present effect as Maggie had absolutely never yet seen them" that "the question of the amount of correction to which Charlotte had laid herself open rose and hovered for the instant only to sink conspicuously by its own weight; so high a pitch she seemed to give to the unconsciousness of questions, so resplendent a show of serenity she succeeded in making." James recognizes, as

Maggie says, that "it's *always* terrible for women," but he also makes it clear at the end of *The Golden Bowl* that the description of Charlotte's return to America as her "doom" in Book Fifth is hyperbolic, as indeed it was when it referred to her giving herself away and to her arranging appearances in Volume I. For the two marriages to last, all four partners have to help hold a cracked—finally broken—bowl together. Consequently, one may finally allow Charlotte at least the possibility of *some* upward progress, though it is not, of course, comparable to Maggie's, Adam's, or Amerigo's (*GBI*, 50; *GBII*, 287, 346, 349, 357).

A very long book might be devoted to exegesis of *The Golden Bowl* and still leave many important matters undiscussed. Even within my particular focus on the dialectic of Henry James, much more might be said. I have omitted, in the present discussion, detailed analysis of the polar oppositions that govern the rhetoric and imagery in this novel as much as in *The Wings of the Dove* and *The Ambassadors*, for which I did try to demonstrate the incorporation in stylistic and structural details of the dialectic. Such transactions between extremes as operate, for example, in the oxymoronic phrase "possible, impossible" (repeated several times in *The Golden Bowl*; see *GBI*, 111, and *GBII*, 281) and in Adam's elaborate image of the myriad curves within the larger angularity of the Prince are ubiquitous in the novel and embody on a small scale the same disposition to pose and to try to reconcile oppositions that is the vital principle of the spiral dialectic. For readers who find the converting power of Adam Verver's imagination incredible or the spiritual beauty that James attributes to Maggie repugnant, my argument about the spiral dialectic in the novel obviously will not dispel a sense that the ambiguities at the end, in the description of the Prince and Charlotte, for instance, as "human furniture" (see p. 104, above) and in the closing phrase about "pity" and "dread," work ironically against affirmation of the "success" (*GBI*, 366) the Ververs claim for themselves:

> It kept him before her therefore, taking in—or trying to—what she so wonderfully gave. He tried, too clearly, to please her—to meet her in her own way; but with the result only that, close to her, her face kept before him, his hands holding her shoulders, his whole act enclosing her, he presently echoed: " 'See'? I see nothing but *you*." And the truth of it had with this force after a moment so strangely lighted his eyes that as

for pity and dread of them she buried her own in his breast. (*GBII*, 368–69)

On the other hand, for readers willing to suspend the sort of disbelief that arises from disagreement with particular articles of the novelist's faith, I hope I have shown how the spiral dialectic is the very form of the affirmation that James intended of the fusion achieved by Maggie and the Prince, by Adam, and, possibly, at the very end, though this is much less certain, by Charlotte. It may be, as Krook argues, that Maggie's feeling of pity and dread is her horror that the Prince "might want, or feel obliged, to 'confess' to her," exemplifying "the same impulse to 'spare' the Prince" she has acted upon in "other crucial places in the story" or it may be that the words mean, as Krook allows, what R. P. Blackmur suggests, "that Maggie 'pities' the Prince because she knows that this moment marks his final subjugation to her moral 'tyranny,' and 'dreads' her own remorse about what she had done."[39] But there are other possibilities—that the light in the Prince's eyes concentrates for Maggie the truth of the grim knowledge they have shared together (that, as he tells her, "everything's terrible, cara—in the heart of man" [*GBII*, 349]), that the pity and dread are of the sheer intensity of the Prince's love for Maggie, or that the phrase indicates the high cost in human suffering that they, and the others too, have paid to achieve the final synthesis. One may have one's pick; as is so often the case with this most poetically organized of novels, the choice is a litmus test of the reader's subjective chemistry. It seems to me that we would do well to rest content with less specific interpretations of the mysterious final chord on which *The Golden Bowl* resolves. Pity and dread so closely resemble the Aristotelian description of the emotions purged by tragic drama as "pity and terror" that the general conclusion that James means to tap the tragic undertones of the novel seems to me sensible. A comedy the form of which is the dialectic of spiral return must necessarily violate generic decorum by swerving through tragic possibilities on its way to an affirmative resolution. The form of *The Golden Bowl*, it is clear, is that of a comedy or, perhaps even better, of a romance. After the peripety, the protagonist, Maggie, works toward success, not failure. Marital harmony is restored, and the res-

39. Krook, *The Ordeal of Consciousness*, 318, 323.

toration is celebrated in the closing scene, as is generation, in the exhibited person of the Principino, brought out for a farewell with his grandfather and step-grandmother.[40] The tragic chord at the end is subsumed within the whole description of the final embrace of Maggie and the Prince, which is a long-delayed expression of the sexual desire that the pair only just manage to repress, by mutual agreement, at the end of the penultimate chapter. Their embrace embodies their union and at the same time symbolizes the synthesis they achieve between the appreciation of surfaces and of how much may be hidden beneath them, which Maggie learns from the Prince, and the moral sense, without the aid of which, as Amerigo learns from Maggie, the aesthetic sense is inadequate, dangerous, potentially diabolical. In the end, when each has, by such indirections as I have outlined, found directions out, their embrace is eloquent, above all, of their mature passion and love, under the reign of which the Princess becomes truly royal and Amerigo truly rich.

40. For a full treatment of the comedic elements in *The Golden Bowl*, see Ronald Wallace, *Henry James and the Comic Form* (Ann Arbor, 1975), 136–47.

CHAPTER FOUR

The Spiral Dialectic in the Career of Henry James

In asking when James began to give significant expression to his disposition to the dialectical ordonnance of his fictions—in asking how and when he started to build even the smallest details of his art on polarities and to construct total works according to the Romantic design of spiral return that I have described in his late novels—I am raising questions that verge on the biographical. But if my undertaking in the present essay is a sort of biography, it is intentionally a narrow one, concerned only with the growth of one aspect of James's art as evidenced only in his fiction and in his explicit comments about it. Rather than attempt an exhaustive survey of James's vast *oeuvre*, I shall restrict my commentary to representative works, to those that seem to me to exemplify the growth of James's dialectical habit of mind and to offer substantial rewards to analysis in terms of dialectical models. Because the Jamesian dialectic is already prominent in the fiction of James's first decade as a writer, the artifacts of which are almost exclusively short stories, I shall focus on them, citing the text of the first serial publication of each tale discussed. I will then take up two of James's earliest long fictions, *Roderick Hudson* and *The American*, proceeding thereafter to the conclusion of this study, a synoptic account of the evolution of the oppositional element in James's novels throughout the phases of his career leading up to the late period that we have already considered. My underlying concern—or better, perhaps, my overriding one—is akin to that to which James himself confessed, with some trepidation, in relation to the persons in his fiction: his "irrepressible and insatiable, his extravagant and immoral, interest in personal character and in the 'nature' of a mind."[1] Without, I hope, either extravagance or immorality, my aim is to contribute to our understanding of the consciousness of Henry James, an interest that seems, among many of the best recent commentators on James—Mull, Ward, Yeazell, and Rowe (to name only a few)—practically irrepressible and insatiable.

"In James's time," Leon Edel observes, "a dedicated artist rarely committed his inexperience, however precocious, to a long work." James conscientiously passed his apprenticeship writing tales, over two dozen short fictions appearing in the decade before *Roderick Hudson* (1875), "my first attempt at a novel," he says in his preface (though in fact his short novel *Watch and Ward* had come out serially in the *Atlantic Monthly* in 1871, his seventh year as a publishing writer of fiction). James's theoretical distinctions among the varieties of short fictions have been ably discussed by Krishna Baldev Vaid and by James Kraft, among others, and yet many questions linger about the critical theory itself and especially about its relation to James's practice. From the novel, "a long fiction with a 'complicated' subject," James discriminates the *nouvelle*, "of which the main merit and sign is the effort to do the complicated thing with a strong brevity and lucidity," intensity being sought through pursuit of an "ideal of economy" (*AN*, 4, 231). From the *nouvelle* in turn he discriminates the tale (or short story), which deals with the simple rather than the complicated thing in one of two fashions, as "picture" or as "anecdote." The difficulties one may have in sorting out these often "delicate" distinctions—as Kraft calls the last, between "picture" and "anecdote"—and in carrying them over to criticism of James's fiction itself are suggested in the introductory remarks to the studies of James's tales by Vaid and Kraft. Vaid, for example, pronounces certain questions, such as that of the "maximum dimensional reach of a Jamesian nouvelle" as "definitively settled," but on other matters, such as the difference between the anecdotal and the developmental, he concludes that "James's practice does suggest that there is no method whereby you can lay down hard and fast rules," and he quotes Murdock and Matthiessen

1. *AN*, 156.

in their introduction to the *Notebooks*: "Short stories became *nouvelles*, and *nouvelles* became novels." Thus, though James provides characteristically antithetical descriptions of his procedures in tales of allegedly different types, declaring, for example, that an anecdotal subject was to be followed "as much as possible from its outer edge in" while the subject "comparatively demanding 'development'" was to be pursued "from its center outward" (*AN*, 232–33), his practice subverts his own categories. James's apprenticeship writing tales prepared him to write novels, and his earliest ventures in storytelling, as Vaid observes, "contain in seed form his later technical, thematic, and artistic preoccupations" in his fictions of whatever length.[2]

From James's second story on, "The Story of a Year" (the first to appear under his own name), a variety of stylistic, rhetorical, thematic, and structural traits embodying the young writer's preoccupation with antitheses and with resolving them begin to appear in his fiction with increasing frequency and complexity. All of the aspects of the dialectic of the late novels are present in the early tales, from oxymoronic phrasing, formal rhetorical antithesis, and dialogues that turn upon opposing terms to the concept and design of the ascending, synthesizing spiral journey. James's first decade of fiction writing may be said to climax in 1875 with three works governed to an unprecedented degree by antitheses: *Roderick Hudson*, completed before James's departure for Europe in mid-autumn, 1875; "Benvolio," a tale written immediately after *Roderick Hudson*; and *The American*, which was published in 1877 but which was already under way by November 30, 1875, when James announced its title in a letter to the editor of *The Galaxy*.[3] Before taking up these works—and before considering the psychobiographical discussions by Leon Edel and S. Gorley Putt of the dualities in *Roderick Hudson* and "Benvolio"—I should like to point out the dialectical elements of greatest salience in the tales written before 1875.

Elements of opposition and synthesis are prominent throughout the first half dozen tales James published. In "The Story of a Year," for

2. Leon Edel, Introduction to Henry James, *Roderick Hudson* (Boston, 1977), v; James Kraft, *The Early Tales of Henry James* (Carbondale, 1969), xii; Krishna Baldev Vaid, *Technique in the Tales of Henry James* (Cambridge, Mass., 1964), 6–9; Matthiessen and Murdock (eds.), *The Notebooks of Henry James*, xvi.

3. Edel, *The Conquest of London*, 202.

example, demonstrating, as Kraft observes, that James "knew what direction he wanted his fiction to take," the narrator states that he has "no intention of following Lieutenant Ford to the seat of the war," for "the exploits of his campaign are recorded in the public journals of the day" and "my own taste has always been for unwritten history, and my present business is with the reverse of the picture."[4] The two men between whom the capricious heroine Lizzie Crowe vacillates are "the *data* of her problem," standing "like opposing knights, (the black and the white,) foremost on the great chessboard of fate." Her original ardor of devotion to Lieutenant Ford is a "pensive ecstasy" of knowing that "the golden sands are dropping one by one," making "servitude freedom, and poverty riches," but when Lizzie's ardor cools, the image undergoes a transformation, for the golden sands "run out," only to be replaced by "leaden sands" that also "dropped one by one." Abroad in a "dim landscape that had been brightening all day to the green of spring" but which "was now darkening to the grey of evening," Lieutenant Ford and Lizzie witness a vision, in clouds radiant with sunset, of bloody war, of "a country of blackened villages and crimsoned pastures" in which "opposing squadrons bore each other down" and then were "scattered, bowling with equal velocity towards north and south." Ford suggests that the vision "is an allegory" of "the end of the war." When Lizzie expresses her fear that "it means a shabby compromise" in which "light disappears, too, and the land is in darkness," Ford's reply expands the allegory, giving it the form of an ascending spiral: " 'Only for a season,' answered the other. 'We mourn our dead. Then light comes again, stronger and brighter than ever. Perhaps you'll be crying for me, Lizzie, at that distant day.' " Ford's words are prescient and ironic; for, parallel to the passage from light through darkness back to stronger and brighter light, Lizzie passes from devotion to Ford through her infatuation with Mr. Bruce, the "opposing knight"—whose proposal she accepts when she thinks the absent Ford is on the point of death from a war wound—back to a renewal of her allegiance to her first lover, who has returned from the front to die at home. Just before he dies, he renounces his own

4. Kraft, *Early Tales*, 5; Henry James, "The Story of a Year," in Maqbool Aziz (ed.), *The Tales of Henry James, 1864–1865* (Oxford, 1973), Vol. I of Maqbool Aziz (ed.), *The Tales of Henry James* (2 vols. to date; Oxford 1973–), 30. Following parenthetic citations of *TJ* are to tales James published between 1865 and 1869, collected in their original serial versions in this volume.

claims upon Lizzie and blesses her union with Mr. Bruce. Ford's forgiveness and benevolence, in their power to secure a posthumous devotion, prefigure the deathbed forgiveness and generosity of that later wronged lover, Milly Theale. Presumably, the serenely lucid selflessness of the dying Ford brings home to Lizzie the capricious vanity with which she has betrayed him, inspiring her with the resolve she declares to do "justice to my old—old love." True to the lieutenant's prediction, her access to a light on herself "stronger and brighter than ever" coincides with her mourning for him. We should note, however, that the contempt with which James has persistently treated Lizzie—"She was sorry," he writes early in the tale, that "she knew so little: as sorry, that is, as she might be, for we know that she was shallow"—makes it almost impossible for the reader to care about her or to believe in her ability to sustain this final resolve. One may well wonder if her shriek, when she at last forbids Mr. Bruce to follow her, expresses her horror of her past infidelity or her fear of yielding to Mr. Bruce and thus of committing a second one. Nevertheless, James's first signed story contains, in the allegory of light and darkness, the concept and, in the chronicled development of Lizzie Crowe, the design of the Romantic dialectic of spiral return (*TJ*, 21–22, 30–33, 42, 44, 56).

James's next two stories depict characters unable to move successfully between the polarities according to which they define their situations. Locksley, in "A Landscape Painter," seeks in anonymity "to abjure for a while my conventional self, and to assume a simple, natural character." This is an opposition, however, in which the terms are unequal. Locksley cannot escape the "conventional self," for despite his concealment of his considerable wealth, his fiancée reads his diary when he is ill, discovers the deception, and resolves to marry him for his money. The story climaxes with a typical Jamesian reversal—Locksley discovers the truth to be the precise contrary of his belief that he has been accepted for his "simple, natural character" and not for his "hundred thousand a year" (*TJ*, 61). That the heroine, appropriately named Miss Blunt, has told him quite early on that "I mean to marry the first rich man who offers" emphasizes that Locksley's delusion about the motives of her behavior comes about at least in part from his own willingness to be deceived. He has neither the courage nor the imaginative clarity to transcend his "conventional self," and James's point about him, as Mull suggests, is that his "romantic notion of an independent self is unrealizable."[5]

Similarly, in "A Day of Days," Adela Moore seeks to put "the world," "human nature," and her own "excessive intellectual growth" behind her by burying "herself in the country" in order to live in "the society of nature" and "in her feelings." She succeeds at least to the extent of losing enough of her illusions about the conventional "world" to undergo a reversal of her feelings toward a friend who is very much of that world: "Laura B., for whom a year ago she had entertained a serious regard, now impressed her as a very flimsy little person, who talked about her lover with almost indecent flippancy." But though she is sufficiently liberated from social constraints to entertain on her own for one "day of days" an attractive young stranger who has come to visit her conveniently absent brother, she is too timid, when the question of romance arises between them, to step farther beyond the bounds of conventionality by bidding him to drop, for her sake, an imminent voyage to Europe. She too, like Locksley, is incapable of realizing the independent, natural self for which she yearns. The conventional self to which it is opposed is too strong, though the failure of the possible marriage of true minds that both young people glimpse is as much his as hers, as James Kraft points out in an excellent discussion to which my remarks here are indebted.[6] Although neither "A Day of Days" nor "A Landscape Painter" achieves a broad thematic synthesis or an overall structural one, both tales contain prominent, vivid oppositions, not only in the large, general issues that the stories pose but also in their stylistic details. For instance, the setting of "A Landscape Painter" "is certainly at once the brightest and the blackest spot in New England," and Tom Ludlow, Adela's visitor in "A Day of Days," is "at once one of the best liked and one of the best hated of men" and "a common fellow but . . . a very uncommon one." "A Day of Days" also contains, in Adela's initial mistaking of Ludlow for a familiar companion, the local Unitarian minister, the first of those characteristically dialectical scenes of delayed recognition of which I took note in my discussion of *The Ambassadors* (*TJ*, 65, 89–90, 92, 105).

5. Mull, *Henry James's "Sublime Economy,"* 24.
6. See Kraft, *Early Tales*, 11–16.

In James's fifth story, "My Friend Bingham," two other typically bipolar motifs discussed in my treatment of *The Ambassadors* make their first appearances in the tales. One of these is the idea that polarities set up fields within which one may swing, almost violently, from one pole to the other. In *The Ambassadors*, Strether refers to this concept several times as one of "reaction," and Maria Gostrey has the same notion in mind when she refers to Strether's possible "revulsion in favour of the principles of Woollett."[7] The hero of "My Friend Bingham" embodies "so violent a reaction" against the people among whom he has been born and bred—"people in whom the hereditary possession of a large property . . . had extinguished all intelligent purpose and principle"—that he has become "*par excellence* a moralist, a man of sentiment," a devotee of spiritual as opposed to material goods. Bingham is also the first in that long line of Jamesian protagonists, culminating in Strether, whose scrupulousness and "a certain fastidiousness of mind" (like that of Bingham) animate within them "the oddity of a double consciousness" (like that of Strether).[8] The "certain diffident enthusiasm" that stands foremost among the traits that "redeemed him [Bingham] from vulgarity" is a notable forecast of the indifference in Strether's curiosity and, more immediately, of the full-blown emergence two years later, in 1869, of the dualistic "New England conscience" in a tale we shall consider shortly, "A Light Man" (*TJ*, 108–10).

That "My Friend Bingham" is a tale of sin, suffering, and redemption conceived in the high Romantic mode is emphasized by a dramatic allusion to *The Rime of the Ancient Mariner*. Bingham and the narrator, his close friend, are duck-hunting along a stretch of seashore when Bingham decides to take aim at a standing gull with the same sort of sublimely unmotivated carelessness with which the ancient mariner shoots, unexpectedly even to himself, the portentous albatross. As Bingham prepares to fire, the narrator recites:

> God save thee, ancient mariner,
> From the fiends that plague thee thus!
> Why look'st thou so? "With my cross-bow
> I shot the albatross."

7. *AM*, 132, 202.
8. *Ibid.*, 18.

Bingham's duck shot, like the bolt from the mariner's crossbow, flies forth with unforeseen and terrible consequence, killing a little boy who has been concealed by the gull—he had been trying to catch it from the opposite side of the rock on which it had perched—and who takes Bingham's volley full in the face as the bird rises into the air unharmed. This "damnable" act, as Bingham himself calls it, occasions such remorse in him, which evokes such pity, in turn, from the dead boy's widowed mother, that Bingham and she fall in love and marry (*TJ*, 113, 117).

The parallels with Coleridge's poem are numerous. Bingham has been alienated not only from his family's vulgar materialism but also from the "graces" of civilized family life, "its good humour" and "home-keeping benevolence," and, following a "genuine romance" in which he "had been cruelly jilted," he had resolved, as the narrator makes out, upon "a solemn act of renunciation," "had forsworn marriage" altogether (*TJ*, 109–110). The narrator urges, and events make clear, that the renunciation violates Bingham's nature. His withdrawal from life is at base a failure of self-awareness, similar to the mariner's initially ignorant—and thus culpable—innocence; Bingham's detachment at any rate seems at one with the carelessness of his fatal volley, just as the mariner's unconsciousness of himself and of his proper relation to the natural order is a condition of his killing of the albatross. Bingham's suffering as a result of his manslaughter effects a spiritual revolution in him; the man who had forsworn marriage comes to propose it, and he is apparently reconciled to the "home-keeping benevolence" that his ample means make possible (though we should note that his marriage to an impecunious Baptist minister's widow is not at all the sort of alliance approved by the society against which his earlier abjuration of family ties had been indeed an overreaction). Bingham's love and marriage are like the love with which Coleridge's mariner, becoming reconciled to God and to the natural order, blesses the watersnakes, creatures that have been disgustingly ugly to him but that come to seem transcendently beautiful; at the same time, the childlessness of Bingham's marriage is parallel to the eternal debt of penitence that the mariner owes regardless of his growth in self-knowledge and spiritual harmony. One notes also that the marriage from which the wedding guest is detained in Coleridge's poem functions not only as a contrast of community and conventionality with the isolation and extraordinariness of the mariner's ordeal but also as the natural equivalent of the mariner's supernatural reconciliation with the world. Similarly, for Bingham, marriage functions both as the embodiment of the conventional and as the act and sign of reconciliation. The line of Bingham's development, like that of the ancient mariner, is a spiral ascent, and the same design is apparent in the story of his bride. For her, too, the way down has been the way up, and "the proper conclusion of my story lies in the highly dramatic fact that out of the depths of her bereavement—out of her loneliness and her pity—this richly gifted woman had emerged, responsive to the passion of him who had wronged her all but as deeply as he loved her." The reference to Coleridge, finally, is by no means unusual; in fact, by far the greatest number of explicit literary allusions in James's early stories—and throughout the first two decades of his fiction—are to the English Romantic poets. In "A Landscape Painter," for example, Locksley reads Wordsworth aloud, and in "Poor Richard," James's sixth tale, occurs the first of his inveterate allusions to Keats, a quotation from "The Eve of St. Agnes" (*TJ*, 81, 126, 155).

"Poor Richard," a story built on dramatic contrasts and reversals and on rhetorical and thematic antitheses, is perhaps the best example among these earliest tales by Henry James of conformity to the *Bildungsweg* paradigm of progress from a point of origin through its antitheses and back to the origin on a higher level. Generically, "Poor Richard" is a miniature of that most Romantic of forms, the *Bildungsroman*. We first meet Richard Clare, the title character, when he is attempting to reform his hitherto shiftless and dissolute ways in order to make himself worthy of Gertrude Whittaker, a parentless, wealthy, and thus extraordinarily independent young woman of high moral character. Clare is a rustic, a farmer who has mismanaged his inherited land, irresponsibly piling up debts while drinking heavily, "so wanton in his errors as almost to impugn his sanity." Utterly devoid, moreover, of social grace or subtlety, he is nevertheless full of strong, instinctive feeling, and he loves Gertrude truly, for herself alone and not for her wealth. In the dialogue with which the story opens, she offers him friendship instead of love, taking upon herself, for the sake of pity and of her old friendship with his sister, the work of his "redemption." The Richard of the first of the three sections of the story has been sufficiently inspired by Gertrude, despite her rebuffs of him as a lover, to feel the "process" of his association with her not merely as "salutary" but even as "aesthetic," and in his resolve to prove that "he was good enough to be better" he gives up liquor and launches into a conscientious effort to make a going concern of his farm. He perseveres in his reformation despite what he takes to be major setbacks dealt him by two rivals for Gertrude's affections. But, near the end of the second section of the story, the rivalry leads him to tell a lie impulsively, a lapse for which he becomes, almost at once, greatly ashamed. His regimen breaks down. He tries to drown his remorse, goes to bed "miserably drunk," and wakes up with typhoid. When he recovers, in the third section of the story, after weeks of illness during which his survival is for some time doubtful, his conversion, as it were, is complete. The unregenerate boy has become "abundantly a man." In the pattern of Richard's boyishly earnest but inadequate reformation, followed by a moral collapse and then by what is virtually a physical as well as a spiritual rebirth into wholly adequate and assured manhood, James has dramatized a typically Romantic journey of spiral return (*TJ*, 134–35, 137, 160, 178).

The *Bildungsweg* design in "Poor Richard" is supported by oppositions in every aspect of the tale. Richard's willingness to take emotional risks is opposed to the timidity of Gertrude and to that of the more attractive of his two rivals, Captain Severn, for Severn and Gertrude fail to make anything of their attraction to each other because each has "too much pride" and "too little imagination." Richard's passionate sincerity is opposed to the exploitative, calculated deceptions of his other rival, Major Luttrel. His dying into his new life of achieved manhood brings about a fundamental reversal in the terms of his relations with Gertrude and with the world in general. Between the opening and closing scenes, for example, Richard and Gertrude exchange positions—he had been the unrequited lover, too desperately confused and immature for the then formidable Gertrude, but in the end, come into his mature awareness of himself and of her, he has grown beyond her, and he does not respond when Gertrude, recognizing his strength and health, is ready to love him. His remark when he first sees the physical deterioration that expresses "the misery of her soul" because of her engagement to Luttrel, whom she does not love, might well stand for the dynamic of their relation: "I've got my strength again—and meanwhile you've been failing." It is possible to take this as symptomatic of the psychopathology of sex in James's fiction, a "first glimpse, in James," as S. Gorley Putt suggests, "of emotional cannibalism" or "the operation," as Donald Mull argues, "of a corollary of what John Bayley calls 'Proust's Law' (in this case, that A never loves B until B has ceased loving A)," but it would be well to note too that reversals such as the one undergone by Richard and Gertrude occur throughout James's fiction, even between characters between whom there is no question of sexual relations, love, or marriage, between, for example, Strether and Chad Newsome (*TJ*, 149, 173).[9]

In the design of his very first tales, as we have seen, James uses polarities in a characteristically Romantic way. The tales that followed "Poor Richard" in the sixties and in the first half of the seventies contain many further examples of dialectical organization. This is less the case in some of the stories, to be sure, than in others. The Jamesian dialectic is not prominent, for instance, in James's experiments in Hawthornian tales of the supernatural, in, for example, "The Romance of Certain Old Clothes" and "De Grey: A Romance" (both of 1868) or in "The Last of the Valerii" (1874). But even in these inferior and generally derivative—indeed almost parodic—tales there are flashes of what we have come to know as typically Jamesian art. In "De Grey: A Romance" an exchange of dialogue that turns upon opposing terms forecasts, as Putt points out, the late tale "The Beast in the Jungle" (1903):

> "My adventures?" said Margaret. "I have never had any."
> "Good!" cried Paul; "that in itself is an adventure." (*TJ*, 293)

In "The Last of the Valerii," the marriage of an American girl and a Roman aristocrat foreshadows the fusion of America and Europe in Maggie Verver's marriage to Prince Amerigo. In the vignette upon which the story closes, Count Valerio, who has been saved by his wife from his enthrallment to a statue of Juno recently unearthed on his ancestral grounds, takes in her forgiveness for his having neglected her in his reversion to paganism and buries his head in her lap—a remarkable prefiguration of the concluding vignette in *The Golden*

9. Putt, *Henry James: A Reader's Guide*, 36; Mull, *Henry James's "Sublime Economy,"* 23. For a discussion of distinctively American adaptations of the *Bildungsroman*, see C. Hugh Holman, *Windows on the World: Essays on American Social Fiction* (Knoxville, 1979), 170–76.

Bowl. That Count Valerio is rescued from his unnatural obsession with the Juno by his American wife suggests an opposition similar to the one posited by Prince Amerigo when he sees himself as pursuing, in his marriage to Maggie, a "scientific" modernity antithetical to his inherited prejudices, "the antidote to superstition."[10]

A detailed analysis of the ways in which the best of the tales James wrote from 1868 through 1874 express the young writer's dialectical vision would extend the present chapter far beyond its intended length. The play of oppositions underlies all of the most promising stories of the period, including, especially, "Osborne's Revenge" (1868), "A Light Man" (1869), "A Passionate Pilgrim" (1871), and "Madame de Mauves" and "Eugene Pickering" (both 1874). For example, "Osborne's Revenge," the last of the six tales James published in 1868, is built on a thoroughgoing reversal of the narrator's expectations; his pursuit of the "wicked girl" whose heartlessness he has incorrectly concluded to have been responsible for the suicide of a close friend leads him only to "a charming one" who is clearly innocent, and the passage in which he first encounters her is a delayed recognition scene of considerably greater sophistication, subtlety, and dramatic effect than the similar scene taken note of in my remarks above about "A Day of Days" (*TJ*, 317).

Of the numerous oppositional elements in "A Light Man," one, at least, should not be permitted to pass without comment, James's imputation of a Strether-like double consciousness to the first character to whom he attributed a "New England conscience."[11] Here the first-person narrator, Max, expresses his puzzlement about his friend Theodore, whom Max is cynically trying to supplant in the affections and bequests of a childless old millionaire, Mr. Sloane:

10. Putt, *Henry James: A Reader's Guide*, 34; *GBI*, 17.

11. Austin Warren, in "The New England Conscience," 149, reported that the first use known to him of the phrase "the New England Conscience" was by Henry James in his first notebook entry on *The Ambassadors* in 1895. Taking up "Mr. Warren's implicit challenge," Raymond Thorberg pointed out, in 1969, that the phrase may be found in James's minor novel *Confidence* (1879); two years later, in a single paragraph, Thorberg reported the presence of the "New England conscience" in the passage from "A Light Man" quoted below (see "Henry James and the 'New England Conscience,'" *Notes and Queries*, n. s., XVI [1969], 222–23, and "The New England Conscience," *ibid.*, n. s., XVIII [1971], 264). After 1895, James used the phrase once more, in his "Project for *The Ambassadors*" (see n. 14, below).

> He [Theodore] is troubled, too, about Mr. Sloane. His attitude toward the *bonhomme* quite passes my comprehension. It's the queerest jumble of contraries. He penetrates him, contemns him—yet respects and admires him. It all comes of the poor boy's shrinking New England conscience. He's afraid to give his perceptions a fair chance, lest, forsooth, they should look over his neighbor's wall. He'll not understand that he may as well sacrifice the old man for a lamb as for a sheep. His view of the gentleman, therefore, is a perfect tissue of cobwebs—a jumble of halfway sorrows, and wide-drawn charities, and hair-breadth 'scapes from damnation, and sudden platitudes of generosity; fit, all of it, to make an angel curse.

Theodore, whose character is an antithesis to Max's—"I don't believe," Max says at one point, "in disinterested service; and Theodore is too desperately bent on preserving his disinterestedness"—has given up serious theological study because "instead of faith full-armed and serene, there sprang from the labour of his brain a myriad abortive doubts, piping for sustenance"; Theodore can now delight in Voltaire as well as in Emerson.[12] "So deucedly conscientious" and "so scrupulous" a man could scarcely feel anything other than "a jumble of contraries" in having his disinterestedness put on the line, as it were, by Max's rivalry for Sloane's favor. Theodore does indeed betray a desire for the inheritance, as the reward, we should add, of apparently loyal, upright service. But to argue that "Theodore is really no better than Max" is to ignore his outburst of tears when he recognizes his part "in this filthy contest."[13] He feels, as he roundly declares, "shame," and we may gauge the force of his insight into himself and of his reaction to it by the act of renunciation he has just committed, for we have seen him burn—only moments before Sloane's death—a will that would have passed the old man's wealth on to him (*TJ*, 352, 360, 361, 371). In recovering his scrupulousness after the unconscionable contest with Max, Theodore completes a spiral evolution. Strether's double consciousness is of course far more complicated and far richer than Theodore's, in part because Strether's is an expression of his being "a man of imagination" as well as a man "ridden by his 'New

12. This description of Theodore's crisis of faith echoes, perhaps, Matthew Arnold's description in "Thyrsis" (1866) of Arthur Hugh Clough's spiritually troubled departure from Oxford: "He went; his piping took a troubled sound / Of storms that rage outside our happy ground."

13. Kraft, *Early Tales*, 46. On the same page, Kraft remarks that "Theodore seems a very early and undeveloped Lambert Strether."

England conscience,'" but the association of the New England conscience in Theodore with a mind afflicted by contraries is an even more striking development toward James's conception of the pilgrim of Woollett than the "diffident enthusiasm" of the hero of "My Friend Bingham" (*AN*, 310).[14]

"A Passionate Pilgrim," the earliest of his tales included by James in the New York Edition of his works, is a chronicle of failure brought about by the delusions of the protagonist. The contrast between illusion and reality, the perceived and the actual, is fundamental to the story. It stands, moreover, as a signal instance of James's international theme in its earliest form, "a sop," as he wrote in his preface, "instinctively thrown to the international Cerberus" (*AN*, 194). The passionate American pilgrim Clement Searle, deeply interested in his possible accession to an English estate upon which he has remote claims of ancestry, has been "nursed at the opposite pole" from the distant English cousins who now hold the property.[15] Himself a jumble of contraries, "full of that perplexing interfusion of refinement and crudity which marks the American mind," his perceptions "delicate; his opinions, possibly, gross," he is the first character to fall prey to that characteristically Jamesian obsession with an alternative life, with what he might have been had he been to the English manor born.[16] Searle yearningly believes that the terms of his life would have been reversed for his English self: "here my vulgar idleness would have been—don't laugh now—elegant leisure."[17] Eventually, in the delirium of his fatal illness, he confuses himself with an ancestral namesake of the previous century, baffling the narrator, who finds "it hard to distinguish between the play of fancy and the labor of thought, and to fix the balance between perception and illusion."[18] A reference in the narrative to the self as a haunted tenement (see the *Atlantic Monthly*, XXVII [1871], 362) seems to prefigure the ordeal of Spencer Brydon in "The Jolly Corner," and indeed this early tale is nearly the precise reverse of that later, highly dialectical one:

14. "Project for *The Ambassadors*," in Matthiessen and Murdock (eds.), *The Notebooks of Henry James*, 375.
15. Henry James, "A Passionate Pilgrim," *Atlantic Monthly*, XXVII (1871), 493.
16. *Ibid.*, 358.
17. *Ibid.*, 361.
18. *Ibid.*, 491.

Clement Searle's obsession with his alternative life as an Englishman leads to his fatal delusion, foreclosing, at the same time, any possible development of the affection that has grown between him and Miss Searle, one of his English cousins; the Europeanized Brydon's obsession with his alternative life had he remained in his native America leads to the nearly fatal encounter with his other self in the house on the jolly corner, a trial from which he emerges sufficiently whole to accept for the first time the love of his devoted friend Alice Staverton and to return it. In relation to Alice and in relation to his native land as well, Brydon develops according to the familiar Romantic spiral, but Clement Searle is too weak a character to survive the transaction between extremes to which he subjects his being. This way of describing Searle's predicament, moreover, suggests some hitherto unnoticed affinities he has with other James characters, with, for example, Hyacinth Robinson in *The Princess Casamassima*, who dies—by his own hand—because the growth of his imagination and sensibility makes him increasingly susceptible to the powerful forces at work in the field of oppositions drawn around him, drawn, for that matter, by James in such a way that the oppositions become, for Hyacinth, tragically irreconcilable.

In "Madame de Mauves," the third of James's stories included in the New York Edition and one of the most widely discussed of the early fictions, Longmore may at first appear to develop according to the pattern of spiral return. There can be little doubt that in this *nouvelle* James blazed a trail he would follow with greater subtlety and with a finer talent for complication in *The Ambassadors* some thirty years later, as Robert McLean has shown in persuasive detail.[19] Like Strether, Longmore has a double consciousness, never choosing "the righthand road without beginning to suspect after an hour's wayfaring that the left would have been the interesting one."[20] Longmore's oddity, moreover, is connected with his American puritanism, and thus he is a descendant of Theodore in "A Light Man" as well as a harbinger of Strether. "Madame de Mauves," indeed, is a tale that

19. See Robert C. McLean, "The Completed Vision: A Study of *Madame de Mauves* and *The Ambassadors*," *Modern Language Quarterly*, XXVIII (1967), 446–61.

20. Henry James, "Mme. de Mauves," *The Galaxy*, XVII (1874), 216. This story has been known as "Madame de Mauves" (not "Mme.") since its second appearance, in *A Passionate Pilgrim* (1875).

pursues the international contrast with a vengeance, so much so that it approaches at times the allegorical, seeming to lie, so far as mode is concerned, midway between the fundamental realism of the international tales of the late seventies—of "Daisy Miller," for instance, and of "An International Episode"—and the essential allegory of contrast (albeit not the preeminent international one) in "Benvolio," James's fourth tale after "Madame de Mauves." Longmore, at any rate, begins in innocent and detached admiration for the American wife of a French baron, falls in love with her—so far as he is capable of that high passion—entertains for a while with mounting excitement her husband's hints that Longmore should make love to her (for the baron hopes thus to accommodate her to *his* penchant for love affairs), and at last takes the morally straight path of renunciation, deciding to return to America in order to rise to the "ideal of conduct" she has conceived "for him."[21]

But Longmore's enactment of the dialectic of spiral return, as close as it seems to the affirmative pattern of development undergone by Strether, is drastically undercut by James's suggestions that Longmore is incapable of genuine passion and, even more importantly—as McLean, Kraft, and others have noted—that the ostensible uprightness of Madame de Mauves is in fact a cruelly inhumane, cold, insensitive rigidity. Both Longmore and Madame de Mauves habitually set up antitheses in attempting to describe their predicaments, but the oppositions are either falsely conceived or else, for these characters at least, irreconcilable. For example, when he meets a French artist and the artist's mistress in the course of a pastoral excursion strikingly similar to the rural outing that leads to Strether's encounter with Madame de Vionnet and Chad on the river, Longmore sits "brooding and asking himself whether it was better to cultivate an art than to cultivate a passion." His inability to achieve for himself the fusion of passion and art that the artist and his companion have apparently realized is brought home to us by his subsequent dream, "a rather striking allegory" in which Longmore, in a wood "divided by the murmuring stream he had left an hour before," is unable to arrive on the same bank as Madame de Mauves, despite the assistance of the baron as boatman:

21. *Ibid.*, 369.

> She made him no motion that he should cross the stream, but he wished greatly to stand by her side. He knew the water was deep, and it seemed to him that he should have to plunge, and that he feared that when he rose to the surface she would have disappeared. Nevertheless, he was going to plunge, when a boat turned into the current from above and came swiftly toward them, guided by an oarsman, who was sitting so that they could not see his face. He brought the boat to the bank where Longmore stood; the latter stepped in, and with a few strokes they touched the opposite shore. Longmore got out, and, though he was sure he had crossed the stream, Mme. de Mauves was not there. He turned with a kind of agony and saw that now she was on the other bank—the one he had left.

Similarly, Madame de Mauves, who reads Wordsworth to her husband, poses an opposition between her own "taste for poetic fitness" and "life," which "is hard prose, which one must learn to read contentedly." Her inability to find some point of moderation between these extremes amounts to a kind of brutality of idealism that at last does her husband in, as Longmore learns from a mutual acquaintance two years after his return to America, where he has failed to " 'devote' himself to anything" because he has "intently, constantly" thought of her:

> "M. de Mauves had *fait quelques folies*, which his wife had taken absurdly to heart. He had repented and asked her forgiveness, which she had inexorably refused. She was very pretty, and severity, apparently, suited her style; for whether or not her husband had been in love with her before, he fell madly in love with her now. He was the proudest man in France, but he had begged on his knees to be readmitted to favor. All in vain! She was stone, she was ice, she was outraged virtue. People noticed a great change in him: he gave up society, ceased to care for anything, looked shockingly. One fine day they learned that he had blown out his brains."

The terrible cost of Madame de Mauves' "rigid taste for poetic fitness" having thus been spelled out, Longmore does not act upon his "first impulse . . . to return to Europe," for he has now become "conscious of a singular feeling, for which Awe would hardly be too strong a name."[22]

22. *Ibid.*, 356, 364, 366, 374. Longmore, incidentally, is a notable exception—like Alice Staverton in "The Jolly Corner"—to Ruth Bernard Yeazell's observation that James's characters do not dream; see her *Language and Knowledge in the Late Novels of Henry James*.

By contrast with "Madame de Mauves," "Eugene Pickering," James's only other story of 1874 that may in any sense be termed major, presents a straightforward, unironic, almost schematic version of the design of spiral return. Pickering is a naïve American, kept unnaturally innocent up to his twenty-seventh year by the "muffling and coddling" of a "really almost monastic" education under the guidance of his astoundingly protective father, whose death precedes the opening of the story by five months. Pickering's father has even arranged for him to marry the daughter of a business acquaintance, a young woman who is nine years Pickering's junior and whom he has never met. The father's system, "persistently and uninterruptedly applied," has been so successful that the narrator, who has not seen the son since they were boyhood companions fifteen years before, recognizes him easily on their chance meeting in Hamburg, for Pickering, though physically matured, has been virtually untouched by experience, displaying a "candid, unsophisticated, cloister face" "like certain young monks I had seen in Italy." Pickering has come for the first time, however, to sense the potential in himself for fuller development:

> "I find I'm an active, sentient, intelligent creature, with desires, with passions, with possible convictions—even with what I never dreamed of, a possible will of my own. I find there is a world to know, a life to lead, men and women to form a thousand relations with. It all lies there like a great surging sea, where we must plunge and dive and feel the breeze and breast the waves. I stand here on the brink, staring, longing, wondering, charmed by the smell of the brine and yet afraid of the water. The world beckons and smiles and calls, but a nameless influence from the past, that I can neither wholly obey nor wholly contemn, seems to hold me back. I'm full of impulses, but somehow, I'm not full of strength. Life seems inspiring at certain moments, but it seems terrible and unsafe."

Thus torn, Pickering affirms that he will keep the engagement to be married—as he has promised his dying father he would—but, as he declares, "I want to *live* first!"[23]

Live first he does, through a love affair with a German *femme fatale*, the beguiling Madame Blumenthal, whose "imagination is lodged where her heart should be"—a widow, novelist, playwright, and rafinée. So exquisite is Madame Blumenthal's polished presenta-

23. Henry James, "Eugene Pickering," *Atlantic Monthly*, XXXIV (1874), 401, 403, 405.

tion of herself that even the worldly narrator is taken in by her charm, commending himself as "a very competent philosopher" for his balancing of "the account between nature and art in my affable hostess." Pickering falls utterly in love with Madame Blumenthal, proposes to her, receives her acceptance and, then, abruptly, her dismissal:

> "I give you ten minutes," she had said, pointing to the clock. "Make your scene, tear your hair, brandish your dagger . . . I led you on, if you will. I received your visits in season and out. Sometimes they were very entertaining. Sometimes they bored me fearfully. But you were a curious case of—what shall I call it?—of enthusiasm . . . I wanted to make you commit yourself unmistakably . . . Of course I can't marry you; I can do better."

Jarred out of his innocent, romantic illusions, Pickering almost instantaneously accomplishes a quantum leap in maturity: "he had tasted of the cup of life . . . turned . . . so suddenly to bitterness" and now "his face was five years older." After a brief, enervating plunge into despair, Pickering recovers himself: "He had had a fever and then he had had a chill; the pendulum had swung right and left in a manner rather trying to the machine; but now, at last, it was working back to an even, natural beat." Now he chooses, freely, on his own account, to resume his original project: he will pursue the arranged marriage, and, if his intended accepts him, she too will have freely chosen, for he has recently learned in a letter from her father that she has violently rejected the arrangement, hitherto unknown to her, and has released Pickering from his obligation. The story concludes with an effect of ineptness in James's hasty, contrived denouement. The narrator has suggested to Pickering that his intended—aptly named Miss Vernor—must be "a lovely creature, and six months afterwards he wrote me that I was right." Pickering develops, then, according to the Romantic paradigm of spiral return, moving from extreme innocence through the antithetical phases of his involvement and disillusion with Madame Blumenthal and back at last to his original commitment on a level that is higher, as his newly discovered maturity and assurance in the end make clear.[24]

24. *Ibid.*, 514, 519, 522–23, 525–26. I would speculate that James may well have named the *femme fatale* of this tale Madame Blumenthal after Blumine in *Sartor Resartus*: Carlyle's Diogenes Teufelsdröckh is of course an exemplary late-Romantic embodiment of the paradigm of spiral development, and Blumine plays a role in his history parallel to Madame Blumenthal's in Picker-

In his first decade of publishing fiction, then, James developed two general, antithetical methods of treating the polarities prevalent in the best of his tales: in stories dealing with weak protagonists—characters deficient in stability, imagination, or capacity for feeling (like Locksley, Adela Moore, Clement Searle, and Longmore)—the oppositions remain unresolved; in stories dealing with strong protagonists—characters qualified for affirmative development by their common sense and moral fiber, combined with imagination, and by strength and clarity of feeling (like Bingham, Richard Clare, Theodore, and Eugene Pickering)—the oppositions are resolved through the dialectical process of spiral return. We shall soon find James turning, in the critical year 1875, from the first of these alternatives to the second as he moves in the late autumn from two works just completed, *Roderick Hudson* and "Benvolio," to a new undertaking, *The American*.

Roderick Hudson presents an intense and complicated play of oppositions that generally prove—and particularly so for Rowland Mallet and Hudson himself, the principal figures in the novel—irreconcilable. As Leon Edel has observed, "James knew he was writing a kunstlerroman . . . in the high romantic tradition." The rootedness of the work in Romantic literary tradition is emphasized not only in the depiction of Hudson as the type of the Byronic artist and in James's making the chief setting, as Edel says, "the Rome of Goethe, of Shelley, of Keats," but also in explicit references in the novel to Romantic poets, to Coleridge, for instance, when Hudson complains that his "mind is like a dead calm in the tropics, and my imagination as motionless as the phantom ship in the Ancient Mariner" and to Wordsworth, probably, when Hudson says he saw "*la beauté parfaite* . . . before I was born—in another state of being" and, certainly, when Mallet enjoys the Alps with " a volume of Wordsworth in his pocket."[25] The contraries opera-

ing's, for Blumine first enamors Teufelsdröckh in the ardor of his innocence and then, in unaccountably and precipitously throwing him over for another, initiates the dark night of his soul. That Teufelsdröckh first encounters Blumine in a flowery valley is consonant with James's Blumenthal, literally *flower valley*, and there is probably resonance too between the given names of Carlyle's protagonist (Diogenes–God-born) and James's (Eugene–well-born).

25. Edel, Introduction to James, *Roderick Hudson,* vi; Henry James, *Roderick Hudson* (Boston, 1876), 209, 247, 421, hereinafter cited parenthetically as *RH*. Of course, it is not the phantom ship that is becalmed in Coleridge's poem but the Mariner's own, actual vessel; accordingly, in his final revision James substituted "blighted" for "phantom" in Hudson's allusion.

tive in *Roderick Hudson* are as insistently juxtaposed as any in the great dialectical poems of Coleridge and Wordsworth. America is opposed to Europe, passion to art, prudence to recklessness, an idealistic theory of art to a materialistic one, and so on. Thus, for example, only in "the old imperial and papal city" of Rome does Hudson find "what he had been looking for from the first—the complete antipodes of Northampton [Massachusetts]." Accommodation of such complete antipodes is of the most extreme difficulty; otherwise Hudson (and his patron and observer Mallet, too) might well have been redeemed from the fates to which their antithetical defects of character consign them. But, as Hudson tells an apprehensive Mallet when the "gradual process" of his "disintegration" (*AN*, 12) is already irreversibly advanced, "To reconcile Northampton and Rome is rather a problem"—a problem devised by James, furthermore, to be practically insoluble, for among the principal terms of what he called "my little plan . . . was the projection, for my fable, at the outset, of some more or less vivid antithesis to a state of civilization providing for 'art' " (*AN*, 8; *RH*, 84, 157).

Hudson's disintegration is the subject of the novel, but "the centre of interest . . . is in Rowland Mallet's consciousness, and the drama is the very drama of that consciousness" (*AN*, 16). Mallet is a further development of the characters in the early tales (Bingham, Theodore, Longmore) who seem to be forerunners of Lambert Strether: he is a New England artist manqué, endowed with "an uncomfortably sensitive conscience," with intelligence, and with a fund of imaginative appreciation of aesthetic values, but with no creative ability of his own and with no more than a highly circumscribed, modest capacity for feeling. Like the other forerunners of Strether, Mallet has a double consciousness:

> His life had been a singular mixture of the rough and the smooth. He had sprung from a rigid Puritan stock, and had been brought up to think much more intently of the duties of this life than of its privileges and pleasures. His progenitors had submitted in the matter of dogmatic theology to the relaxing influences of recent years; but . . . he had at least been made to feel that there ran through all things a stream of right and wrong, as different, after all, in their complexions as the texture, to the spiritual sense, of Sundays and week-days. His father was a chip of the primal Puritan block . . . and if the lad had not been turned

> to stone himself, it was because nature had blessed him, inwardly, with a well of vivifying waters.
>
> He had frequent fits of extreme melancholy, in which he declared that he was neither fish nor flesh nor good red herring. He was neither an irresponsibly contemplative nature nor a sturdily practical one, and he was forever looking in vain for the uses of the things that please and the charm of the things that sustain. He was an awkward mixture of strong moral impulse and restless aesthetic curiosity.

Accordingly, Mallet's consciousness steadily generates polarities. For example, he follows his dialectical remark that "a passive life in Rome . . . takes on a very respectable likeness to activity" with the antithetical and equally oppositional "prevision . . . that if Roman life doesn't do something substantial to make you happier, it increases tenfold your liability to moral misery" (*RH*, 1, 6, 8–9, 15).

The characters in the novel are all opposed to each other dialectically, usually in twos, occasionally in threes. The central antithesis of characters is between Mallet and Hudson. Mallet, we learn early on, often "wished he were a vigorous young man of genius, without a penny." In Roderick Hudson he finds just such a young man, and in becoming Hudson's patron, in spiriting the promising sculptor from the culturally suffocating, narrow provinciality of Northampton to the rich, artistically stimulating cosmopolitanism of Rome, he hopes to see brought to fruition in Hudson the very qualities he knows himself to lack, above all the great creative passion that turns out to coexist in Hudson with an irrepressible impulse toward self-destruction. The contrasts between Mallet and Hudson are consistently sharp. For instance, shortly after their arrival in Rome—when they have already undergone a characteristically Jamesian reversal of roles, with Mallet, who had been Hudson's initiator into things European, becoming instead Hudson's student in high civilization—Mallet feels "something akin to envy" because of his uncomfortable sense of the way "the young sculptor's day passed in a single sustained pulsation, while his own was broken into a dozen conscious devices for disposing of the hours" (*RH*, 15, 91).

The other important antithesis of characters is between Mary Garland and Christina Light. James attributed what he later took to be the failure of Mary Garland as a character to his own inability to create "the ideal antithesis," for the very "difficulty had been from the first that I required my antithesis—my antithesis to Christina Light, one of the main terms of the subject": "Directness seemed to fail unless Mary should be, so to speak, 'plain,' Christina being essentially so 'coloured'; and completeness seemed to fail unless she too should have her potency. She could, moreover, by which I mean the antithetic young woman could, perfectly have had it; only success would have been then in the narrator's art to attest to it" (*AN*, 18). James's intention with the two women is, at any rate, clear enough. When they meet at Madame Grandoni's, for example, "the almost dramatic opposition of these two keenly interesting girls touched Rowland with a nameless apprehension." In the same scene, Miss Light observes that she is able to "appreciate" Miss Garland "because I have imagination. She has none" (*RH*, 344, 348).

There are, in addition, a series of secondary but significant antitheses of characters, foremost among which are those between Hudson and Gloriani and between Hudson and Prince Casamassima. From time to time, to refine and intensify such oppositions, James brings a third figure into the dialectic. At the dinner party that Mallet gives to celebrate the first triumphs of Hudson's art in Rome, the modest little watercolorist Singleton, "an embodiment of aspiring candor, with feeble wings to rise on," is grouped with Hudson, "a genius which combined sincerity with power," and with Gloriani, who incarnates "art with a worldly motive, skill unleavened by faith, the mere base maximum of cleverness." Similarly, Mallet at one point falls "a-thinking that a certain natural ease in a woman was the most delightful thing in the world: There was Christina Light, who had too much, and here was Miss Blanchard, who had too little, and there was Mary Garland (in whom the quality was wholly uncultivated), who had just the right amount" (*RH*, 112–13, 340).

That *Roderick Hudson* is as fully imbued with the oppositional principle as James's late novels might be demonstrated in exhaustive detail. As in the late novels, oxymorons abound. A notable example is the description of the "artless artfulness" of Hudson's early work, a description the terms of which are reversed when Christina Light is said to speak with "artful artlessness." Other characters besides Mallet are most strikingly portrayed in sentences that pose oppositions. Thus, as Madame Grandoni tells Mallet, Miss Light "is a mixture of good and bad, of ambition and indifference." Shortly after arriving in Rome, Hudson impresses Mallet with his ability to ride "his two horses at once with extraordinary good fortune," establishing "the happiest *modus vivendi* between work and play," but after Mallet comes to see that the sculptor's "beautiful faculty of production was a double-edged instrument, susceptible of being dealt in back-handed blows at its possessor" and that "men of genius, accordingly, were alternately very enviable and very helpless," he sends the following description of the artist to Mary Garland:

> He is the most extraordinary being, the strangest mixture of qualities. I don't understand so much force going with so much weakness—such a brilliant gift being subject to such lapses . . . Sometimes I think he hasn't a grain of conscience, and sometimes I think that, in a way, he has an excess. He takes things at once too easily and too hard; he is both too lax and too tense, too reckless and too ambitious, too cold and too passionate . . . and for good and evil alike he takes up a formidable space.

The ideas entertained by the characters in *Roderick Hudson* are similarly dialectical. Gloriani's cynical, materialistic theory of art, for example, is not only diametrically opposed to Hudson's idealistic, spiritual one, but it is also, in and of itself, a tangle of contraries:

> It was the artist's opinion that there was no essential difference between beauty and ugliness; that they overlap and intermingle in a quite inextricable manner; that there is no saying where one begins and the other ends; that hideousness grimaces at you suddenly from out of the bosom of loveliness, and beauty blooms before your eyes in the lap of vileness . . . and that a consummate work is a sort of hotch-potch of the pure and the impure, the graceful and the grotesque. Its prime duty is . . . to savor of a complex imagination.

The savor of James's complex imagination is, at any rate, pervasive in *Roderick Hudson*, and suffice it to add, without further illustration, that the structures of dialogues, of paragraphs, of chapters, and of the large, general stages of development in which the story unfolds are as grounded in opposition as the elements of the novel surveyed in the preceding remarks (*RH*, 34, 94, 98, 144, 149, 200, 267).

Roderick Hudson, nevertheless, however oppositional in design, belongs to that group of James's fictions in which transactions between the extremes depicted seem in the end to be impossible. Perhaps more than other work, *Roderick Hudson* is resonant with Sallie Sears's characterization of James's fictional world "as rent asunder, with half its goods on the left hand of God, half on the right, and no passage in between."[26] The dialectic of the novel proves intractable to resolution because of the incapacity of the central characters. The sheer impetuousness and self-destructiveness of Hudson's passion for Christina Light—even when Mallet breaks through the barrier of the artist's egotism to make it clear that he himself is in love with Hudson's wronged fiancée, Hudson responds with anger at his own obtuseness, not with compassion for Mallet's pain or with appreciation of his sacrifice—make him unable to achieve the self-realization that brings Jamesian heroes like Strether to a higher awareness and to some sort of resolution of the polarities that have hitherto governed their existence. Mallet, conversely, falls so far short of having even a normative capacity for passion (as Hudson rather cruelly suggests in his response to Mallet's confession of love for Mary Garland) that he is unable to pursue his suit with Miss Garland after Hudson's death. The emphasis in the closing pages of the novel on the excessive moderation of Mallet's feelings, moreover, reinforces the impression of his complete want of the creative, imaginative power he has sought to foster and to exercise vicariously in becoming Hudson's patron.

"Benvolio," James's one tale of 1875, is also, as Edel observes, "his sole venture into allegory." In "Benvolio," as in *Roderick Hudson*, oppositions are everywhere, and everywhere irreconcilable. Benvolio, though not a flawed personality like Hudson or Mallet, is "a tissue of absolute contradictions." "The negative, with Benvolio, always implied the positive," and thus he leads "a kind of double life" in pendular alternation between his two mistresses, the worldly, brilliant Countess and the reclusive, contemplative Scholastica. Unable to realize himself fully in association with either of the women, he at last settles on Scholastica, bringing her home from the refuge she has sought in "the antipodes," for, as he puts it to the Countess, "can't you imagine that I cared for you only by contrast? You took the trouble to kill the contrast, and with it you killed everything else." The story concludes with the observation that, after the reunion with Scholastica, Benvolio

26. Sears, *The Negative Imagination*, 145.

"began to produce again; only many people said, his poetry had become dismally dull."[27]

"Benvolio" and *Roderick Hudson* have both occasioned psychobiographical commentaries. *Roderick Hudson*, says Leon Edel, presents "a skillful variation on the familiar Quincy Street problems," problems that Edel has elsewhere in his biography attributed to James's having had a too-feminine, maimed father and a too-masculine mother and to his suffering from a practically pathological case of suppressed sibling rivalry with his brother William. Thus, for example, Edel remarks that "in Rome, Rowland and Roderick wander about very much as Henry and William had recently wandered" and that "in contemplating the two men, so romantically named and so involved in a kind of emotional duel—Rowland, the rational, with no real sense of what it means to be an artist, and Roderick the impulsive, with no sense of how to curb his artist's ego—it seems as if James has abstracted the incandescence of his genius and placed it beside his decorous, cautious, restrained self . . . He treats them as irreconcilable . . . It was as if a wall of glass stood between Henry James and his desires . . . In this novel the *feeling* self had to die. It was too great a threat to the rational self." Similarly, Edel remarks that the allegory of "Benvolio" "has in it less of the universal than of the autobiographical," and he proposes that James in effect posed a question about himself in the tale: "How to reconcile . . . those two natures within himself—the inner America and the inner Europe—the Roderick and the Rowland, that duality which every issue of the *Atlantic* was revealing?" In a kindred spirit, S. Gorley Putt treats "Benvolio" and *Roderick Hudson* in a chapter titled "Everyone Was a Little Someone Else': *Roderick Hudson*, *Confidence*, and Parables of the Split Personality." The basis of James's duality, according to Putt, is his "endless fascination in the contrast between those whose vocation was 'to be' and those whose ambition was 'to do'."[28]

Now there is much in the approach to Jamesian duality in these

27. Edel, *The Conquest of London*, 190; Henry James, "Benvolio," *Galaxy*, XX (1875), 209, 223, 226, 235. For pendulum images in descriptions of Benvolio, see pp. 214 and 233.

28. Edel, *The Conquest of London*, 175–78, 190, 193; Putt, *Henry James: A Reader's Guide*, 104.

remarks by Edel and by Putt that is clearly congenial with the understanding of James advanced throughout the present study. Edel concludes his discussion of "Benvolio" by stressing the extremes that generally delimited James's imaginative universe:

> It was precisely by contrast, by the vision of the old and the new, the two great worlds between which he shuttled, the American in Europe, the European in America, the polarities of the parochial and the cosmopolitan, that Henry was to live. Contrast and comparison was to be the law of his life; and in the performance of this, an act of critical judgment was necessary as well as an artistic function. He reconciled both; and he paid his price. He became at once the most intellectual of artists, and the most passionate of critics. And he led always the double life of Benvolio: he courted Europe and he never forgot America.

And Edel goes on to suggest James's moderation of the extremes: "What strikes the reader in this fantasy is the fact that the two personages dwelling within Benvolio, although quite different, nevertheless manage to enjoy peaceful coexistence. . . . The two selves might be different, but they were different parts of a harmonious self. This suggests that in certain fundamental areas Henry was an individual without conflict." Putt, too, stresses the ubiquity of duality in James's fiction: "there is hardly one novel or tale which does not to some degree strike the geminian notes of antithesis or parallel, dissonance or assonance, contradiction or compensation," and throughout "the fiction from *Benvolio* . . . to the later mellower versions of that same diptych . . . there may also be perceived the degree to which this same problem, like exasperated Siamese twins or the warring words of an oxymoron, first shapes, then develops, and finally comes near to disintegrating James's prose style."[29]

Setting aside my strong dissent from Putt's irritable denigration of James's late style, I want nevertheless to make clear a fundamental objection to these psychobiographical accounts of the Jamesian dialectic.[30] Despite their partial congeniality with my argument, analyses like Edel's and Putt's, though admittedly plausible on their own

29. Edel, *The Conquest of London*, 193–94; Putt, *Henry James: A Reader's Guide*, 87.

30. My objections here would, of course, also apply to other psychobiographical accounts of the Jamesian dialectic, to, for example, the biographical implications of Manfred Mackenzie's view of James's "binary form" in *Communities of Honor and Love in Henry James*.

grounds, incur the obvious risks of oversimplification and reductiveness. Many of James's tales deal with "split personality," but most do not. According to Putt, practically all of the fiction strikes "notes of antithesis." Is it not a probable oversimplification, then, to suggest that the dialectical structure of most of James's work has its genesis in a fascination with the "geminian" theme expressed explicitly in a mere—if significant—fraction of his *oeuvre*? The reductive implications of psychogenetic thematic and stylistic analysis seem to me the most troubling of all. We are asked to believe that James's characteristic concerns and the forms in which he embodies them are best considered as arising from divisions of one sort or another within his own psyche. James's art becomes, in this view, a record of psychological compulsion, not of conscious artistic design. Putt's implication, especially, is that we are dealing here with a defect in James: the "unresolved problem" of the geminian obsession "finally comes near to disintegrating James's prose style." More and more, Putt seems to be saying, James's art was diseased, the record of a sick, "split" personality. Such suggestions point up, by way of contrast, what I would argue is an advantage of the alternative perspective offered here, the description of the Jamesian dialectic as having its provenance in the literature of the Romantic age. Instead of referring James's literary practice to his psychological history, it is referred, in my account, to a specifically literary influence. His use of polarities thus becomes not a compulsion arising from psychic division—a flaw for which "he paid his price" even in Edel's deeply sympathetic account—but a legitimate attribute of a richly meaningful imaginative tradition.

The closing months of 1875 saw the inception of a new novel, *The American*, which may be said to mark a decisive break with the years of apprenticeship and to initiate the first great phase of James's achievement, the early period extending from 1876 through the publication of *The Portrait of a Lady* in 1881. For in the story of Christopher Newman, James presents as complete an enactment of the dialectic of spiral return as is to be found in any of his works. In doing so, he establishes the course he was to follow in all of the major works of the early period. With *The American*, James turned from the first of the alternative methods developed in his earliest tales for dealing with polarities, the method whereby he dramatized irreconcilable extremes, to the second, whereby he worked toward a resolution of extremes in the maturing awareness of his protagonists.

In the details of its construction, *The American* is thoroughly dialectical, far more so, indeed, than *Roderick Hudson*. Consider, for example, this early description of Christopher Newman: "It was our friend's eye that chiefly told his story; an eye in which innocence and experience were singularly blended. It was full of contradictory suggestions. . . . Frigid and yet friendly, frank and yet cautious, shrewd yet credulous, positive yet skeptical, confident yet shy, extremely intelligent and extremely good-humored, there was something vaguely defiant in its concessions, and something profoundly reassuring in its reserve."[31] Claire de Cintré is similarly described in antithetical terms. She makes Newman wonder "where, in so exquisite a compound, nature and art showed their dividing line." Here is how he sees her on their second meeting: "In her whole person there was something both youthful and subdued, slender and yet ample, tranquil yet shy; a mixture of immaturity and repose, of innocence and dignity." And here is how he describes her later, when he has become an intimate of her parlor and has had opportunities to observe her social manner: "She was so tall and yet so light, so active and yet so still, so eloquent and yet so simple, so frank and yet so mysterious." In her speech, Newman is delighted to hear "soft roughnesses." The descriptions of all the characters, with the exception of the extraordinarily simple Mrs. Bread, are invested with such polarities, but the dialectic is most intense and consistent in the portrayal of the two central figures, particularly in that of Newman (*TA*, 79, 84, 100, 114).

The issues that confront Newman throughout his passionate pilgrimage on the Continent are best summarized as bipolar: work and leisure, duty and pleasure, surface and depth, the commercial and the aesthetic, the class of commercial persons and the aristocracy, revenge and forgiveness—such antitheses, along with the obvious, central one of America and Europe (present in every major work of the early period except *Washington Square*) govern the dynamic form of Newman's experience. Like other characters in the novel, Newman foreshadows prominent figures in the late fiction. Thus, just as Claire

31. Henry James, *The American*, ed. Joseph Warren Beach (New York, 1949), 3; hereinafter cited parenthetically as *TA*. The text of this edition is that of the first—Boston: Houghton, Osgood and Company, 1877.

de Cintré looks forward to Madame de Vionnet, Mrs. Tristram to Fanny Assingham and to Miss Gostrey, Mr. Tristram to Colonel Bob and Jim Pocock, so Newman looks forward to Lambert Strether and Adam Verver. Like Strether's experience in *The Ambassadors*, Newman's in *The American* develops as a reaction to his past life, and in the early novel, as in the later one, this idea is expressed several times with the image of a pendulum. When Tristram asks if he has "retired from business," Newman replies that "I dare say that a twelve month hence the operation will be reversed. The pendulum will swing back again" (*TA*, 23). Like Strether, too, Newman at last chooses renunciation and a return—a changed, new man—to America.

Newman's resemblance to Adam Verver is far more striking, going well beyond the correspondence of their similarly suggestive names. Each, of course, is an American businessman in Europe. Each has turned his back on the commercial for the aesthetic. Adam has seen his career specifically as a spiral ascent. Newman, if in a slightly different fashion, also senses the circularity of his experience. As he tells Claire de Cintré when he makes his second marriage proposal midway through the novel, "I'm going back to where I began. I *am* back there. I have been all around the circle." Adam's peculiar sensibility is in part developed for the reader through James's allusion to "Upon First Looking Into Chapman's Homer." The Keatsian vibrations set up around Newman are practically inescapable when James tells us that his "tenderness turned very often into a positive heart-ache" and speaks of times "when the heart has a heavy weight upon it . . . when, at any rate, happiness passes into that place in which it becomes identical with pain." Here one recognizes the same complex of emotions and images—the heavy aching of the heart, the intermingling of pleasure and pain—that occurs in the first stanza of the "Ode to a Nightingale," in the twenty-third stanza of "The Eve of St. Agnes," and in the Elgin Marbles sonnet. When Mrs. Tristram, in Newman's presence, says she sees a resemblance between Valentin de Bellegarde and the hero of Keats's "La Belle Dame Sans Merci," there is the prospective irony that Newman himself will come to resemble the ailing "knight at arms / Alone and palely loitering" near the close of his adventure, outside the house of the Carmelites where Claire has withdrawn forever (*TA*, 163, 179).

As I argued in the preceding chapter, Adam Verver's conscientious development takes the form of a spiral return. So does Christopher Newman's. His starting point in the novel is the antithesis of the foregoing stage of his life—from public and commercial affairs he has turned to the private and aesthetic spheres. Experienced in the former, he is innocent in the latter. With the utmost good faith, he believes that the Bellegardes will accept him as Claire's husband. When that belief is destroyed, he passes through a period in which he contemplates revenge, a period during which he strongly flirts, so to speak, with the antitheses of his original, innocent good faith and benevolence. In the end, having traversed the extreme opposite of his point of origin, he renounces revenge, returning to his first innocence on a higher level of awareness, and planning, simultaneously, a literal return to his starting point, America. Thus Newman fulfills the Romantic dialectic of spiral return.

Most strikingly, so far as the comparison with Adam Verver is concerned, Newman too experiences intense, sudden, characteristically Romantic moments of visionary illumination at the critical turning points in his spiritual evolution. Two such moments frame the portion of Newman's life chronicled in *The American*. The first is related retrospectively; Newman recalls how he came to give up an opportunity for doing an enemy out of a deal worth sixty thousand dollars. He had made his decision in a hack that came to resemble a "hearse," suggesting the death of his established selfhood. The renunciation of revenge leads, moreover, to Newman's spiritual rebirth ("I seemed to feel a new man inside my old skin"), to his abandonment of business ("I wanted to throw it all up and break off short"), and to his journey to Europe ("I longed for a new world"):

> "It was a hack like any other, only a trifle dirtier, with a greasy line along the top of the drab cushions, as though it had been used for a great many Irish funerals. It is possible I took a nap. . . . At all events I woke up suddenly, from a sleep or from a kind of reverie, with the most extraordinary feeling in the world—a mortal disgust for the thing I was going to do. It came upon me just like that!"—and he snapped his fingers—"as abruptly as an old wound that begins to ache. . . . The idea of losing that sixty thousand dollars . . . seemed the sweetest thing in the world. And all this took place quite independently of my will, and I sat watching it as if it were a play at a theatre. I could feel it going on inside me. You may depend upon it that there are things going on inside of us that we understand mighty little about."

The second, intentionally parallel illumination occurs for Newman in two stages. Having gone to the house of a great lady to begin his revenge by revealing the secret of the Bellegarde parricide, he finds himself unexpectedly silent: "A singular feeling came over him—a sudden sense of the folly of his errand . . . Wherein would it profit him to tell her that the Bellegardes were traitors and that the old lady, into the bargain, was a murderess? He seemed morally to have turned a somersault." The somersault, however, is at that time only partly completed. Newman has matured radically, to be sure: "never yet," for example, "had he seemed to himself to have outgrown so completely the phase of equal comradeship with Tom Tristram." But as for his revenge, he is only "able to say that it was provisionally pigeon-holed in a very safe place; it would keep till called for." He still carries the letter incriminating the Bellegardes, and he still enjoys "their suspense as to what he would do yet." He pays a final visit to the house of the Carmelites on the Rue d'Enfer (a possible allusion to the moment on the Rue St. Thomas de l'Enfer when Carlyle's Diogenes Teufelsdröckh records his protest to "The Everlasting No": "*I* am not thine, but Free") and there feels "his own release from ineffectual longing."[32] But the conversion is only fully achieved when he goes into Notre Dame on his way home, not because he wants to pray but "because while he was there he was out of this world":

> He leaned his head for a long time on the chair in front of him; when he took it up he felt that he was himself again. Somewhere in his mind a tight knot seemed to have loosened . . . He gave a groan as he remembered what he had meant to do; he was annoyed at having meant to do it; the bottom, suddenly, had fallen out of his revenge. Whether it was Christian charity or unregenerate good nature . . . I don't pretend to say; but Newman's last thought was that of course he would let the Bellegardes go. . . . He was ashamed of having wanted to hurt them. . . . At last he got up and came out of the darkening church; not with the elastic step of a man who has won a victory or taken a resolve, but strolling soberly, like a good-natured man who is still a little ashamed.

That Newman's culminating epiphany takes place in the great cathedral emphasizes, finally, the traditional ethical sanctions for his rejection of revenge and strongly suggests the resonance of his spiral

32. Thomas Carlyle, *Sartor Resartus: The Life and Opinions of Herr Teufelsdröckh*, ed. Charles Frederick Harrold (New York, 1937), 168.

ascent—from the first refusal to take revenge on his business rival, to the studied contemplation of revenge on the Bellegardes, to the final decision to let them off too—with the received Christian paradigm of salvation (*TA*, 22–23, 338, 341, 343, 353, 356–57).

James's major fictions from *The American* through *The Portrait of a Lady* show him working consistently toward resolutions of polarities. Two of the novels of the period, *The Europeans* and *Washington Square*, stand outside the main line of James's stylistic development. The light satiric and ironic mode James practiced in both of them seems to have called for little of the detailed dialectical ordonnance typical of the author. Though they are now widely regarded as minor masterpieces, they were omitted by James from the New York Edition. Nevertheless, both *The Europeans* and *Washington Square* exemplify James's tendency in this phase of his career to resolve the dialectic in his tales harmoniously. In *The Europeans*, the marriage of Gertrude Wentworth and Felix is a symbolic reconciliation of the central antithesis in the novel of Europe and America. In *Washington Square*, the pattern of spiral return supplies the form of Catherine Sloper's moral heroism, for she progresses from the defenseless, sentimental innocence of her girlhood through her infatuation with the unscrupulous Morris Townsend to the higher innocence she attains in the difficult integrity of her rejection of Townsend when he renews his suit after her father's death. In "Daisy Miller," Winterbourne undergoes a similar spiral evolution. When he first meets Daisy, he believes her to be innocent, however vulgarly she comports herself by European standards: "it was a wonder to Winterbourne that, with her commonness, she had a singularly delicate grace," for she seems to him "an extraordinary mixture of innocence and crudity." When scandal surrounds Daisy because of her independent gallivanting with Mr. Giovanelli in Rome, Winterbourne makes the error of disbelieving in her innocence. In the end, however, when Giovanelli assures Winterbourne at Daisy's funeral that she was "most innocent," he returns to his original faith in her innocence and comes to a deeper appreciation of its incorruptibility and value. He sees at last, though too late, the love that might have been his, and he takes from the American girl the lesson that he has "lived too long in foreign parts."[33]

33. Henry James, "Daisy Miller: A Study," *Cornhill Magazine*, XXXVII (June, 1878), 692, 698, and *ibid.*, (July, 1878), 67.

I have already commented, in the first chapter of this study, on the way the Jamesian dialectic operates in the crowning achievement of the early period, *The Portrait of a Lady*. I just want to comment very briefly here on John Carlos Rowe's unsympathetic treatment of Isabel Archer in his brilliant book *Henry Adams and Henry James*. Rowe suggests that Isabel's Romantic transcendentalism is utterly at odds with James's mature wisdom. Thus, for example, he sees "the dialectical movement" of the debate between Isabel and Madame Merle about the nature of personal identity as exposing "the hollowness of the philosophical dualism of both Isabel and Carlyle." For Rowe, Madame Merle clinches her side of the debate when she ends it by asking if Isabel should like to go without the social clothes she disdains. Trenchant as it undoubtedly is, this analysis seems to me to ignore the obvious, particularly that James likes Isabel very much and Madame Merle very little, that he exposes the youthful follies of the younger woman but also unveils far worse attributes of the other—her hypocrisy and deceit, her ability and willingness to use people as things. One notes, too, that Madame Merle's description of personal identity (it is "one's expression of one's self; and one's house, one's furniture, one's garments, the books one reads, the company one keeps—these things are all expressive") comes equipped with sanctions for her viciously manipulative intrigues; after all, if other people, "the company one keeps," are regarded as materials for "one's expression of one's self," is one not justified in working those materials for all they are worth? What is wanted to counterbalance Professor Rowe's sense of James as a philosophical modernist allied with Madame Merle in the debate with Isabel is a fuller appreciation of the broadly Romantic bias throughout *The Portrait of a Lady*. Consider, for example, the Wordsworthianism of Isabel's "remarkably active imagination," which has among its principal effects "her deepest enjoyment," that of feeling "the continuity between the movements of her own soul and the agitations of the world," and also her seeking her spiritual home, as she turns down suitor after suitor, "with something," in Wordsworth's phrase, "evermore about to be." James, one should note, both celebrates and criticizes Isabel's "nobleness of imagination," for if it "rendered her a good many services" it also "played her a great many tricks." But there is no mistaking that James values Isabel for her imagination above all and that, against Osmond's cold self-promoting rationalism (and Madame Merle's), he would have his readers' sympathies wholly with his heroine. Contrast with James's, for a moment, Jane Austen's very different, typically Neoclassical treatment of a similar configuration, her criticism of Emma Woodhouse's fancifulness and her sympathetic portrayal of the rational Mr. Knightly. James practically turns Austen's criteria of value upside down, thus registering, yet again, the effects of the Romantic revolution on his own sensibility and art.[34]

The eighties and the first half of the nineties were unusually difficult years for James. Shortly after *The Portrait of a Lady* came out, both his parents died. At the close of the eighties, when disturbingly low sales of his latest novels nearly brought about a rupture with his publisher of many years, Macmillan, James embarked upon his unfortunate venture into the theater. The three ambitious novels of the eighties, *The Bostonians* and *The Princess Casamassima* (both 1886) and *The Tragic Muse* (1890), have been aptly described by F. W. Dupee as exhibiting "an inverted idealism." All three depict irresoluble clashes of polarities. In *The Bostonians*, with its dominant note of caustic satire, Olive Chancellor and Basil Ransom, the northern feminist and the southern male supremacist, are far too rigid to assay any moderation of the extremes they represent. Ransom's marriage to the feminist orator Verena Tarrant is not at all the symbolic fusion of opposing values dramatized in other marriages in James. The passive Miss Tarrant has simply been relinquished by one pole and captured by the other. The union she has entered with Ransom is bound to bring her many more tears than she sheds in the tearful closing episode, as the final sentence in the novel assures us. In *The Princess Casamassima*, Hyacinth Robinson encompasses the polarities central to the novel, but they are nonetheless irreconcilable. Divided in his very origins—the illegitimate child, probably, of a French working-girl and an English aristocrat—Robinson finds Christina Light (the Princess Casamassima) as fatal as she proved to be for Roderick Hudson, for she encourages the growth in him of a Keatsian, aesthetic sensibility that increasingly alienates him from his anarchist affiliations. Hyacinth is neither a rigid, fixed character like Olive and Ransom

34. John Carlos Rowe, *Henry Adams and Henry James: The Emergence of a Modern Consciousness* (Ithaca, 1976), 32, 34; *PLI*, 45, 66, 68, 287–88; William Wordsworth, *The Prelude*, VI, 608.

nor an incomplete and thus flawed, weak one like Hudson and Mallett, each tragically lacking what the other has in dangerous abundance. In some respects, his is an impressively strong character; he may well be seen as bearing his essential innocence and integrity intact through a welter of troubles and betrayals. But Hyacinth's turning upon himself of the gun that it has been his anarchist assignment to use in the assassination of a government minister makes for a ruthless clarification of the despair into which he plunges because of the disloyalty of his friends on every hand and even more because of the impossibility of resolving the conflict between his class allegiance and his remarkably enlarged affinity for the fine arts, for culture, and generally for refinements in the quality and grace of life. His radical part in the class struggle commits him to the destruction of civil society, whereas the development of his sensibility entails recognition of the value of tradition, order, and privilege in making an advanced civilization possible.[35]

In detail, both *The Bostonians* and *The Princess Casamassima* are unremittingly oppositional. *The Tragic Muse* is so much more so that it threatens to fly apart. The world (especially polite society and the political community) is absolutely at odds with art; love for other human beings (but not passionate self-involvement) is at odds with art; even art is at odds with art (the secluded, solitary world of the painter being contrasted throughout with the public, crowded one of the actress). A remark about the art of portraiture by Gabriel Nash, "the great explainer," is emblematic of the doubleness of the novel in stylistic detail and in the ideas it treats: "unlike most other forms, it was a revelation of two realities, the man whom it was the artist's conscious effort to reveal and the man (the interpreter) expressed in the very quality and temper of that effort. It offered a double vision, the strongest dose of life that art could give, the strongest dose of art that life could give."[36] The marriages that are finally made at the end of the various intrigues in the novel symbolize not a fusion of the opposed values of life and art but rather resignation to the impossibility of a fusion: Miriam Rooth, the actress, suppresses her love for Nick Dormer and settles on a union with the actor Dashwood pri-

35. Dupee, *Henry James,* 128. For a fine discussion of "Keats and James and *The Princess Casamassima,*" see Adeline R. Tintner's essay of that title.
36. Henry James, *The Tragic Muse* (London, 1891), 257, 259.

marily because of its efficacity for her career; Peter Sherringham similarly gives up his passion for Miriam to wed Biddy Dormer, a marriage of convenience for the sake of *his* career; and the possibility raised at last that Nick, too, will bury his love for Miriam in a conventionally appropriate marriage with Lady Julia only suggests another shabby compromise. James's short stories immediately preceding and throughout the suspension of his career as a novelist display, again in Dupee's apt phrase, the same "inverted idealism" seen in the novels of the eighties—one might point here, especially, to "The Author of Beltraffio" (1884), "The Aspern Papers" and "The Lesson of the Master" (1888), "The Pupil" (1891), "The Real Thing" (1892), "The Middle Years" (1893), and "The Coxon Fund" (1894).

James's notebook entry of January 23, 1895, is a justly famous record of the enormous impetus he carried out of his failure in the theater, of the astounding artistic and personal courage with which he rose from defeat: "I take up my *own* old pen again—the pen of all my old unforgettable efforts and sacred struggles. To myself—today—I need say no more. Large and full and high the future still stands. It is now indeed that I may do the work of my life. And I will. x x x x x I have only to face my problems."[37]

In a notable series of experimental works, he went on to dramatize not the compromised, defeated innocence to which the fictions of the middle period had been a troubling plaint but the triumphant innocence of three incorruptible heroines, Fleda Vetch, in *The Spoils of Poynton* (1896), Maisie Farange, in *What Maisie Knew* (1897), and Nanda Brookenham, in *The Awkward Age* (1898). Fleda and Maisie both possess virtually unwavering integrity. Unless one stretches the case by taking Fleda's lie to Mrs. Gereth (in which she honors a promise to Owen) or Maisie's encouragement of the affair between her stepparents (in which she acts with innocent good will) as antithetical to their initial spotlessness, one cannot say that either of these heroines undergoes a spiral evolution. But both grow in integrity and awareness, and James strongly affirms their moral heroism, their remaining true to the moral sense that Fleda always possesses and that Maisie gradually acquires. In *The Awkward Age*—which, as I argued in my first chapter, incorporates the spiral dialectic into the

37. Matthiessen and Murdock (eds.), *The Notebooks of Henry James,* 179.

disposition of its "Books"—there is irony, to be sure, in that the direction of the spiral may even appear to be downward; but Nanda Brookenham herself is incorruptible, however much her exposure to improprieties has compromised her in the eyes of convention. Her withdrawal with Mr. Longdon, like Maisie's with Mrs. Wix, is an act of self-preservation and of moral courage. There are disturbing notes, no doubt, in these works; and in a few other works of the late nineties, notably in "The Turn of the Screw" and *The Sacred Fount*, James's virtuosity and his anxiety about the fate of meaning and the grounds of knowledge create irresoluble suspensions in brilliant parables of ambiguity. But in his heroic young women, whose integrity he affirms in spite of the often terrible knowledge they must grow into, he goes a long way toward returning to the idealism of his early period, now freed, for the most part, from the brooding pessimism of the middle works.

That return, the taking up of the "old pen again," was substantially completed in the three masterpieces James produced in the dawn of the present century. In *The Ambassadors*, *The Wings of the Dove*, and *The Golden Bowl*, he dramatized, as he had not done since *The American* and *The Portrait of a Lady*, preponderantly positive enactments of the Romantic dialectic of spiral return. That he was able to do so at a time when his insights into the complexities of conduct, of morality, and of epistemology were more numerous and acute than ever is as extraordinary as it is moving. James's recovery of his powers of affirmation following the dark middle period gives his career itself the form of an ascending spiral. In sustaining himself against the sort of despair that had debilitated American novelists as different as Melville and Twain, in returning in late middle age to the Romantic humanism of his early years, James built more than ever "large and full and high," accomplishing what must be accounted among the greatest sustained acts of literary heroism.

Bibliography

Abrams, M. H. *Natural Supernaturalism: Tradition and Revolution in Romantic Literature*. New York: Norton, 1971.

———. "Rationality and Imagination in Cultural History: A Reply to Wayne Booth." *Critical Inquiry*, II (Spring, 1976), 447–64.

Allott, Miriam. "Symbol and Image in the Later Work of Henry James." *Essays in Criticism*, III (July, 1953), 321–26.

Anderson, Quentin. *The American Henry James*. New Brunswick: Rutgers University Press, 1957.

Andreas, Osborn. *Henry James and the Expanding Horizon*. Seattle: University of Washington Press, 1948.

Aziz, Maqbool, ed. *The Tales of Henry James*. Oxford: Clarendon Press, 1973.

Bailey, N. I. "Pragmatism in *The Ambassadors*." *Dalhousie Review*, XXX (Spring, 1973), 143–48.

Barzun, Jacques. "Henry James, Melodramatist." In *The Question of Henry James*, edited by F. W. Dupee, pp. 254–66. New York: Henry Holt, 1945.

Bayley, John. *The Characters of Love: A Study in the Literature of Personality*. New York: Basic Books, 1960.

———. *The Romantic Survival: A Study in Poetic Evolution*. London: Constable, 1957.

Beach, Joseph Warren. *The Method of Henry James*. Philadelphia: Albert Saifer, 1954.

Bell, Millicent. "The Dream of Being Possessed and Possessing: Henry James's *The Wings of the Dove*." *Massachusetts Review*, X, No. 1 (1969), 97–114.

———. "Henry James: The Man Who Lived." *Massachusetts Review*, XIV, No. 2 (1973), 391–414.

Bewly, Marius. *The Complex Fate: Hawthorne, Henry James and Some Other American Writers*. London: Chatto and Windus, 1952.

Blackall, Jean Frantz. *Jamesian Ambiguity and "The Sacred Fount"*. Ithaca: Cornell University Press, 1965.

Blackmur, R. P. Introduction. Henry James. *The Golden Bowl*. New York: Grove Press, 1952.

———. *The Lion and the Honeycomb: Essays in Solicitude and Critique*. New York: Harcourt, Brace, 1955.

———, ed. *The Art of the Novel: Critical Prefaces of Henry James*. New York: Charles Scribner's Sons, 1934.

Bloom, Harold. *The Ringers in the Tower: Studies in Romantic Tradition*. Chicago: University of Chicago Press, 1971.

Booth, Wayne C. *The Rhetoric of Fiction*. Chicago: University of Chicago Press, 1961.

———. "M. H. Abrams: Historian, Critic, Pluralist." *Critical Inquiry*, II (Spring, 1976), 411–45.

Bowden, Edwin T. *The Themes of Henry James: A System of Observation Through the Visual Arts*. New Haven: Yale University Press, 1956.

Buitenhaus, Peter. *The Grasping Imagination: The American Writings of Henry James*. Toronto: University of Toronto Press, 1970.

Byrd, Scott. "The Fractured Crystal in *Middlemarch* and *The Golden Bowl*." *Modern Fiction Studies*, XVIII (Winter, 1972–73), 551–54.

———. "The Spoils of Venice: Henry James's 'Two Old Houses and Three Young Women' and *The Golden Bowl*." *American Literature*, XLIII (November, 1971), 371–84.

Cargill, Oscar. *The Novels of Henry James*. New York: Macmillan, 1961.

Carlyle, Thomas. *Sartor Resartus: The Life and Opinions of Herr Teufelsdröckh*. Edited by Charles Frederick Harrold. New York: Odyssey Press, 1937.

Chartier, Richard. "The River and the Whirlpool: Water Imagery in *The Ambassadors*." *Ball State University Forum*, XII (Spring, 1971), 70–75.

Chase, Richard. *The American Novel and Its Tradition*. Garden City: Doubleday, 1957.

Chatman, Seymour. *The Late Style of Henry James*. Oxford: Basil Blackwell, 1972.

Coleridge, Samuel Taylor. *Biographia Literaria or Biographical Sketches of My Literary Life and Opinions*. Edited by George Watson. New York: Dutton, 1965.

Cook, Albert. *The Meaning of Fiction*. Detroit: Wayne State University Press, 1960.

Cox, C. B. *The Free Spirit: A Study of Liberal Humanism in the Novels of George Eliot, Henry James, E. M. Forster, Virginia Woolf, and Angus Wilson.* London: Oxford University Press, 1963.

Crews, Frederick C. *The Tragedy of Manners: Moral Drama in the Later Novels of Henry James.* New Haven: Yale University Press, 1957.

Dumitriu, Gheorghita. "Henry James's Use of Imagery in 'The Wings of the Dove.'" *Analele Universitatii, Bucuresti, Limbi Germanice,* II (1973), 67–74.

Dupee, F. W. *Henry James.* New York: Delta, 1965.

Durr, Robert A. "The Night Journey in *The Ambassadors.*" *Philological Quarterly,* XXXV (January, 1956), 24–38.

Edel, Leon. *Henry James: The Untried Years, 1843–1870.* Philadelphia: Lippincott, 1953.

———. *Henry James: The Conquest of London, 1870–1881.* Philadelphia: Lippincott, 1962.

———. *Henry James: The Middle Years, 1882–1895.* Philadelphia: Lippincott, 1962.

———. *Henry James: The Treacherous Years, 1895–1901.* Philadelphia: Lippincott, 1969.

———. *Henry James: The Master, 1901–1916.* Philadelphia: Lippincott, 1972.

———. Introduction. Henry James. *The American Scene.* Bloomington: University of Indiana Press, 1968.

———. Introduction. Henry James. *Roderick Hudson.* Boston: Houghton Mifflin, 1977.

———. Review of *The American Henry James. American Literature,* XXIX (January, 1958), 493–95.

Edel, Leon, and Dan H. Laurence. *A Bibliography of Henry James.* London: Rupert Hart-Davis, 1961.

Erdman, David V., ed. *The Poetry and Prose of William Blake.* Garden City: Doubleday, 1970.

Fergusson, Francis. "The Drama in *The Golden Bowl.*" *Hound and Horn,* VII (April–May, 1934), 407–13.

———. "*The Golden Bowl* Revisited." *Sewanee Review,* LXIII (Winter, 1955), 13–28.

Finn, C. M. "Commitment and Identity in 'The Ambassadors.'" *Modern Language Review,* LXVI (July, 1971), 522–31.

Firebaugh, J. J. "The Ververs." *Essays in Criticism,* IV (October, 1954), 400–410.

Forster, E. M. "Pattern in *The Ambassadors.*" In *Aspects of the Novel* (London: Edward Arnold, 1927).

Friedman, Norman. "Imagery: From Sensation to Symbol." *Journal of Aesthetics and Art Criticism,* XII, No. 1 (1953), 25–37.

Frye, Northrop. Introduction. William Shakespeare. *The Tempest.* Baltimore: Penguin, 1959.

Gale, Robert L. *The Caught Image: Figurative Language in the Fiction of Henry James.* Chapel Hill: University of North Carolina Press, 1964.

———. *Plots and Characters in the Fiction of Henry James.* Hamden: Archon Books, 1965.

Gargano, James W. "*The Ambassadors* and *Louis Lambert*." *Modern Language Notes*, LXXV (1960), 211–13.

———. "The Theme of Salvation in *The Awkward Age*." *Texas Studies in Language and Literature*, IX (Summer, 1967), 273–87.

Gibson, Priscilla. "The Uses of James's Imagery: Drama Through Metaphor." *PMLA*, LXIX (December, 1954), 1076–84.

Girling, H. K. "The Function of Slang in the Dramatic Poetry of 'The Golden Bowl.'" *Nineteenth-Century Fiction*, II (September, 1956), 130–47.

Gordon, Caroline. "Mr. Verver, Our National Hero." *Sewanee Review*, LXIII (Winter, 1955), 29–47.

Graham, Kenneth. *Henry James, The Dream of Fulfillment: An Approach to the Novels.* Oxford: Clarendon Press, 1975.

Hartman, Geoffrey. *Beyond Formalism: Literary Essays 1958–1970.* New Haven: Yale University Press, 1970.

Hocks, Richard A. *Henry James and Pragmatistic Thought: A Study in the Relationship Between the Philosophy of William James and the Literary Art of Henry James.* Chapel Hill: University of North Carolina Press, 1974.

Hoffman, Charles G. *The Short Novels of Henry James.* New York: Bookman, 1957.

Holder-Barell, Alexander. *The Development of Imagery and Its Functional Significance in Henry James's Novels.* Bern: Francke Verlag, 1959.

Holman, C. Hugh. *Windows on the World: Essays on American Social Fiction.* Knoxville: University of Tennessee Press, 1979.

Holland, Laurence Bedwell. *The Expense of Vision: Essays on the Craft of Henry James.* Princeton: Princeton University Press, 1964.

Hueffer, Ford Maddox. *Henry James: A Critical Study.* London: Martin Secker, 1913.

James, Henry. *The Ambassadors.* Edited by S. P. Rosenbaum. New York: Norton, 1964.

———. *The American.* Edited by Joseph Warren Beach. New York: Holt, Rinehart, and Winston, 1949.

———. "The Aspern Papers." *Atlantic Monthly*, LXI (March–May, 1888), 296–315, 461–82, 577–94.

———. "The Author of Beltraffio." *English Illustrated Magazine*, I (June–July, 1884), 563–73, 628–39.

———. *The Awkward Age.* New York: Charles Scribner's Sons, 1908.

———. "The Beast in the Jungle." In *The Better Sort.* London: Methuen, 1903.

———. "Benvolio." *Galaxy*, XX (August, 1875), 209–35.

———. *The Bostonians.* London: Macmillan, 1886.
———. "The Coxon Fund." *The Yellow Book,* II (July, 1894), 290–360.
———. Daisy Miller: A Study." *Cornhill Magazine,* XXXVII (June, 1878), 678–98; XXXVIII (July, 1878), 44–67.
———. "Eugene Pickering." *Atlantic Monthly,* XXXIV (October–November, 1874), 397–410, 513–26.
———. *The Europeans.* London: Macmillan, 1878.
———. *The Golden Bowl.* 2 vols. New York: Charles Scribner's Sons, 1909.
———. "The Jolly Corner." *English Review,* I (December, 1908), 5–35.
———. "The Last of the Valerii." *Atlantic Monthly,* XXXIII (January, 1874), 69–85.
———. "The Lesson of the Master." *Universal Review,* I (July 16 and August 15, 1888), 342–65, 494–523.
———. "The Middle Years." *Scribner's Magazine,* XIII (May, 1893), 609–20.
———. "Mme. de Mauves." *Galaxy,* XVII (February–March, 1874), 216–33, 354–74.
———. "A Passionate Pilgrim." *Atlantic Monthly,* XXVII (March–April, 1871), 352–71, 478–99.
———. *The Portrait of a Lady.* 2 vols. New York: Charles Scribner's Sons, 1908.
———. *The Portrait of a Lady.* Boston: Houghton, Mifflin, 1882.
———. "The Pupil." *Longman's Magazine,* XVII (March–April, 1891), 512–31, 611–32.
———. "The Real Thing." *Black and White,* III (April 16, 1892), 502–507.
———. *Roderick Hudson.* Boston: James R. Osgood, 1876.
———. *The Sacred Fount.* New York: Charles Scribner's Sons, 1901.
———. *A Small Boy and Others.* New York: Charles Scribner's Sons, 1913.
———. *The Spoils of Poynton.* New York: Houghton Mifflin, 1897.
———. *The Tragic Muse.* London: Macmillan, 1891.
———. "The Turn of the Screw." In *The Two Magics.* New York: Macmillan, 1898.
———. *Washington Square.* New York: Harper & Brothers, 1881.
———. *What Maisie Knew.* Chicago: Herbert S. Stone, 1897.
———. *The Wings of the Dove.* 2 vols. New York: Charles Scribner's Sons, 1909.
Jefferson, D. W. *Henry James.* New York: Grove Press, 1961.
Jones, Granville H. *Henry James's Psychology of Experience: Innocence, Responsibility, and Renunciation in the Fiction of Henry James.* The Hague: Mouton, 1975.
Kelley, Cornelia Pulsifer. *The Early Development of Henry James.* Urbana: University of Illinois Press, 1965.
Kermode, John Frank. *The Romantic Image.* New York: Macmillan, 1957.
Kimball, Jean. "The Abyss and *The Wings of the Dove*: The Image as

Revelation." In *Modern Judgments: Henry James*, edited by Tony Tanner, pp. 266–82. Nashville: Aurora, 1970.

———. "Henry James's Last Portrait of a Lady: Charlotte Stant in *The Golden Bowl.*" *American Literature*, XXVIII (January, 1957), 449–68.

Kornfeld, Milton. "Villainy and Responsibility in *The Wings of the Dove.*" *Texas Studies in Language and Literature*, XIV (Summer, 1972), 337–46.

Kraft, James. *The Early Tales of Henry James.* Carbondale: Southern Illinois University Press, 1969.

Krook, Dorothea. *The Ordeal of Consciousness in Henry James.* Cambridge: Cambridge University Press, 1967.

Labrie, Ross. "Henry James's Idea of Consciousness." *American Literature*, XXXIX (January, 1968), 517–29.

Langbaum, Robert Woodrow. *The Poetry of Experience: The Dramatic Monologue in Modern Literary Tradition.* London: Chatto & Windus, 1957.

Leavis, F. R. *The Great Tradition: George Eliot, Henry James, Joseph Conrad.* New York: New York University Press, 1973.

Le Clair, Robert C. *Young Henry James, 1843–1870.* New York: Bookman, 1955.

Levy, Leo B. "Henry James and the Jews." *Commentary*, XXVI (September, 1958), 243–49.

———. *Versions of Melodrama: A Study of the Fiction and Drama of Henry James, 1865–1897.* Berkeley: University of California Press, 1957.

Lewis, R. W. B. "The Vision of Grace: James's *The Wings of the Dove.*" *Modern Fiction Studies*, III, No. 1 (1957), 33–41.

Leyburn, Ellen Douglass. *Strange Alloy: The Relation of Comedy to Tragedy in the Fiction of Henry James.* Chapel Hill: University of North Carolina Press, 1968.

Lindenberger, Herbert. "Lawrence and the Romantic Tradition." In *A D. H. Lawrence Miscellany*, edited by Harry T. Moore, pp. 326–41. Carbondale: Southern Illinois University Press, 1959.

Lubbock, Percy. *The Craft of Fiction.* New York: Scribner's, 1921.

———, ed. *The Letters of Henry James.* 2 vols. New York: Scribner's, 1920.

McLean, Robert C. "The Completed Vision: A Study of *Madame de Mauves* and *The Ambassadors.*" *Modern Language Quarterly*, XXVIII (December, 1967), 446–61.

Mackenzie, Manfred. *Communities of Honor and Love in Henry James.* Cambridge: Harvard University Press, 1976.

Markow-Totevy, Georges. *Henry James.* Translated by John Cumming. New York: Funk & Wagnalls, 1969.

Marks, Robert. *James's Later Novels: An Interpretation.* New York: William Frederick, 1960.

Matthiessen, F. O. *Henry James: The Major Phase.* New York: Oxford University Press, 1944.

Matthiessen, F. O., and Kenneth B. Murdock, eds. *The Notebooks of Henry James*. New York: Oxford University Press, 1947.

Maynard, Reid. "The Irony of Strether's Enlightenment." *Lockhaven Review*, No. 11 (1969), 33–44.

Merrill, Robert. "What Strether *Sees*: The Ending of *The Ambassadors*." *Bulletin of the Rocky Mountain Modern Language Association*, XXVII (June, 1973), 45–52.

Mooney, Stephen L. "James, Keats, and the Religion of Consciousness." *Modern Language Quarterly*, XXII (December, 1961), 398–401.

Mull, Donald L. *Henry James's "Sublime Economy": Money as Symbolic Center in the Fiction*. Middletown: Wesleyan University Press, 1973.

Nettels, Elsa. "*The Ambassadors* and the Sense of the Past." *Modern Language Quarterly*, XXXI (June, 1970), 220–35.

———. *James and Conrad*. Athens: University of Georgia Press, 1976.

Nuhn, Ferner. *The Wind Blew From The East: A Study in the Orientation of American Culture*. New York: Harper, 1942.

Owen, Elizabeth. " 'The Awkward Age' and the Contemporary English Scene." *Victorian Studies*, XI (September, 1967), 63–82.

Paterson, John. "The Language of 'Adventure' in Henry James." *American Literature*, XXXII (November, 1960), 291–301.

Pearce, Howard. "Henry James's Pastoral Fallacy." *PMLA*, XC (October, 1975), 834–47.

Pearson, Gabriel. "The novel to end all novels: *The Golden Bowl*." In *The Air of Reality*, edited by John Goode, pp. 301–362. London: Methuen, 1972.

Poirier, Richard. *The Comic Sense of Henry James: A Study of the Early Novels*. London: Chatto & Windus, 1960.

Poulet, Georges. *The Metamorphoses of the Circle*. Translated by Carley Dawson and Elliot Coleman. Baltimore: Johns Hopkins University Press, 1967.

———. *Studies in Human Time*. Translated by Elliot Coleman. Baltimore: Johns Hopkins University Press, 1956.

Putt, S. Gorley. *Henry James: A Reader's Guide*. Ithaca: Cornell University Press, 1967.

Rahv, Philip. *Image and Idea: Fourteen Essays on Literary Themes*. New York: New Directions, 1949.

Ricks, Beatrice. *Henry James: A Bibliography of Secondary Works*. Metuchen: Scarecrow Press, 1975.

Rimmon, Shlomith. *The Concept of Ambiguity—the Example of James*. Chicago: University of Chicago Press, 1977.

Rowe, John Carlos. *Henry Adams and Henry James: The Emergence of a Modern Consciousness*. Ithaca: Cornell University Press, 1976.

———. "The Symbolization of Milly Theale: Henry James's *The Wings of the Dove*." *ELH*, XL (Spring, 1973), 131–64.

Samuels, Charles Thomas. *The Ambiguity of Henry James.* Urbana: University of Illinois Press, 1971.

Sandeen, Ernest. "*The Wings of the Dove* and *The Portrait of a Lady*: A Study of Henry James's Later Phase." *PMLA*, LXIX (December, 1954), 1060–75.

Schneider, Daniel J. *Symbolism: The Manichean Vision, A Study of James, Conrad, Woolf & Stevens.* Lincoln: University of Nebraska Press, 1975.

Schug, Charles. *The Romantic Genesis of the Modern Novel.* Pittsburgh: University of Pittsburgh Press, 1979.

Sears, Sallie. *The Negative Imagination: Form and Perspective in the Novels of Henry James.* Ithaca: Cornell University Press, 1968.

Segal, Ora. *The Lucid Reflector: The Observer in Henry James's Fiction.* New Haven: Yale University Press, 1969.

Short, R. W. "Henry James's World of Images." *PMLA*, LXVIII (December, 1953), 943–60.

Shucard, Alan R. "Diplomacy in Henry James's *The Ambassadors.*" *Arizona Quarterly*, XXIX (Summer, 1973), 123–29.

Snow, Lotus. "The Disconcerting Poetry of Mary Temple: A Comparison of the Imagery of *The Portrait of a Lady* and *The Wings of the Dove.*" *New England Quarterly*, XXXI (September, 1958), 312–39.

Spencer, James L. "Symbolism in James's 'The Golden Bowl.'" *Modern Fiction Studies*, III (Winter, 1957–58), 333–44.

Spender, Stephen. *The Destructive Element: A Study of Modern Writers and Beliefs.* Philadelphia: Albert Saifer, 1953.

Stallman, R. W. "'The Sacred Rage': The Time-Theme in *The Ambassadors.*" *Modern Fiction Studies*, III (Spring, 1957), 41–56.

Stevenson, Elizabeth. *The Crooked Corridor: A Study of Henry James.* New York: Macmillan, 1949.

Swingle, L. J. "Wordsworth's Contrarieties: A Prelude to Wordsworthian Complexity." *ELH*, XLIV (Summer, 1977), 337–53.

Tanner, Tony, "*The Golden Bowl* and the Reassessment of Innocence." *London Magazine*, New Series, I (November, 1961), 38–49.

Thorberg, Raymond. "Henry James and the 'New England Conscience.'" *Notes and Queries*, New Series, XVI (June, 1969), 222–23.

———. "The New England Conscience." *Notes and Queries*, New Series, XVIII (July, 1971), 264.

Thorburn, David. *Conrad's Romanticism.* New Haven: Yale University Press, 1974.

Tintner, Adeline R. "Keats and James and *The Princess Casamassima.*" *Nineteenth-Century Fiction*, XXVIII (September, 1973), 179–93.

———. "The Spoils of Henry James." *PMLA*, LXI (March, 1946), 239–51.

Tuttleton, James W. *The Novel of Manners in America.* Chapel Hill: University of North Carolina Press, 1972.

Vaid, Krishna Baldev. *Technique in the Tales of Henry James.* Cambridge: Harvard University Press, 1964.

Van Doren, Carl. *The American Novel.* New York: Macmillan, 1921.

Veeder, William. *Henry James—The Lessons of the Master: Popular Fiction and Personal Style in the Nineteenth Century.* Chicago: University of Chicago Press, 1975.

Vincec, Sister Stephanie. "A Significant Revision in *The Wings of the Dove*." *Review of English Studies,* New Series, XXIII (February, 1972), 58–61.

Wallace, Ronald. "Comic Form in *The Ambassadors*." *Genre,* V (March, 1972), 31–50.

———. *Henry James and the Comic Form.* Ann Arbor: University of Michigan Press, 1975.

———. "Maggie Verver: Comic Heroine." *Genre,* VI (December, 1973), 404–15.

Ward, J. A. "*The Ambassadors* as a Conversion Experience." *Southern Review,* New Series, V (April, 1969), 350–74.

———. *The Imagination of Disaster: Evil in the Fiction of Henry James.* Lincoln: University of Nebraska Press, 1961.

———. "James's Idea of Structure." *PMLA,* LXXX (September, 1965), 419–26.

———. *The Search for Form: Studies in the Structure of James's Fiction.* Chapel Hill: University of North Carolina Press, 1967.

Warren, Austin. "The New England Conscience: Henry James and Ambassador Strether." *Minnesota Review,* II (Winter, 1962), 149–61.

Watanabe, Hisayoshi. "Past Perfect Retrospection in the Style of Henry James." *American Literature,* XXXIV (May, 1962), 165–81.

Watt, Ian. "The First Paragraph of *The Ambassadors*: An Explication." *Essays in Criticism,* X (July, 1960), 250–74.

Wegelin, Christof. *The Image of Europe in Henry James.* Dallas: Southern Methodist University Press, 1958.

Weinstein, Philip M. *Henry James and the Requirements of the Imagination.* Cambridge: Harvard University Press, 1971.

Wellek, René. "Henry James's Literary Theory and Criticism." *American Literature,* XXX (1958), 293–321.

Winters, Yvor. *Maule's Curse: Seven Studies in the History of American Obscurantism.* Norfolk: New Directions, 1938.

Wise, James N. "The Floating World of Lambert Strether." *Arlington Quarterly,* II (Summer, 1969), 80–110.

Wright, Walter F. *The Madness of Art: A Study of Henry James.* Lincoln: University of Nebraska Press, 1962.

Yeazell, Ruth Bernard. *Language and Knowledge in the Late Novels of Henry James.* Chicago: University of Chicago Press, 1971.

Index